D0916304

FOUR ILLUSIONS

FOUR ILLUSIONS

Candrakīrti's Advice for Travelers on the Bodhisattva Path

Translation and Introduction by
KAREN C. LANG

OXFORD
UNIVERSITY PRESS

2003

OXFORD
UNIVERSITY PRESS

Oxford New York
Athens Auckland Bangkok Buenos Aires Cape Town Chennai
Dar es Salaam Delhi Hong Kong Istanbul Karachi Kolkata
Kuala Lumpur Madrid Melbourne Mexico City Mumbai Nairobi
São Paulo Shanghai Taipei Tokyo Toronto

Copyright © 2003 by Oxford University Press, Inc.

Published by Oxford University Press, Inc.
198 Madison Avenue, New York, New York 10016

www.oup.com

Oxford is a registered trademark of Oxford University Press

All rights reserved. No part of this publication may be reproduced,
stored in a retrieval system, or transmitted, in any form or by any means,
electronic, mechanical, photocopying, recording, or otherwise,
without the prior permission of Oxford University Press.

Library of Congress Cataloging-in-Publication Data
Candrakirti.
[Bodhisattvayogacaracatuh'sataktika. English. Selections]
Four illusions : Candrakiriti's advice for travelers on the Bodhisattva path ; translations and introduction by Karen C. Lang.
p. cm.
Includes bibliographical references and index.
ISBN 0-19-515112-7; ISBN 0-19-515113-5 (pbk.)
1. åryadeva, 3rd cent. Catuòââtaka. 2. Mådhyamika (Buddhism) I. Lang, Karen C. (Karen Christine), 1947- II. Title.
BQ3300.B6222 E522 2002
294.3'85—dc21 2002070911

9 8 7 6 5 4 3 2 1

Printed in the United States of America
on acid-free paper

ACKNOWLEDGMENTS

This book has had a long gestation period. Its origins began with my work on Āryadeva's *Catuḥśataka*. During my stay in Dharamsala, India, in 1978, supported by a Fulbright-Hays doctoral dissertation fellowship, I benefited greatly from the opportunity to hear Geshe Ngawang Dhargyey's illuminating lectures on the *Catuḥśataka* and rGyal tshab rje's commentary. In addition to commenting on many of the stories Candrakīrti included in his text, Geshe Dhargyey supplemented his oral commentary with some well-chosen stories of his own. Support from an American Institute of Indian Studies short-term senior fellowship enabled me to return to India in the fall of 1988 to begin work on a translation of Candrakīrti's *Catuḥśatakaṭīkā*. During this time, I was affiliated with the Central Institute of Higher Tibetan Studies at Sarnath, and I am grateful for the support rendered by Venerable Samdhong Rimpoche and Professor K. N. Mishra. The first draft of the translations of the first four chapters of this text was completed during the years 1989–90, thanks to the generous support of a National Endowment for the Humanities Translation Grant. This grant enabled me to return to Dharamsala in the fall of 1989, where I was able once again to have the pleasure of discussing Madhyamaka philosophy with Geshe Sonam Rinchen and Ruth Sonam.

Over the last ten years, parts of the introduction were presented at various conferences and colloquiums in India, Europe, and the United States. I cannot give credit to all the people who have enriched my own understanding of Madhyamaka thought and Indian philosophy, but I would especially like to thank my mentor David Seyfort Ruegg and two friends from my graduate school days, Edeltraud Harzer Clear and William Ames. Other friends and colleagues who have contributed much to my understanding of Indian and Tibetan Buddhist thought include Georges Dreyfus, Jeffrey Hopkins, Christian Lindtner, Elizabeth Napper, and Tom J. F. Tillemans. Thanks also to Cynthia Read for her support in seeing this book through the press, to Margaret Case for her patient and painstaking editing, and to two anonymous readers, whose perceptive comments have made this a much richer book.

CONTENTS

ABBREVIATIONS

A *Aṅguttara Nikāya*, edited by R. Morris and E. Hardy. 5 vols. 1885–1900. Reprint, London: Pali Text Society, 1955–61.

AK *and* AKB *Abhidharmakośa and Bhāṣya*, edited by Swami Dwarikas Shastri.Varanasi: Buddha Bharati,1970–73.

AS *Arthaśāstra*, edited by R. P. Kangle. Bombay: University of Bombay, 1960–1965.

AV *Atharvaveda*, edited and translated by Satya Prakash Sarasvati. New Delhi: Veda Pratishthana, 1992.

BC *Buddhacarita*, edited by E. H. Johnson. Lahore: University of Punjab, 1936. Reprint, New Delhi: Oriental Books Reprint Corporation, 1972.

BG *Bhagavad-Gītā*, edited and translated by R. C. Zaehner. London, New York, Oxford University Press, 1969.

BU *Bṛhadāraṇyaka Upaniṣad*, edited and translated by S. Radhakrishnan. *The Principal Upaniṣads*. London: George Allen & Unwin, 1978.

CŚ *Catuḥśataka*, edited by Karen Lang. *Āryadeva's Catuḥśataka: On the Bodhisattva's Cultivation of Merit and Knowledge.* Copenhagen: Akademisk Forlag, 1986.

CŚṬ *Catuḥśatakaṭīkā*, edited by Haraprasād Shāstrī, "Catuḥśatika of Ārya Deva," *Memoirs of the Asiatic Society of Bengal*, 3 no. 8 (1914): 449–514.

D *Dīgha Nikāya*, edited by T. W. Rhys-Davids and J. Estlin Carpenter. 1890. Reprint, London: Pali Text Society, 1960–67.

Dhp *The Dhammapada*, eds. John Ross Carter and Mahinda Palihawadana. New York: Oxford University Press, 1987.

Ja *Jātakāṭṭhakathā*, edited by V. Fausbøll. 6 vols. London: Pali Text Society, 1877–96. Reprint, London: Pali Text Society, 1962–64.

JM *Jātakamālā*, edited by P. L. Vaidya. Buddhist Sanskrit Texts 21. Darbhanga: Mithila Institute, 1959.

KP *Kaśyapaparivarta*, edited by A. von Stael-Holstein. Shanghai, 1926. Reprint, Tokyo: Meicho-fukyu-kai, 1977.

M *Majjhima-nikāya*, edited by V. Trenckner and R. Chalmers. 3 vols. 1888–1902. Reprint, London: Pali Text Society, 1960–64.

MĀ *Madhyamakāvatāra*, edited by Louis de La Vallée Poussin. Bibliotheca Buddhica, 9. St. Petersburg, 1912. Reprint, Osnabrück: Biblio Verlag, 1970.

Mbh *Mahābhārata*, edited by Vishnu S. Sutthankar et al. 5 vols. Poona: Bhandarkar Oriental Research Institute, 1971–76.

MDŚ *Mānavadharmaśāstra*, edited by J. Jolly. London: Trübner, 1897.

Miln *Milindapañho*, edited by V. Trenckner, London: Williams and Norgate, 1880. Reprint, London: Pali Text Society, 1962.

MKV *Prasannapadā Madhyamakavṛtti*, edited by Louis de La Vallée Poussin. Bibliotheca Buddhica 4. St. Petersburg, 1903–13. Reprint, Osnabrück: Biblio Verlag, 1970.

MMK Mūlamadhyamakakārikāḥ, edited by J. W. de Jong. Madras: Adyar Library, 1977.

P *Peking Edition of the Tibetan Tripiṭaka*, edited by D. T. Suzuki. 168 vols. Vol. 98 (Ya). Tokyo-Kyoto: Tibetan Tripiṭaka Research Institute, 1956–61.

RĀ *Ratnāvalī*, edited by Michael Hahn. Vol. 1. Bonn: Judica et Tibetica, 1982.

RV *Rig Veda*, edited by Barend A. van Nooten and Gary B. Holland. Cambridge, Mass: Dept of Sanskrit and Indian Studies, Harvard University, 1994.

S *Saṃyutta Nikāya*, edited by L. Feer. 5 vols. 1884–98. Reprint, London: Pali Text Society, 1973–90.

SB *Śatapatha Brāhmaṇa*, edited by W. Caland and revised by Raghu Vira. Delhi: Motilal Banarsidass, 1983.

SL *Suhṛllekha. bShes pa'i spring yig*, edited by A. Sonam. Sarnath: Pleasure of Elegant Sayings Printing Press, 1971.

Sn *Saundarananda*, edited by E. H. Johnston. Lahore, 1928. Reprint, Delhi: Motilal Banarsidass, 1975.

SN *Suttanipāta*, edited by D. Anderson and H. Smith. London: Pali Text Society, 1948.

SR *Samādhirājasūtra*, edited by P. L. Vaidya. Darbangha: The Mithila Institute of Post Graduate Studies and Research in Sanskrit Learning, 1961.

Thag. *and* Thīg. *Thera- and Theri-Gāthā*, edited by H. Oldenberg and R. Pischel. 2d ed. by London: Pali Text Society, 1966.

Uv *Udānavarga*, edited by F. Bernhard. 2 vols. Göttingen: Vandenhoeck and Ruprecht, 1965–68.

Vin *Vinaya-piṭakam*, edited by H. Oldenberg. 5 vols. London: Pali Text Society, 1879–83.

NOTES ON THE TRANSLATION

Candrakīrti wrote in Sanskrit, but with the exception of the *Prasannapadā* and some fragments of his commentary on the *Catuḥśataka*, his works no longer exist in the language in which he composed them. Haraprasād Shāstrī discovered fragments of Candrakīrti's *Bodhisattvayogācāracatuḥśatakaṭīkā* among some old palm leaf manuscripts he had acquired. Three years later, in 1914, he published an edition of the text in the *Memoirs of the Asiatic Society of Bengal*. Unfortunately these fragments represent less than a third of the original text. This pioneering edition contains numerous doubtful readings that can be corrected through a careful comparison of the text with the available Tibetan translations.

The Tibetan Translation

The Tibetan translator, sPa tshab Nyi ma grags, working together with Sanskrit scholar Sūkṣmajana, translated Candrakīrti's commentary on the *Catuḥśataka* along with several other Madhyamaka texts. The Tibetan historian Go lo tsa ba records Nyi ma grags's birth in the sPa tshab district of Tibet in the year 1055. Nyi ma grags traveled to Kashmir, where he remained for twenty-three years, studying the Sanskrit language and Buddhist texts with Kashmiri Buddhist scholar Sajjana and his sons Mahājana and Sūkṣmajana in the town of Anupamahapura, the present-day Śrinagar. The colophon to Nyi ma grags's translation of the *Bodhisattvayogācāracatuḥśatakaṭīkā* indicates that the work was done during the reign of the Kashmiri king Harṣadeva (1089–1101). When Nyi ma grags returned to Tibet, two of the Indian scholars he had worked with in Kashmir, Kanakavarman and Tilakakalaśa, accompanied him. At the Ramoche monastery in Lhasa, he and Kanakavarman compared earlier translations with the original Sanskrit texts that they brought from central India and made the appropriate revisions. Nyi ma grags, in collaboration with several Indian scholars, worked on the revision of his own earlier translations as well as on the translations of Madhyamaka texts prepared by earlier generations of Buddhist scholars. Nyi ma grags continued to teach these texts for many years, until he was well into his eighties (Lang 1990, 132–36).

Four editions of the Tibetan translation exist: Chone vol. Ya, 30b–239b, published in microfiche by the Institute for the Advanced Studies of World Religions, Stonybrook, N.Y., 1974; Derge, vol. Ya, 30b–239a, published by the Faculty of Letters, Tokyo University, 1981; and Peking, vol. Ya, 33b–273b, published by the Tibetan Tripitaka Research Institute, Tokyo and Kyoto, 1956–61. A block-print edition of the Narthang edition is kept at the Library of Tibetan Works and Archives in Dharamsala, India. Many of the variant readings of the four editions are attributable to errors in carving the blocks or differences in orthography, which confirm the close connection between the Peking and Narthang editions and the Derge and Chone editions (Schoening 1995, 1:132–34). Most of these variants involve miscarved letters, added letters, or omissions of vowel signs that would not affect the translation. More significant are variants that indicate the correction of a difficult reading by a simpler one. In the footnotes to the translation I have noted these variations.

Modern Editions, Translations and Studies

Translations into French, Japanese, and English of several chapters from Candrakīrti's commentary have been published. Jacques May (1980–84) has translated chapter 9 into French. Susumu Yamaguchi (1964) has translated chapter 9 into Japanaese, and Ikkyo Ogawa (1977) has translated chapter 11 into Japanese (not seen). Koshin Suzuki (1989) has translated the first part of chapter 1 into English, and Tom Tillemans (1990) has translated chapters 12 and 13 into English. Ruth Sonam (1994) has translated Gyeltsap's commentary on the *Catuḥśataka* into English, along with Geshe Sonam Rinchen's contemporary commentary on the text.

On the English Translation

In addition to the problems caused by the fragmentary nature of the Sanskrit text, the translation of the fragments that have survived presents its own problems. Sanskrit philosophical prose was written for and by an educated elite familiar with the standards of Sanskrit literary style, which prized brevity. This spare style of composition omits not only parts of the sentence but even parts of the argument that could be supplied from the context. The readers of medieval Indian philosophical texts were well acquainted with a common heritage of arguments and illustrations and had access to an oral tradition that explained puzzling points and references. Candrakīrti, in the first half of his commentary, draws upon this common heritage for many of the analogies and short tales that he uses to augment his philosophical points. More than a thousand years later, we are left with parts of a philosophical puzzle that have become increasingly difficult to piece together. We can sometimes recover the meaning of a troublesome passage from the context of connected passages, from similar statements expressed elsewhere in the same text, and from parallel passages in other works by the same author or in subsequent followers of his tradition.

Although the majority of the *Bodhisattvayogācāracatuḥśatakaṭīkā* exists only in Tibetan, Nyi ma grags systematically reproduces in his translations the syntactical patterns of Sanskrit. The precision and consistency of his translation style often make it possible to discern the underlying Sanskrit structure of Candrakīrti's text. I have not, however, followed his example in translating Candrakīrti into English. My intention is to avoid an unnatural "hybrid English" that imitates Sanskrit syntax and taxes the patience of readers unfamiliar with Sanskrit or Tibetan terms. I occasionally transform passive constructions into active ones (and vice versa) and split long, cumbersome sentences into shorter and more manageable ones. Although I cannot claim a translation that renders every passage literally word for word, I have tried not to sacrifice accuracy for a clear and readable text. In particular, I have taken some liberties in translating the stories so that their humor and vigor are not lost. Where parentheses do occur, they mark the addition of words that make the meaning clearer, or they indicate the Sanskrit term when I adopt a nonstandard translation. I have not translated Āryadeva's and Candrakīrti's verses into English equivalents, since such an attempt would emphasize my limitations as a poet. I have used instead an indented four-line format to separate the verses from the prose commentary. The paragraphs into which Candrakīrti's text is divided are not numbered in the original; the section numbers were added to make cross-referencing between the English translation and the Introduction easier. To make the debate format of the text clear, I have identified with "objection" and "response" the relevant sections of the text. The section headings of the translation also have been added to help clarify the topics under discussion.

There is the temptation when translating an old text to make it more relevant to a contemporary audience. Much of what Candrakīrti has to say about mortality, sexuality, pain, and how people create their identities applies universally to people in different times and different places. It is also evident that Candrakīrti's views reflect the culture of his times and are addressed to a specific and more limited audience. His advice on curbing sexual desire, for example, assumes an audience that is primarily male and heterosexual. Whenever possible, I have used gender-neutral and inclusive language. All translations of Sanskrit, Pāli, and Tibetan texts included in the introduction are my own, unless otherwise noted.

I

Introduction

1

TRAVELERS ON THE BUDDHA'S PATH

Stories of Gautama Buddha's life say that he left behind his home and family in search of an answer to the question of why people suffer. Neither his experience of sensual pleasures as a rich man's son nor his experience of harsh austerities as a homeless wanderer brought relief. After he found the answer to his question, he chose the active life of teaching over a quiet life of meditative silence. When asked to teach, he responded with compassionate concern for the well-being of others.[1] He sought out his former companions and told them about a middle path that avoided both self-indulgence and self-torture. In this first discourse (S V 421), the Buddha identified the demands of desire as the basic cause of human suffering: "And this, O monks, is the truth of the arising of suffering. It is this desire, which leads to repeated existence, which is associated with pleasure and passion, and which finds pleasure everywhere." He prescribed a course of treatment to alleviate the pain and restore sufferers to health. The recommended treatment is concerned with alleviating not just physical pain. Equally important is treatment of the mental pain that comes from wanting what is unattainable (immortality) or transient (happiness, beauty, power). The Buddha prescribed a path of action based on ethical conduct, on meditation, and on insight into erroneous beliefs. Erroneous beliefs about gods and heavens perpetuate the illusion of immortality. Erroneous beliefs about acquiring endless quantities of food, drink, sex, and wealth perpetuate the illusion that happiness or beauty or temporal power can endure. The Buddha took his therapeutic message on the road and found converts in the cities and rural areas he traveled through. The new community (*saṃgha*) he formed was linked not by blood ties but by a vision of this world as a disturbing and dangerous place.

The Mahāyāna Movement

The Buddha's teachings became the vehicle that assured people safe passage through the dangers of this world and the next. The preservation and proper interpretation of the Buddha's words were of paramount importance for the first generation of his followers. As the Buddha lay dying, he advised his grieving disciples that they must look to his words for inspiration and guidance after he had gone. Traditional accounts of early Buddhist history record that five hundred of these disciples who had attained the status of saints (*arhat*) met to recite and collect what they had remembered of the Buddha's teachings.[2] These disciples and their students carried his word into new areas and formed new communities. Within a hundred years of the Buddha's death, these diverse monastic communities, led by teachers with their own opinions on the interpretation of his teachings, had developed sectarian identities (Bareau 1955; Dutt 1977).

Around the first century C.E., debate over the interpretation of the Buddha's teachings contributed to the writing and rewriting of discourses (*sūtra*) and scholastic texts (*abhidharma*) with new analyses of the Buddha's teachings. The authors of Abhidharma works shared certain fundamental assumptions about the world and the practice of the Buddha's path. They believed that things (*dharma*) have an inherent existence or nature of their own (*svabhāva*) and that arhats experience Nirvana through their insight into the nature of these things. The movement now known as Mahāyāna (Great Vehicle) criticized the arhats' path as focusing too intently on their self-centered pursuit of Nirvana. Bodhisattvas begin their path with their intention of working for the enlightenment (*bodhi*) of all beings (*sattva*). Mahāyāna supporters claimed that the vehicle of the Bodhisattva is greater because that path balances the individual pursuit of insight with great compassion for others. The authors of Mahāyāna texts rejected the Abhidharma assumption that mental health is associated with the skillful pigeonholing of things into categories, such as healthy and unhealthy (*kuśala, akuśala*). They believed that insight into the empty nature of all things frees the Bodhisattvas' mind from discouragement or depression and enables them to remain actively working in the world. Although the origins of the Mahāyāna movement remain obscure, most scholars agree that it developed in monastic circles. It was not a sectarian movement, since Chinese pilgrims reported that the monks who supported its vision lived in the same monastic institutions as other monks whom they criticized for supporting an inferior path (Williams 2000, 96–111).

Chinese and Tibetan pilgrims followed the trade routes to India, the holy land of Buddhism, visited its sacred sites, and collected texts, which they brought back to their native lands. The fragmentary nature of the few Mahāyāna texts that survive in medieval Sanskrit manuscripts and the piecemeal translation of others into Chinese and Tibetan compound the difficulty of determining the circumstances under which the Mahāyāna movement arose. No historical records attest to the emergence of a charismatic leader. No early Mahāyāna scriptures (*sūtra*) bear an author's name, since the Buddha, seen in visions or revelations, inspired their composition. The unsystematic and diverse teachings in these texts suggests that they were composed in monastic communities separated by geography, language, and philosophy. Monks who traveled from one monastery or pilgrimage place to another carried copies of these scriptures, which became part of an institution's library. The duplication of these scriptures was itself a meritorious act. Learned monks in these institutions around the first century C.E. began to compose Mahāyāna treatises (*śāstra*), which explained the teachings of these scriptures and incorporated them into a systematic philosophy.

Nāgārjuna's Middle Way

Nāgārjuna (ca. second to third centuries C.E.), the best known of these early Mahāyāna philosophers, lived in a monastic community in southern India. In addition to his philosophical works, Nāgārjuna wrote letters to one of the Śatavāhana Dynasty kings encouraging him to adopt the vision of the Mahāyāna.[3] In his most important work, the *Mūlamadhyamakakārikāḥ* (Root Verses on the Middle Way), he uses reason to defend the position that things are empty of any inherent existence of their own and cannot create themselves or sustain themselves without depending on other causes and conditions. The Madhyamaka (Middle Way) school of Buddhist philosophy takes its name from his belief that emptiness (*śūnyatā*) is the middle way between the extreme positions of nihilism and eternalism. Nihilists reject belief in a transmigrating self that experiences the results of actions (*karma*); eternalists believe in the eternal existence of such a self. Nāgārjuna concedes that the eternalist view, which motivates people to do good in hope of a heavenly reward, is better than the nihilist view, but better still is the liberating insight that repudiates both views (RĀ I.43–45). This liberating insight is the proper understanding of emptiness, as explained in Mahāyāna scriptures.

In the *Mūlamadhyamakakārikāḥ*, Nāgārjuna refers to an early Mahāyāna scripture, the *Kāśyapaparivarta* in which the Buddha speaks of the therapeutic value of emptiness. In this text, the Buddha asks Kāśyapa to determine if a patient would be cured under these circumstances: a doctor gives medicine to a patient, but after it cures his symptoms it remains in his bowels without being expelled (KP §95–97). If it remains, Kāśyapa replies, the patient's problems would become worse. The Buddha encourages him to regard emptiness in the same way. Nāgārjuna similarly regards emptiness as a therapeutic antidote to the ill effects of attachment to views:

> The Buddhas have said that
> Emptiness is a purgative for all views.

> But they have said that those who hold
> Emptiness as a view are incurable. (MMK XIII.8)

Emptiness functions like a laxative to free blockages of the mind. After it has accomplished its purpose, there is no reason to continue using it. Nāgārjuna caustically suggests that people who hold on to emptiness will be no better off than the unfortunate patient with chronic constipation. He further condemns the destructive psychological effects of attachment to views in his *Yuktiṣaṣṭīkā* (Sixty Verses on Logic). He warns (vv. 47–51) that engaging in divisive debates makes people vulnerable to attack by the "snakes of the afflictions (*kleśa*)." The snake of desire poisons debaters who want their own views to succeed and the snake of anger attacks them when their opponents' views prevail.

Many of the Buddha's discourses collected in the *Aṭṭhakavagga* condemn the negative consequences of attachment to views. These discourses indicate that by eradicating egotism and remaining constantly mindful, the serious practitioner can calm the mind's development and expansion of concepts and views. The encyclopedic work of Madhyamaka philosophy attributed to Nāgārjuna, the *Ta-chih-tu Lun* (**Mahāprajñāpāramitopadeśa*), quotes the *Aṭṭhakavagga*.[4] The *Aṭṭhakavagga* and the works of Nāgārjuna support restraint of the senses as a means of calming the disruptive effects of the mind's unrestrained activity: "Peace is the calming of all that is perceived, the calming of conceptual development (*prapañca*)" (MMK XXV.24ab). This verse advocates yogic practices that withdraw the mind from all sensory stimuli as a means for calming the mind and controlling its tendency to develop concepts. Insight into the emptiness of things also brings conceptual development to a halt (MMK XVIII.5).

The Bodhisattva's Practice of Yoga

The mental discipline of yoga is an integral part of the Buddha's path. Generations of disciples followed this discipline and created their own guides for fellow travelers on the path. Nāgārjuna's disciple, Āryadeva (ca. 170–270 C.E.)[5] in his *Catuḥśataka* (Four Hundred Verses) charts a gradual course that begins with the Bodhisattva's practice of virtuous actions and culminates in the liberating knowledge of a Buddha. In the *Catuḥśataka*, Āryadeva compares Buddhas and Bodhisattvas with teachers and physicians to illustrate his belief that both skillful teaching techniques and all-encompassing compassion are essential to the task of rescuing people trapped in the vicious cycle of death and rebirth (*saṃsāra*). Their teaching is progressive and tailored to the specific needs and capabilities of each suffering individual. Like physicians who know different remedies for treating their client's complaints, Buddhas and Bodhisattvas also know various methods of treating illnesses and select the most appropriate and most effective one (CŚ V.12–13). They treat with compassion even sick and disturbed patients who abuse them, since, as Āryadeva points out, they see "the mental affliction as the enemy not the person who has the affliction" (CŚ V.9cd). The therapeutic treatment Āryadeva advocates calms all who are disturbed by the fear of death, angered by painful feelings, tormented by sexual desire, and afflicted by arrogance. The *Catuḥśataka's* discussion of Bodhisattvas and their path prepares the ground for the later and better known discussion of this topic in the *Bodhicaryāvatāra* (Introduction to the Practices of a Bodhisattva) of Śāntideva.

Several hundred years after Āryadeva's death, the Madhyamaka philosopher Candrakīrti (ca. 550–650 C.E.)[6] wrote the first full-length commentary on the *Catuḥśataka*. In the full title of Candrakīrti's commentary, the *Bodhisattvayogācāracatuḥśatakaṭīkā*[7] (Commentary to the Four Hundred Verses on the Bodhisattva's Practice of Yoga), the expression "practice of yoga" (*yogācāra*) refers to the mental training of a Bodhisattva and not to the contorted positions of a well-trained and supple body in the strenuous practice of Haṭha Yoga. This mental discipline requires a supple and flexible mind capable of discerning all the contorted positions that an agile imagination might assume. This training, as well as the active pursuit of compassion for people who hold these contorted positions, enables Bodhisattvas to dive in, rescue these people from the "whirlpool of birth in the Lord of Death's realm," and help them cross to safety "in the boat of the Mahāyāna" (§207).

The mental discipline of yoga is necessary to cut through and expose the erroneous beliefs and illusions (*viparyāsa*) that endanger people and keep them trapped in the whirling cycle of death and rebirth (*saṃsāra*). The Buddha identifies four basic illusions that distort reality: the belief that an impermanent thing is permanent, the belief that a painful thing is pleasurable, the belief that an impure thing is pure, and the belief that what is not a self is an enduring self. These verses summarize his teaching:

> People who perceive the impermanent as permanent
> The painful as pleasant, what lacks a self as a self,
> And the pure as impure are assailed by illusions,
> Their minds disturbed and distracted.
> These people harnessed to Māra's yoke, far from a secure state,
> Wander around in the cycle of death and rebirth.
> But when the Buddhas, bearers of light, appear in the world,
> They reveal this teaching that calms all suffering.
> Hearing this will restore these people's minds
> And with insight they perceive the impermanent as impermanent,
> The painful as painful, the selfless as selfless, and the impure as impure.
> Endowed with the right view they transcend all suffering. (A II. 52)

These verses emphasize the painful outcome of adhering to illusions. People whose minds these four illusions disturb remain in perpetual bondage to Māra, the Lord of Death. Only the healing power of the Buddhas' teachings can alleviate their suffering. The Buddhas light the path for people to escape from Māra's yoke. Guided by the light of his path, the Buddha's disciples transform themselves and no longer fear the Lord of Death's power (§10).

"While people's thoughts are upset by the four illusions," the Buddha says (quoted by Candrakīrti in MKV 296), "they will never cross over this unreal cycle of death and rebirth." Candrakīrti explains that these illusions appear as the direct opposite of what disciplined practitioners (*yogin*) know to be true. Ignorant people "think that a young woman's body, the source from which impurities emerge, is pleasurable and that she delights their eyes and their minds. They are pleased because they suppose their thoughts are true in nature. But to yogins her purity is an illusion" (§229). Yogins understand that a woman's body is impure and lust will bring fools pain instead of pleasure. Their superior understanding is related to their practice of meditation. "Yogins reject the illusion of permanence and develop the habit of meditating on impermanence" (§231). They know that impermanent things can never provide any enduring satisfaction and that neither ordinary perception nor logical assertions can prove the existence of a permanent self (§234).

The Lives of Āryadeva and Candrakīrti

The Buddhist tradition regards Āryadeva and Candrakīrti as Bodhisattvas whose compassion and insight help others travel the path that crosses over the ocean of death and rebirth. Sacred biographies or hagiographies of important Buddhist teachers combine facts and historical details about real people with myths, legends, and folktales that often include fictional characters. Much like early legends of the apostles and the saints in the Christian tradition, these hagiographies have their roots in oral tradition and in the art of the storyteller. The Buddha's life has generated numerous hagiographies compiled by pious Buddhists over the millennia and nearly as many modern scholars' attempts to sort out the facts of his life from the storyteller's embellishments. "It is difficult to write a biography of the Buddha that will meet modern criteria," Karen Armstrong writes, "because we have very little information that is historically sound. There is not a single incident in the scriptures which we can honestly affirm to be historically true" (2001, xiii).[8] Although many Buddhists would contest the claim that no incident is historically true, hagiographies are not historical documents. They may contain historically valuable information, but this information is limited. Since multiple accounts of a Buddhist saint's life story contain different, and in some cases contradictory, details, the historian has to look to other sources to confirm this evidence. Hagiography "is to be read as an ideological document, reflecting the religious interests of the community which put the hagiography together" (Williams 2000, 26–27). Hagiographies of Buddhas and Bodhisattvas illustrate the moral values and religious ideals of the Buddhist community.

The hagiographies of Buddhist saints take the Buddha's life as their inspiration and develop its characteristic themes and dramatic structures. The same structural pattern of miraculous feats and rhetorical strategies that emphasize specific moral and intellectual qualities occur in the life stories of Āryadeva and Candrakīrti. The sage Asita's prediction that the young prince would become either a universal monarch or a Buddha (BC I.81) exposes the tension between the highest goals of secular and religious life that persist throughout the multiple versions of the Buddha's life, in the lives of other Buddhist saints, and in the scholastic treatises of Āryadeva and Candrakīrti.[9] In particular, Prince Siddhārtha's choice of the open spaces of the forest over the confines of his palatial home and his adoption of pure (nonsexual) behavior over the impure (sexual) behavior of a householder corresponds to much of the advice given in the first four chapters of Āryadeva's *Catuḥśataka* and in Candrakīrti's commentary on it. The hagiographies of Āryadeva and Candrakīrti present complementary versions of the religious beliefs and practices that their scholastic treatises advocate.

The Life of Āryadeva

The earliest information we have about the life of Āryadeva occurs in the hagiography translated into Chinese by the Central Asian monk Kumārajīva (344–413 C.E.). It tells us that he was born into a Brahmin family in south India and became the spiritual son of Nāgārjuna. Āryadeva became so skilled in debate that he could defeat all his opponents and convert them to Buddhism. One defeated teacher's student sought him out and murdered him in the forest where he had retired to write. The dying Āryadeva forgave him and converted him to Buddhism with an eloquent discourse on suffering (Robinson 1967, 27; Yamakami 1912, 187–94). We see the storyteller's influence clearly in the final episode of the dramatic conflict between the compassionate Buddhist monk and his embittered assailant. This hagiography depicts Āryadeva as a Bodhisattva, whose final act demonstrates his great compassion and his insight into Buddhist teachings on suffering.

The Chinese pilgrim Hsüan-tsang's record of his journey to India in the seventh century C.E. relates several similar legends (Beal [1884] 1984, 1.188–9; 2.97–99, 209–12). He reports that Āryadeva came to south India from the island of Siṃhala because of his compassion for the ignorant people of India. He met the aging Nāgārjuna at his residence on Black Bee Mountain, located southwest of the Śatavāhana capital, and became his most gifted student. Nāgārjuna helped Āryadeva prepare for debate against Brahmanical teachers who had defeated Buddhist monks in the northeastern city of Vaiśali for the previous twelve years. Āryadeva went to Vaiśali and defeated all his opponents in less than an hour.

The Tibetan religious histories of Bu ston (1290–1364) and Tāranātha (b. 1575) augment the brief biographical information in Candrakīrti's commentary: "Āryadeva was born on the island of Siṃhala as the son of the

Siṃhala king. In the end he renounced his status as crown prince and entered the religious life. He then traveled to southern India and became Nāgārjuna's disciple" (§4). According to Bu ston, Āryadeva was miraculously born inside a lotus on the island of Siṃhala and adopted by its king. After he grew up, he renounced his position as crown prince and traveled to India, where he studied with Nāgārjuna and mastered all the teachings of Buddhist and Brahmanical schools. Because of his mastery over these texts, the monks at Nālandā requested his help in defeating in debate Mātṛceṭa, a follower of the Hindu god Śiva (Obermiller 1931–32, 2.130–31). Tāranātha rejects as fictional Bu ston's description of Āryadeva's miraculous birth. He reports that Āryadeva was born to the Siṃhala king, Pañcasṛṅga, renounced his claim to the throne, and was ordained by Hemadeva. While on pilgrimage to India, he met Nāgārjuna, who entrusted to him all his teachings. Tāranātha's version of Mātṛceṭa's defeat indicates that Āryadeva used oil to rub out the chalk answers on Mātṛceṭa's slate, a cat to devour a parrot trained to debate, and a brazen layman who exposed himself to prompt Mātṛceṭa's learned female associate to leave. Deprived of all help, the defeated Mātṛceṭa was confined in a temple library and converted by the Buddha's word. Āryadeva returned to teach in southern India and passed on his knowledge to his student, Rahulabhadra, before his death near the city of Kāñcī (Chimpa and Chattopadhyaya 1970, 23–26; Sonam 1994, 19–15). Other hagiographies add new details to these stories and supplement them with new episodes:

> Mātṛceṭa and his followers were performing ritual ablutions in the Ganges for the purposes of purification. Āryadeva came down to the river carrying a golden pot and ostentatiously began to wash the outside of it. Mātṛceṭa asked him why he was washing the outside of it when the inside was full of excrement. Āryadeva replied, "What is the use of washing your body with water from the Ganges, when you are full of defilements?" (Thurman 1984, 37–38; cf. Sonam 1994, 13–15)

This encounter of Āryadeva with Brahmins obsessed with their purity corresponds to his views on purity in the *Catuḥśataka* (III.18–24) and with the amusing stories Candrakīrti tells about people who are full of excrement (§20, §318, §326, §330).

The Life of Candrakīrti

Stories about Candrakīrti's amazing abilities were in circulation when his works were first translated into Tibetan in the eleventh century. The colophon to his *Madhyamakāvatāra* (Introduction to the Middle Way) tells of his drawing milk from a painting of a cow (MĀ 409).[10] The religious histories of Bu ston and Tāranātha tell this story and others, which depict him as being able to move his hand through stone pillars and walk unimpeded through walls. According to Bu ston and Tāranātha, Candrakīrti was born in south India and entered a monastery, where he mastered all the Buddhist scriptures. Tārānātha adds that he was born in Samanta during the reign of King Śīla, the son of Śrīharṣa (Chimpa and Chattopadhyaya 1970, 206). He took a special interest in Nāgārjuna's treatises and studied them with the disciples of two rival interpreters, Bhāvaviveka and Buddhapālita. He preferred Buddhapālita's interpretations of Madhyamaka teachings and defended them in a famous debate with the grammarian Candragomin, who supported the idealist position of the Vijñānavāda (Doctrine of Consciousness) school (Obermiller 1932, 2.134–35; Chimpa and Chattopadhyaya 1970, 198–99, 203–6; Thurman 1984, 40–41).

Geshe Wangyal's contemporary retelling of these stories emphasizes Candrakīrti's skill in persuading skeptical fellow Buddhists to adopt his way of thinking:

> One day, while circumambulating the main temple at Nālandā, Candrakīrti hit his head on a pillar. A scholar who was with him asked, "You are the believer in the self-naturelessness of both persons and phenomena. Why, then, does anything happen when your head hits the column?" The Bodhisattva replied, "Column? What column?" and put his hand through the column as though it were not there. Another time there was an extremely heavy rainy season, and all the cows sought shelter deep in the jungle. The monks wanted milk and said to Candrakīrti, "If everything is really without an intrinsic nature of its own, why don't you get us some milk from that picture of a cow?" Candrakīrti milked the cow in the picture and presented the milk to the Sangha. In such ways he led many followers of the other Mahayana schools to the Prāsaṅgika-Mādhyamika. (Wangyal 1978, 28)

Geshe Wangyal's version of the stories provides the philosophical subtext to Candrakīrti's actions. Candrakīrti's actions demonstrate in a concrete and dramatic form the Madhyamaka position that things have no immutable nature of their own. Candrakīrti repudiates a skeptical monk's belief that solidity is the inherent nature of stone when he thrusts his hand through a stone column. He further proves his point that all things lack any inherent nature when he procures milk from the picture of a cow. All versions of Candrakīrti's life story describe how he converts both Buddhist and Brahmanical skeptics to the Madhyamaka point of view through his ability to perform miraculous feats that undermine the false solidity on which people base their beliefs. These extraordinary stories have survived for centuries because they can communicate the complex ideas of Madhyamaka philosophy in a uncomplicated manner.

The Claims of Hagiography

The incredible stories found in Tibetan historical sources and biographies prompted Giuseppe Tucci to complain that human events have nothing to do with such biographies and that the historian must resign himself to go through hundreds of pages to find an important piece of information. Most hagiographies are not wholesale fabrications of invented lives. Factual information is mixed with miraculous feats to create a story to educate and encourage its audience. Janet Gyatso, who takes a more charitable view of Tibetan life histories, writes that these stories presume or suggest that their protagonists reached "full liberation," and these life stories are told as examples for others to follow (Gyatso 1998, 103). The hagiographies portray exemplary individuals whose lives embody moral and intellectual values that make them worthy of admiration, if not veneration. The deliberate reworking and reconstruction of these celebrated lives enables these narratives to remain vital to the life of a religious community.

Hagiography, Edith Wyschogrod observes, is "lived forward." Buddhist accounts of saints with their background assumption of many lives, presuppose that saints' moral and meditation practices are forward-directed, with liberation from rebirth and suffering as their goal. The extraordinary claims of hagiography are, Wyschogrod explains, "rendered believable through the believability of context" (1990, 27–29). The extraordinary claims made in these hagiographies of Āryadeva and Candrakīrti gain credibility through the context in which they occur. Implicit in all these accounts is the believer's conviction that Āryadeva and Candrakīrti are Bodhisattvas, the spiritual exemplars of the Buddhist tradition. The compassion that Āryadeva extends to the man about to take his life and the generosity Candrakīrti demonstrates in feeding the entire monastic community are virtues that Bodhisattvas exemplify and perfect. These idealized life portraits of Āryadeva and Candrakīrti share a common purpose in inspiring the faithful. The variant versions of their life stories concur in their emphasis on their subjects' impressive intellectual abilities, their skill in mastering and teaching Buddhist texts, their compassion for others, and their skill in making converts. These sources portray them as giving unselfishly whatever is requested of them and as willing to use any means (even magical) to introduce others to the truth. Āryadeva and Candrakīrti skillfully use the miraculous powers they have acquired through meditation to convince others to accept the Buddha's liberating message and follow his path to reach full liberation.

Candrakīrti's Commentaries

The medium of the message often took the form of verses or short prose passages that could be easily memorized and passed on from one generation of disciples to the next. The aphoristic prose or verse of the original or "root" texts required oral and written commentaries to clarify and elaborate ambiguous and overly concise wording and to impose a structural unity on the text. An extensive commentarial literature developed around the debate between the various Buddhist and Brahmanical schools over metaphysical theories on the nature of the persons and things that make up the world, as well as on the ethical and psychological practices that were considered most effective in breaking the bonds of this world. These commentaries, modeled on traditional oral explanations of texts, often paraphrase individual words and analyze the components of compounds and the grammatical relations between them before commenting on the philosophical points raised by the statement in question. Candrakīrti exhibits in his commentaries the grammatical prowess the hagiographies attribute to him in his debates with Candragomin. In these commentaries on Nāgārjuna's and Āryadeva's verses, however, he keeps to a minimum these technical explanations of grammatical details and concentrates on exposing the weaknesses of his opponents' positions.

Nāgārjuna and Āryadeva were convinced that they were preserving the true "middle way" of the Buddha's teachings, whereas other Buddhists had strayed from it and adopted extreme positions. Candrakīrti acknowledges his indebtedness to Nāgārjuna in the opening lines of his *Prasannapadā* (Clear Words) commentary on the *Mūlamadhyamakakārikāḥ*:

> I bow before Nāgārjuna,
> Born in the ocean of the Buddhas' wisdom,
> Who has abandoned the abode of the two extremes,
> And with compassion taught the profound nature
> Of the treasury of the true teaching according to his understanding.
> The flames of his philosophy burn his adversaries' opinions as fuel
> And even now they burn away the darkness in peoples' minds.
> Like a shower of arrows, his words of incomparable intelligence
> Completely destroy the enemy army of the cycle of birth and death,
> And reign in splendor over the three realms, over the world
> Of his disciples, including kings. (MKV 1–2)

Candrakīrti characterizes Nāgārjuna's philosophy as a philosophical middle way that avoids the two extremes of nihilism, the position that actions done in this life have no moral consequences in the next, and eternalism, the position that an eternal soul experiences these consequences.

In addition to the *Prasannapadā* Candrakīrti wrote commentaries on two of Nāgārjuna's other works: *Śūnyatāsaptativṛtti* (Commentary on Seventy Verses on Emptiness) and the *Yuktiṣaṣṭīkāvṛtti* (Commentary on Sixty Verses on Logical Reasoning). He also composed two independent works, the *Madhyamakāvatāra* and an Abhidharma text, the *Pañcaskandhakaprakaraṇa* (Five Divisions).[11] We find few clues for determining the chronology of these works. His quotation of the *Madhyamakāvatāra* in both his commentaries on the *Mūlamadhyamakakārikāḥ* and the *Catuḥśataka* suggests that these commentaries were later compositions.

The terse and sometimes enigmatic verses of Nāgārjuna's work has led to divergent interpretations among the classical schools of Madhyamaka thought and has also produced a spate of modern books and articles proposing various interpretations of his philosophy that literally run the gamut from a (absolutism) to z (zerology).[12] Candrakīrti's own work indicates that he is familiar with the divergent interpretations of Nāgārjuna's and Āryadeva's verses set forth by Buddhapālita (470–540 C.E.) and Bhāvaviveka (500–70 C.E.)—rival interpreters of the Madhyamaka school—and Dharmapāla (530–61 C.E.), a teacher of Vijñānavāda.[13] Little is known about Buddhapālita's life; his major work was his extensive commentary on Nāgārjuna's *Mūlamadhyamakakārikāḥ*. Bhāvaviveka, probably born in south India, wrote a lengthy commentary on Nāgārjuna's verses called the *Prajñāpradīpa* (Lamp of Insight). He also wrote several original works, chief among them the *Madhyamakahṛdayakārikāḥ* (Verses on the Heart of the Middle Way) and his own commentary on this work, the *Tarkajvāla* (Blaze of Reason).[14]

Candrakīrti's Methods of Argument

The distinction now taken for granted in discussing the views of Buddhapālita and Bhāvaviveka and in classifying their works—Svātantrika versus Prāsaṅgika—developed late in Buddhist textual history, perhaps not until the eleventh century, when sPa shab Nyi ma grags began to translate and teach the *Prasannapadā* and Candrakīrti's other major works in Tibet (Lang 1990). These two classifications refer to the Svātantrika school's acceptance of independent (*svatantra*) inferences in philosophical debate and the Prāsaṅgika school's rejection of such inferences in favor of reducing opponents' arguments to absurd consequences (*prasaṅga*). Although Candrakīrti did not use these terms himself, they provide convenient labels for his ideas and those of Buddhapālita. He contends that the reductio ad absurdum method only shows the absurd consequences to which his opponents' propositions invariably lead and does not require that he prove a competing thesis of his own. Candrakīrti's rejection of philosophical propositions does not indicate his ignorance of the rules that determine whether one side or another prevails in debate. He knows the formal criteria set down in the works of the Buddhist logicians and in the manuals of the Brahmanical Nyāya school for judging the soundness of an argument. He uses these criteria to demonstrate the technical flaws in his opponents' inferences and arguments.

Nāgārjuna says that when an argument or an explanation based on emptiness is put forth, an opponent's attempt to refute or criticize it will fail, since any reason that an opponent might employ to refute the Madhyamaka thesis of emptiness will have the same uncertain status as the proposition he wants to prove (MMK IV.8–9). Candrakīrti explains that the opponent cannot prove the existence of the form aggregate by using as his reason the existence of other four aggregates, because they are as much in need of proof as form (MKV 127–28).[15] An unproven reason cannot prove any proposition. Whether this opponent's response is interpreted as a logical fallacy or as a futile rejoinder, as the Indian logician B. K. Matilal (1974) believes, the result is the same: the Madhyamaka thesis of emptiness remains unrefuted. Jay Garfield contends that Nāgārjuna and Candrakīrti claim that once the emptiness of any phenomenon has been proven, any reply will inevitably beg the question (1995, 147–48). In other words, once something is established as being empty of inherent existence (*svabhāva*), the opponent who wants to prove that it has inherent existence must either presuppose that it is independent and uncaused or that some other inherently existent thing has produced it, and the inherent existence of that other thing must also be demonstrated. Matilal disagrees that the logical fallacy of begging the question or circular reasoning is at issue here. Rather than the conclusion being assumed in the premises, he argues that when Nyāya and Madhyamaka authors use the technical expression "having the same predicament with proposition to be proved" (*sādhya-sama*), they mean to say that the reason needs to be established beyond doubt before it could establish any another proposition.[16]

Candrakīrti's rejection of his opponents' methods follows also from his unwillingness to support a philosophical system whose assertions categorize things in dualistic terms. Debate produces in its participants the proponent's attachment to his own thesis and his aversion to that of his opponent. Candrakīrti cites with approval this verse from Nāgārjuna's *Yuktiṣaṣṭikā* that criticizes continuing debates:

> Those who hold that everything is impermanent
> Remain on the Buddha's path.
> It is surprising that one who has analyzed a thing
> Keeps on debating. (§228)

Nāgārjuna, in the *Yuktiṣaṣṭikā,* associates attachment to views with the afflictions of desire and anger. People who take sides in debate are open to attack by the "snakes of the afflictions," but the poison of these afflictions cannot affect people who refuse to take a stand (vv. 51–52). Āryadeva similarly advises against partiality, since there is no peace for people who engage in disputes (CŚ VIII.10). The injunction to reject attachment to views is part of the psychological progress of undermining attachment to the false ideas of "I" and "mine." The ultimate triumph over suffering is a far more worthy goal than the temporary pleasure of triumphing over an opponent in debate.

Candrakīrti's Use of Scriptural Authority

Despite his reservations about the logical and psychological consequences of debates, Candrakīrti acknowledges that inference is one of four commonly accepted means of knowledge. The proper analysis of things, Candrakīrti says, is undertaken with four means of knowledge: perception, inference in cases where things are not directly perceptible, comparison, and scriptural authority, which he defines as the testimony of reliable people who know things that are not accessible to ordinary perception (MKV 71–75). When perception and inference fail to give certain knowledge about things that are beyond the scope of the senses, the scriptural authority of the Buddha should be relied upon.[17] In particular, the empty and illusory character of things can be understood best through scriptural testimony, which provides examples for understanding this profound teaching.

Candrakīrti relies on scriptural testimony as "proof texts" that supplement the reasoned arguments he presents in his commentaries on the verses of Nāgārjuna and Āryadeva. He uses quotations from scripture to provide examples that further clarify and strengthen his position. Toward the end of his commentary to the second chapter of the *Catuḥśataka* (§239), he quotes the following verses from some mainstream version of the Buddha's discourses (= S III 142–43):

> Form is like a mass of foam, feeling is like a bubble.
> Karmic formations are like a banana tree's core.
> And consciousness is like a magical illusion.
> Thus, the energetic monk, fully aware and mindful,
> While he investigates things day and night,
> Should enter the tranquil state,
> The bliss, which is the calming of karmically constructed forces.

Candrakīrti juxtaposes these verses on the nonsubstantial nature of the five aggregates (*skandha*) with similar verses from the Mahāyāna *Samādhirājāsūtra* (§240). In the narrative core of this text, the Buddha answers Prince Candraprabha's questions about how he might attain the perfect knowledge that Buddhas possess. The Buddha responds that such knowledge is attained through meditative concentration, which he describes as a tolerant attitude toward the fact that all things neither arise nor cease, that all things share the same empty nature and are like dreams and illusions. The *Samādhirājāsūtra* employs tolerance or patience in two senses: the patience a person must have when criticized by others and tolerance in the sense of a receptive attitude toward the doctrine that all things share the same empty nature. Eliminating the afflictions of desire, anger, and delusion (*moha*) requires both tolerance and a receptive state of mind. A Bodhisattva becomes skilled in this tolerant attitude by recognizing that all things are like illusions, dreams, mirages, echoes, reflections of the moon in water, mirrored images, magical creations, and so on. With this tolerant attitude, Bodhisattva is not attracted, repulsed, or deluded by things that could be objects of desire, anger, or delusion.

Candrakīrti's Commentary on the *Catuḥśataka*

Āryadeva's *Catuḥśataka* requires a commentary to explain its concise and sometimes cryptic verses. Candrakīrti organizes his commentary around a teacher's traditional oral explanations of texts and the practice of oral debates. He constructs a lively debate between Āryadeva and various opponents on the nature of the people and the things that make up the world. In this commentary, Candrakīrti displays the wide range of his knowledge. In the first half of his commentary, he shows his familiarity with popular literature—stories of the Buddha's past births (*jātaka*) and stories from the Hindu epics, the *Rāmāyaṇa* and the *Mahābhārata*. The last half of his commentary shows his insight into the religious and philosophical literature of his Buddhist, Brahmanical, and Jaina opponents. His commentary provides the model for the much shorter fifteenth-century commentaries of the Tibetan scholars rGyal tshab and Red mda' ba, whose detailed topical outlines add an additional organizational layer to Āryadeva's *Catuḥśataka*. Candrakīrti's influence also extends to the three early-twentieth-century Tibetan commentators on the *Catuḥśataka* (Sonam 1994, 22–27).

The *Catuḥśataka* and its commentary present the path to the attainment of Buddhahood, structured around the accumulation of the two requisites of merit (*puṇya*) and knowledge (*jñāna*). These two accumulations, as Nāgārjuna says in the *Ratnāvalī*, quickly eliminate mental and physical suffering and bring about Buddhahood (III.13, 21). The first eight chapters of Āryadeva's *Catuḥśataka* and Candrakīrti's *Bodhisattvayogācāracatuḥśatakaṭīkā* concern the accumulation of merit; the last eight focus on the acquisition of knowledge. The teachings in the first half of these works gradually prepare aspiring Bodhisattvas to receive knowledge about the empty and nonsubstantial nature of persons and things, which is discussed in greater detail in the last eight chapters. Candrakīrti describes the topic of the first half as "virtuous practices" (*dharma*) and the topic of the last half as "philosophical disputes" (*vivāda*) (§2). In this division of the work, Āryadeva and Candrakīrti recognize that practitioners of different abilities make progress along the path in accordance with their own capacities. They endorse methods and practices that correspond to these individuals' varying abilities. In the *Catuḥśataka*, Āryadeva advises that people of slight abilities should practice generosity, people of middling abilities should engage in moral conduct, and people of the highest ability should cultivate tranquillity (CŚ VIII.14). The teaching itself is gradual and adapted to the capacity of each individual. It is important first, Candrakīrti advises, to reject all nonmeritorious (*apuṇya*) actions; second, to reject all philosophical theories that claim the self is in any way related to the mental and physical aggregates that make up human identity; and finally, it is most important for intelligent people to reject all attachment, even to the aggregates, by understanding that all things are empty of any inherent nature (P 155b–156a).

The Authors' Intentions

Āryadeva's reasons for composing the *Catuḥśataka* come from his aspiration to help others understand the dangers of the world and its transient pleasures. Candrakīrti lends support to the idea that Āryadeva is a Bodhisattva who guides others on the path to reach perfect enlightenment when he describes Āryadeva's motive for writing the *Catuḥśataka*:

> Āryadeva's intention was to make disciples, who are born into the world of the three realms and who are vast as the sky, disenchanted with the cycle of death and rebirth. His intention also was to lead them by means of nondual knowledge toward a pure realm, unsurpassed perfect enlightenment, which has great compassion as its cause. (§203)

Āryadeva intends to expose the illusions that enchant people and keep them trapped in the relentless cycle of death and rebirth. Disenchantment with the world becomes the motivation for disciples to enter the Buddha's path. The path ends with the attainment of a Buddha's perfect enlightenment. Buddhas, as Candrakīrti explains in the *Madhyamakāvatāra* start out as Bodhisattvas, and Bodhisattvas begin their journey with "a compassionate mind, nondual knowledge and a mind directed toward enlightenment (*bodhicitta*)" (I.1). Nondual knowledge (*advaya-jñāna*) steers a middle path between the belief that things exist as they appear to ordinary perception and the belief that things lack even nominal existence.[18]

Candrakīrti explains that the main purpose of his commentary is a gradual exploration of the reality of things: "After first analyzing how ordinary things really exist, gradually, ultimate reality will be explained" (§1). This analysis of the real nature of ordinary things prepares the way for a supple and flexible mind to receive the profound teachings about the nondual and empty nature of all things. Buddhas have the proper remedies for repairing the damage that ignorance had inflicted on ordinary people's perception of things. "Buddhas, skilled in the liberating methods of great compassion," Candrakīrti comments, "teach the views of impermanence, pain, impurity, and nonself as remedies for the four illusions, the views of permanence, pleasure, purity, and self" (§242). This medicinal knowledge removes the veil of ignorance from peoples' eyes and enables them to see things as they really are.

Candrakīrti also criticizes the poet Dharmapāla for separating the text into two parts instead of treating it as a single unified work. When Candrakīrti describes Dharmapāla as a poet, he may be using the term in a derogatory manner.[19] He writes that he intends to take the treatise "as a whole, as it was meant to be" and explain all the verses of the *Catuḥśataka*'s sixteen chapters (§2). He faults Dharmapāla for commenting just on the last eight chapters of Āryadeva's text. Candrakīrti has "the tapestry of the whole" (Griffiths 1999, 96) in mind and occasionally uses verses from the second half of the text to support his comments on individual verses in the first four chapters. He charges Dharmapāla with being "very confused" because he explains Āryadeva's verses from the perspective of Vijñānavāda and fails understand that there is no difference between Nāgārjuna's and Āryadeva's explanations of Madhyamaka philosophy (§4).[20] Dharmapāla's division of the text into two also reveals his ignorance of "the fact that the two truths are interconnected and integral parts of a whole" (Sonam 1994, 22–23). Candrakīrti implies that he is on the wrong path:

> Those outside the path of Nāgārjuna
> Have no means of achieving tranquillity.
> They are misled about conventional and ultimate truth,
> And because they are misled they do not attain liberation.
> Conventional truth is the means
> And ultimate truth is the result of that means.
> Whoever does not know the difference between these two[21]
> Enters the wrong path because of that false conception. (§219)

Candrakīrti supports the position of Nāgārjuna (MMK XXIV.8–10) that the ultimate truth of Nirvana is approached through conventional truth. Conventional truth reflects the experience of ordinary people and is expressed through ordinary language. "Just as it is impossible to make a foreigner understand in a language that is different from his own," Āryadeva says, "it is impossible to make people of this world understand without reference to worldly things," (CŚ VIII.19). Language is the means that shows the path leading to ultimate reality. People who fail to understand that language has no further utility once the goal has been reached, however, remain inextricably trapped within the labyrinth of language. Candrakīrti asserts that exceptional practitioners (*ārya*) regard things that appear real to ordinary people as merely conventionally true; they perceive the emptiness of those things as ultimate truth (MĀ 108). Direct and personal experience (*pratyātmavedya*) enables them to apprehend ultimate truth, which transcends the limits of language and dualistic thought.[22]

The Audience for Candrakīrti's Work

Candrakīrti's work was composed and preserved in monastic circles and even now forms part of the curriculum in Tibetan Buddhist monasteries. The audience for his commentary, like those Paul Griffiths describes as the ideal readers of the Vijñānavāda philosopher, Sthiramati (ca. 470–550 C.E.), were likely to be "people (men almost certainly and monks very probably) being trained in a particular scholastic tradition" (Grififiths 1999, 143). Candrakīrti's explicit criticism of Dharmapāla, Vasubandhu, and Bhāvaviveka suggests that he had in mind fellow monks whose scholastic traditions he did not support. Although the last half of his *Catuḥśatakaṭīkā* concerns philosophical disputes, he launches a lengthy attack on the Abhidharma beliefs of Vasubandhu in the second chapter of this work.

The practical advice Candrakīrti offers the king on politics, as well as the numerous amusing stories and examples he incorporates the first half of this commentary, suggests that his audience may not have been limited to monastic circles. His criticism of people who seek satisfaction and stability in the householder's life addresses neophyte monks susceptible to the lures of lay life, but it could also address educated male householders. The structure of his commentary, its length and sophisticated arguments, assume an educated audience familiar with a broad range of Indian literature. He refers to Buddhist philosophical works known to a small group of educated monastics and to stories of the Buddha's previous lives familiar to both lay and monastic audiences. He also utilizes legal and political treatises, secular love poetry, and the epics—the *Mahābhārata* and the *Rāmāyaṇa*—in his demonstration of the superior merits of Buddhism. The brevity of some of these references indicates that Candrakīrti assumes that his audience is already familiar with the arguments or with the story line.

Candrakīrti's arguments, especially in the first half of his commentary instruct the ordinary person—whether lay or monastic—in *dharma*, the virtuous practices, the generous and moral acts that mark the beginning of the Buddhist path and lead to a good rebirth. The fourth chapter, addressed an unnamed Indian king, suggests that politics is a nasty business (*adharma*) and likely to result in the king's rebirth in hell. In addition to quoting the words of the Buddha as support of his position, Candrakīrti broadens the appeal of his arguments by extending the range of examples he uses to prove them.

Candrakīrti the Storyteller

Like the Buddha before him, Candrakīrti uses both reasoned arguments and persuasive stories to guide people along the path. Arguments in Indian philosophical texts frequently employ analogies. Knowledge about something is inferred from its observed similarity to something else; and the structure of an inferential argument is incomplete without the use of examples, both positive and negative. Given this importance of analogy and example in the Indian philosophical tradition, it is not surprising to find that Āryadeva uses them to reinforce his philosophical arguments in the *Catuḥśataka*. Candrakīrti, in his exegesis of the first half of the *Catuḥśataka*, in place of the standard examples required in the formulation of sound inferences, substitutes stories that provide, in a less formal manner, proof of the validity of Buddhist moral precepts. The commentarial text in which these stories are embedded is organized around an informal debate on the topics of death, pleasure, sensual desire, and egotism.

Candrakīrti's Use of the Narrative Genre

At issue here is why a philosopher known for his learned commentaries on philosophically sophisticated texts should cite curious and often amusing stories about promiscuous women, ruthless kings, and hapless fools. This intrusion of popular stories into philosophical arguments raises the same questions about genre that Wendy Doniger O'Flaherty addresses when she speaks of philosophy's intrusion into the stories of the *Yogavāsiṣṭha.* An Indian audience "sees the philosophical argument as the basic genre and the stories set into it like gems, as focal points, as moments when the philosophy gathers momentum and breaks out of a problem it cannot solve into a mode of thinking that at least allows it to state the problem and share it in a parable" (O'Flaherty 1980b, 128). The lines of demarcation between story and argument for Indian authors and their audience are not sharply drawn. The decision to use stories, in addition to philosophical arguments, may also indicate an author's intention to communicate in a more direct and immediate way. "The story," as Sally McFague points out, "is a public genre, inviting participation, empathy, identification" (1975, 122). A story captures the audience's attention and focuses that rapt attention on a problem more readily than does the detached logic of formal argument. In a tradition that describes the path as a gradual one, the use of stories becomes a skillful means of attracting the ordinary person's interest.

Charles Hallisey draws attention to the scholarly bias against narrative literature. The consensus of scholars is that sophisticated Buddhists employ stories to communicate doctrines that the Buddhist laity could not otherwise understand, and that these stories have frequently distorted Buddhist doctrine and should not be taken as representative of "real" Buddhist thought. Hallisey argues that a restrictive view of story literature as "unimportant folk tales that have little to do with the profoundly philosophical corpus" fails to take into account the ethical significance of the genre or the content of the stories themselves (Hallisey and Hansen 1996, 309–10). Edmund Leach makes a similar point when he suggests that, apart from parables in rabbinical commentaries, Buddhist stories about events in the previous lives of the Buddha offer the closest approximation to the New Testament style of homiletic teaching. Though he concedes that none of the 547 *Jātaka* stories in the Theravāda Buddhist tradition directly parallels in content or structure any of the New Testament parables, he finds the general form and "apparent moral implication" similar in many cases. The Christian definition of parables as plain tales about ordinary human beings would exclude *Jātaka* stories in which animals are the main characters (Leach 1983). Leach leaves unanswered the problems he raises, but a closer look at these stories suggests that these problems are more apparent than real. The *Jātaka* stories in which animals are the main characters tell us nothing at all about animal behavior. Stories that seem to be about rabbits are in fact stories about situations that face human beings. Hallisey suggests that using animals as "ethical exemplars" provides a skillful way of discussing moral virtues without specific references to caste and gender (Hallisey and Hansen 1996, 312–13).

Candrakīrti cites an abbreviated version of the *Kukkura Jātaka* (Ja I 175–78 no. 22) in his *Catuḥśatakaṭīkā* (P 110). The Bodhisattva, reborn as a dog, prevents an angry king from slaughtering all the city's dogs. The dog teaches the king about Buddhism, and from that time on the king protects the lives of all creatures within his kingdom. In this story a dog exemplifies the virtues of compassion and nonviolence (*ahiṃsā*). Most examples and stories that Candrakīrti cites in his commentary illustrate the consequences of foolish behavior. Although Candrakīrti is not at all hesitant to make use of stories that criticize the character flaws of high-caste Brahmins and women, he also uses animal stories to make his point about human weaknesses: "Also, a crow entered the carcass of an elephant. Because it had rained, a flooding river disturbed that corpse; and the crow also died in that very place. That elephant was of little value and the danger was great" (§194). He provides a brief explanatory gloss that identifies "foolish ordinary people" who indulge themselves with sensual pleasures with the hapless crow gorging itself on the elephant's bloated carcass. Like the doomed crow, they fail to see the danger of their greed and will die in "the great ocean of the cycle of death and rebirth."

Candrakīrti's Stories and Their Sources

The stories that Candrakīrti uses to augment his philosophical arguments are not allegorical, with one exception:

> A man chased by an elephant in the wilderness fell into an old well. Halfway down he broke his fall by grabbing hold of a *durva* vine whose roots rats were devouring. On all sides, snakes stretched out; and down below a large python uncoiled itself. Because he had tasted a drop of honey that had fallen from above, he considered himself happy. (§194)

He uses this story to make the point that ordinary people, blinded by the illusion of pleasure, fail to perceive the suffering present in all human existence. Each of the metaphoric elements of this improbable story has an allegorical function. Although each metaphor has a significance of its own, the interrelation of all them delivers the full impact of the story's message. Candrakīrti explains that the man in this story represents all ordinary human beings, and the wilderness represents the cycle of birth and death. The elephant stands for death; the well, old age; the python, hell; and the other snakes, the afflictions of negative thoughts. The vine that prevents the man from falling into hell is the path of virtuous actions. The rats signify the ongoing process of the maturation of karma, which gnaws away at these actions. The drop of honey illustrates the deceptively sweet taste of sensual pleasures.

Some of these stories now appear both obscure and inappropriate. This may be the case because we do not know the original context of these stories, recycled out of the Indian past. Candrakīrti says that he acquired them from Dharmadāsa's earlier work, which unfortunately has not survived (§8).[23] The unknown authors of the *Bodhisattvapiṭaka* (Collected Texts on the Bodhisattva) also made extensive use of examples, parables, and stories about the Buddha's previous births in the chapters of this work that illustrate the Bodhisattva's career. These birth stories illustrate the ideal training of a Bodhisattva by using the model of the Buddha's own spiritual experience (Pagel 1995, 84–89). A few of the stories that Candrakīrti uses have parallels in the canonical collection of stories about the Buddha's previous births. Many of them are part of the common heritage of Indian folklore. Their Buddhist affiliation comes from the *Jātaka* commentary, which clarifies the moral point of the tale and identifies the hero as the Buddha in a past life. Archaeological evidence indicates that some of these stories were well known in the third to second centuries B.C.E. and were carved in bas relief on the monuments at the Buddhist sites of Sāñci, Amarāvati, and Bhārhut.[24] Artisans also painted and inscribed scenes and verses from Ārya Śura's *Jātakamālā* (Garland of Birth Stories) in the Buddhist caves at Ajanta (Khoroche 1980, xi–xix).

In addition to these well-known Buddhist stories, Candrakīrti refers also to popular stories from the *Rāmāyaṇa* and the *Mahābhārata* and to stories as yet unidentified. He uses the familiar story of the demon Rāvaṇa's abduction of Rāma's wife, Sītā (§113). He quotes verses from the *Rāmāyaṇa* that describe how Śunaḥśepa's Brahmin father sold him to King Ambarīṣa for use as a human sacrifice to the gods (§35). Candrakīrti also cites stories from the *Mahābhārata* that show Brahmin priests in an unfavorable light. The ravenous Viśvamitra stole and devoured the flesh of a dog. Consumed by anger at the theft of a calf, Jāmadagnya cut the arms off Arjuna Kārtavīrya and killed him (§407).

The explanatory material at the end of the *Jātaka* stories, which identify the Buddha and his human companions with the main characters, provides the framework for a Buddhist audience to interpret the stories' message. Similarly, Candrakīrti provides a brief explanation that links the story in question with the point he wants to his audience to take. Rāma's anguish at the loss of his wife proves the power of pain. The immoral actions of Viśvamitra and Jāmadagnya prove that Brahmin sages should not be regarded as moral exemplars. Candrakīrti's use of these narratives in his commentary challenges the accuracy of the claim that stories distort Buddhist doctrine and do not reflect "real" Buddhist thought. His inclusion of these instructive stories implies that the intent of his commentary was not solely concerned with explaining abstract and difficult philosophical issues (and arguing against rival interpretations) but also with advocating specific moral behavior.

Cultivating Mindfulness as an Antidote to the Four Illusions

Candrakīrti uses compelling narratives and vivid examples to show the power of illusion to an audience ignorant of its danger. Many of these narratives and examples concern the human body. "No map has been used more widely to chart the terrains of the human imagination," Ariel Glucklich observes "than the human body" (1994, 89). In the first four chapters of his commentary on the *Catuḥśataka*, Candrakīrti makes the human body his map for charting four illusions that the imagination projects onto the body, the first of which is immortality. He uses the body as a map on which he draws the path leading away from the danger of Lord Death's domain. Candrakīrti compares the situation of a unobservant man who ignored the signs, strayed from the main road, and died in the wilderness to the fate of all people who remain unconcerned about their mortal nature (§12). They will all perish at the hands of the Lord of Death. No death should ever be unexpected, he claims, because an observant person will see the signs of illness and aging on the body and know that these signs point to death (§56).

The World of the Body

"In this six-foot-long body, with its mind and its ideas," the Buddha says "there is the world, the arising of the world, the ceasing of the world, and the path that leads to the ceasing of the world" (S I 62). All things in the world undergo constant change. Subtle changes may go unnoticed, but the changes that leave their mark on the body as it ages and moves closer toward death are much harder to ignore. Understanding the body, as the Buddha's statement indicates, is essential to understanding the world.

Buddhist texts often use construction metaphors to characterize humans and the world they inhabit. The constructed nature of the body makes the image of a house an apt comparison: "When a space is enclosed by timbers, vines, grass, and mud, it is called a 'house,' similarly when a space is enclosed by bones, sinews, flesh, and skin, it is called a 'body' (M I 190)." This passage emphasizes the similarities between houses and bodies as enclosed spaces sealed off from the larger world. The image of a house takes on a different character when it is applied to the mind. Attention shifts from the supposed strength of the building materials to their weakness: "Just as rain enters a badly thatched house, so desire enters an uncultivated mind" (Dhp 13). This passage emphasizes the similarities between rain as the destroyer of a neglected house and desire as the destroyer of a neglected mind. In another example of building metaphors, desire is recognized as the builder of the house:[25]

> Housebuilder, you are seen. You will never build the house again.
> All your rafters are broken and your ridge pole destroyed.
> Mind has attained freedom from the forces of construction,
> And achieved the extinction of desires. (Dhp 154)

Careful training of the mind enables it to recognize desire as the contractor who builds houses—the bodies that return to world again and again—and with this recognition of desire comes liberation from the world and its relentless cycle of death and rebirth. Buddhists regard the body as a work in progress: a complex building project that employs myriad mental and physical components as its raw materials.

For Buddhists, understanding the body becomes a crucial step in the larger enterprise of understanding how worlds are constructed and how human beings remain trapped within them. Elaine Scarry uses a similar set of building metaphors to illustrate the relations she sees between the body and self: "like the body, its walls put boundaries around the self preventing undifferentiated contact with the world, yet in its windows and doors, crude versions of the senses, it enables the self to move out into the world and allows the world to enter" (Scarry 1985, 38). Buddhist representations of the wheel of life similarly use a house with six open windows to represent the body and its six senses. As these pictorial representations of the cycle of death and rebirth indicate, the body and the senses are the basis from which contact with the world arises. Immobilizing the body in the act of meditation and stemming the flow of sensory stimulation leads to a meditative experience divested of all disruptive mental content. While the windows and the doors of the senses remain shuttered, they shut out contact with the world and block the disruptive emotion of desire that feeds upon this contact. The Buddhist meditator seeks an ideal state "symbolized by an impermeable, highly controlled body and a watertight mind" (Wilson 1995, 92).

Cultivating Mindfulness of the Body

The images of the body that Candrakīrti evokes indicate his awareness of meditative techniques that take observation of the body as their point of departure. Drew Leder (1990, 1) speaks of the paradoxical nature of the body when he describes it as "the most abiding and inescapable presence," and yet also characterized by absence because bodies are "rarely the thematic object of experience." This paradox is less compelling for Buddhists, whose meditative practice takes the body as its object of observation. The human body, with its regular pattern of breathing in and out, and of taking in food and excreting waste, provides an easily accessible and concrete object of observation. Some of these meditations focus on the gross movements of the body as each successive and deliberate step propels it forward. Other practices focus on the more subtle movements of the breath as it circulates throughout the body.

The Buddha advises monks to observe carefully the body's breathing and its activity while walking, standing, sitting, and lying down, as well as its parts and their functions (D II 290, M I 55).[26] In the *Satipaṭṭhānasutta* (Discourse on the Applications of Mindfulness), the cultivation of mindful awareness of the body begins with observing the breath. Observation of the regular succession of the breath as it flows in and out results in calm and concentrated states of mind. Mindful awareness of all physical actions, those of the body at rest and the body in motion, produces the same beneficial result. The body, when carefully analyzed both inside and out, from the hair of the head down to the toenails, reveals its fundamentally impure constituents. Further analysis of body into four elemental constituents (earth, air, water, fire) erodes belief in personal identity. The mind's quartering of the human body, like the butcher's quartering of a cow, leaves behind no recognizable identity.

Meditation on the decomposition of corpse, as advocated in the *Satipaṭṭhānasutta*, begins with disgust at the beginning of the practice, "while the corpse is still recognizably human and culminates with detachment as the practitioner contemplates a pile of bones crumbling to dust and the fundamental principle that all compounded things are impermanent and lack a permanent self."[27] Although consideration of the body's impure nature is the main focus of the application of mindful awareness to the body, the meditator who takes the body as an object of awareness will also observe that its nature is impermanent, painful, and has no self. This analytical decomposition of the body and autopsy of its parts undermines the body as a stable foundation for personal identity. This discourse concludes with the descriptions of how the meditator's attention turns inward and away from disruptive states of mind caused by the pleasures of the senses. The experience that results is of the more subtle pleasures of meditative concentration. Meditative concentration generates mental states described as pure and clean. A sensation of calm suffuses the meditator's body like lather through a sponge. Calm wraps and protects the meditator's body like a clean white towel. Now there is no entrance through which Māra, the embodiment of death, can gain access. The practice of cultivating mindful awareness of the body reflects the gradual nature of the Buddha's teachings. Mindfulness begins with unenlightened practitioners taking note of the impurity and impermanence of their own bodies. The practice culminates in these meditators' acquiring the liberating insight that all things in the world—even the most subtle states of mind—share the same impure, impermanent, and insubstantial nature.

The Four Arrows of Mindfulness and Their Targets

Aśvaghoṣa (100–200 C.E.) retells the popular story of Nanda, the Buddha's half brother, in *Saundarananda* (Handsome Nanda).[28] His version of the story emphasizes the important role that mindfulness of the body plays in Nanda's gradual transformation into an enlightened monk. After reluctantly agreeing to ordination, Nanda regrets his decision and longs to return home to the welcoming embrace of his lovely young wife. The Buddha, determined to rid Nanda of his obsession with Sundarī's beauty, uses his power to transport Nanda to the heavens and show him the superior beauty of divine women. Nanda concedes that in comparison with these beautiful women his own wife is as ugly as a one-eyed monkey. The Buddha promises him the company of these divine women in his next life if he exercises self-control now (Sn X.1–64). Ānanda (his cousin and fellow monk) points out to Nanda the incongruity of keeping his body chaste while his mind lusts after divine sex (Sn XI.8–30). With a change of mind, Nanda turns his attention to meditation:

> First placing his body in an upright position,
> And concentrating mindful awareness on his body,
> He withdrew all his senses into himself
> And well-prepared, he began his practice of Yoga. (Sn XVII.4)

Aśvaghoṣa's account of Nanda's practice of disciplined meditation begins with mindful attention directed toward the body. Careful observation of the body eradicates the illusion that the body is pleasurable, pure, permanent, and autonomous. He uses the vivid images of war to indicate both the difficulty of the practice and the fierce nature of the opposition:

> With the four arrows of the applications of mindfulness,
> Each engaged on its own sphere of action,
> He destroyed in an instant his enemies,
> The illusions, the causes of suffering. (Sn XVII.25)

With the determination of a warrior preparing for battle, Nanda, armed with the power of mindfulness, takes aim against ignorance. Aśvaghoṣa's verse emphasizes the effectiveness of this potent weapon; each well-aimed arrow quickly finds its target and destroys it.

The Ta-chih-tu Lun *on the Application of Mindfulness*

The *Ta-chih-tu Lun*, a compendium of Madhyamaka philosophy that includes quotations from the works of Nāgārjuna and Āryadeva, similarly considers the applications of mindfulness to be the proper antidote for illusion. The application of mindfulness to the body receives the most attention. First, a meditator reflects on the impurity of the body in five ways: (1) the impurity of the womb, (2) the impurity of the seed, (3) the impurity of the body's nature, (4) the impurity of the body's characteristics, and (5) the impurity of the corpse. The parents' ignorance fuels the fire of their sexual desire, and this desire stimulates the flow of their sexual fluids that combine to form the seed. The seed grows for nine months in the foul environment of the womb and is nourished by the filth inside it. The natural impurity of the body that emerges from the womb is so great that even an ocean of water could not cleanse it. Moreover, impurities characteristic of the body leak out of its nine openings in form of tears, ear wax, snot, saliva, sweat, excrement, and urine. In the end, the corpse's impurity becomes an object of meditation for those who observe the progress of its decomposition. The body's impure nature is the primary focus of the application of mindfulness, although the meditator should also observe its impermanent and painful nature (Lamotte 1949–80, 2.1076; 3.1,150–58). Candrakīrti quotes a verse that speaks of the body's impurity in a similar way:

> There is no purity in the body
> Since its seed,
> Its food and its foul smell are defiling. (§327)

His verse implies that impurity characterizes the human body from the very beginning of its creation until its final end as a putrid corpse.

The *Ta-chih-tu Lun* explains further that the meditator who has applied mindfulness to the body recognizes that pleasurable feelings produce attachment to the body. Application of mindfulness to pleasurable feelings, in turn, leads to the recognition that there are no pleasurable feelings connected with the body. Ignorant people fail to understand that the pleasurable feelings they associate with the body result from their mistaken attachment to impure and impermanent things. Only the pleasure that well-trained meditators experience in meditative concentrations is real, because this pleasure is pure and untainted by attachment. The application of mindfulness to thought reveals that all thought is impermanent and lasts no longer than a moment. The application of mindfulness to all things reveals that they are not autonomous and independent of causes and conditions. This cultivation of mindfulness finally enables meditators to relinquish attachment to the pervasive conception of "I" that shapes personal identity and motivates self-centered thoughts (Lamotte 1949–80, 3.1158–69).

Mindful Travelers on the Path to Buddhahood

Mahāyāna scriptures incorporate Mahāyāna teachings on the Bodhisattva's concern for the welfare of others into their discussion of the application of mindfulness. The *Bodhisattvapiṭaka* explains that the knowledge Bodhisattvas acquire through applying mindfulness to the body has no effect on their resolution to devote that body to the service of others. Although Bodhisattvas understand that the body is impermanent, the cycle of death and rebirth does not discourage them. Although they understand the painful nature of the body, physical suffering does not disturb them. They understand that the body is nonsubstantial, but do not tire of assisting other individuals. The body that Bodhisattvas develop as a result of mindfulness acquires the marks of a Buddha's body and they put it to use in making converts (Pagel 1995, 381–82).

Attaining the body of a Buddha is the end point of the Bodhisattva's path set forth in Āryadeva's *Catuḥśataka*. Candrakīrti comments that the first four chapters analyze ordinary things and reveal their impermanent, painful, impure, and nonsubstantial nature. Only after understanding how the mind has the opposite view of things and then repudiating such illusions, will people become Buddhas (§1). The first chapter counteracts the illusion of impermanent things as being permanent by pointing out the mortal nature of the human body. The second chapter counteracts the illusion of painful things as being pleasant by showing how susceptible the body is to illness and painful feelings. The third chapter counteracts the illusion of impure things as being pure by stripping off the body's covering of clothing and perfumed flesh to uncover underneath the bare bones and foul substances that constitute its true impure nature. The fourth chapter counteracts the final illusion, the mistaken apprehension of the impermanent mental and physical aggregates that form a person as being a permanent self. Because people construct their identity on the foundation of the body, the fourth chapter examines the concept of self in relation to the body and to the social class and status it is born into. The fourth chapter concludes with Candrakīrti's suggestion that the king's pride in his own status and power will vanish once he encounters others with superior power. The people he has in mind are Bodhisattvas and Buddhas.

In the opening chapters of his commentary, Candrakīrti advises people on how they can use their bodies and minds to live moral lives and cultivate the merit and knowledge that leads to Buddhahood. He concedes that frank discussion of its nature might encourage people to question whether there is any use for a body that is so flawed. He reminds his audience that Āryadeva urges people to take care of their bodies and to do good with them:

> Although the body may seem like an enemy,
> It must still be taken care of.
> A moral person who lives for a long time
> Generates much merit from it. (§104)

Candrakīrti believes the religious life is more meritorious than the life of a householder. He urges his audience to leave home and pursue the religious life in the forest. His destination of choice—the forest rather than the monastery—suggests that he favors the ascetic lifestyle celebrated in early collections of Buddhist verses (§§88–93). These verses praise the homeless wanderer who cuts off attachment to wife and children and roams free in the forest "solitary as a rhinoceros horn" (SN I 3). Candrakīrti's views provide further evidence for claim that the Mahāyāna movement began in monastic settings in the forest and represented "a hard-core ascetic attempt to return to the original inspiration of the Buddhism, the search for Buddhahood or awakened cognition" (Harrison 1995, 65).

The path Candrakīrti advises people to pursue resembles the path of renunciation that Steven Collins divides into three stages:

> The act of leaving home has three stages: first, one must leave home physically by abandoning household life for the monkhood. Then, one must abandon home psychologically, by destroying desire for and attach-

ment to the present "individuality." Third and last, one must—at the death of the "body-house"—leave home ontologically by abandoning the forever the village of *saṃsāra*. (Collins 1982, 171)

Candrakīrti argues that leaving home is the right course of action. He strongly condemns people who whine about the difficulty of parting from their relatives and reminds them that death makes such separation inevitable: "What intelligent person would do something because of the Lord of Death's rod? You should put the means of liberation first and adopt an attitude that rejects egotism and selfishness" (§90). He implies that fear of leaving "my home, my family" is ego-centered and selfish behavior. He recommends the practice of being mindful of death. The intelligent person who cultivates the thought "I am subject to the law of death" no longer fears death because all desire—even for life—has been severed. With the fear of death conquered, he asks, how can anyone fear leaving home or parting from family (§96)? On "the third and last stage" of the path of renunciation, Candrakīrti's advice takes a different direction. The path of the Bodhisattva circles back toward the "village of *saṃsāra*." Bodhisattvas choose to be reborn, even in unpleasant places of rebirth, because of their resolution to ease the suffering of others. The great compassion that motivates their actions enables them to take up residence in yet another "body-house" and guide other travelers along the path to enlightenment.

This world is an unpleasant and dangerous place, which Candrakīrti compares to an ocean full of "crocodiles, alligators, sharks, and sea monsters, which represent birth, old age, illness, and death" (§207). Despite the dangers, Bodhisattvas plunge into this ocean again and again, because they are devoted to all beings and wish to make "them happy with the radiant good fortune of heaven and liberation" (§209). The path is a gradual one, and travelers on it have different motivations and different short-term destinies. Bodhisattvas speak to beginners on the path about virtuous practices because the merit accumulated from such practices leads to the good fortune of a rebirth in heaven. Heaven is only a temporary place of rest in this cycle of birth and death. Bodhisattvas encourage other travelers to find the greater happiness of liberation from all of their suffering. It is better still, Candrakīrti advises, to keep on the path of the Bodhisattva because this path ends in Buddhahood (P 116a).

2

MORTAL BODIES

In chapter one of the *Catuḥśataka*, Āryadeva is concerned with demonstrating how and why people should stop believing in the illusion of permanence. He interprets belief in permanence as the desire for immortality and uses the human body to explain the truth of impermanence. The impermanent nature of the human body is visible in the changes that occur as it ages, becomes decrepit, and inevitably dies. Candrakīrti maintains in his commentary on the *Catuḥśataka* that belief in immortality, whether it is defined as eternal life among the gods or as the continuance of life through the procreation of sons, is based upon error. People erroneously believe that they can cheat death by propitiating gods or by producing sons.

The door to immortality or the deathless state that the Buddha opens in his teaching leads away from the household life of the married couple toward the monastic life of celibate monks and nuns (Vin I. 5). The Buddha calls upon his disciples to sever old familial and societal ties and to enter into new relationships that are not determined by birth and class. These new relationships are freely chosen, and the Buddhist community is founded on a shared vision of a religious life that is markedly different from the ideal life extolled in religious texts of Brahmins. The Buddha's teaching developed in response to the views held by other religious teachers of his time, many of them Brahmins. The dominance of the priestly Brahmin class in religious and philosophical discourse was equally strong in the centuries during which Madhyamaka thought developed. Although the sources we have for understanding the Brahmin worldview reflect the narrow perspective of a male upper-class elite, they provide the backdrop against which Buddhists defined their own more inclusive religious values.

Brahmanical Texts on Immortality

Vedic texts describe the ideal religious life of an upper-class married householder whose religious activity centers on ritual action. The proper performance of Vedic rituals demands that a man be married, because an effective sacrifice requires a ritual partnership. Without a wife as his partner in the performance of religious rituals, an upper-class man cannot fulfill his religious obligations. Stephanie Jamison argues persuasively that although the wife's ritual activities are few, they are crucial to its success. Her very presence ensures that her fertile powers can be tapped to assure the ritual's success. The wife's presence creates the necessary contact between the human and divine realms, and she becomes the conduit for divine power (Jamison 1996, 30–149).

The Rig Veda *and Other Early Vedic Texts on Immortality*

Vedic texts explain that human beings can prolong their lives through the proper performance of ritual acts of propitiation. The earliest of the Brahmanical texts, the *Rig Veda*, depicts human beings asking the gods to grant them the gift of prolonged life (RV I.10.11). The word often translated as immortality (*amṛta*) in its earliest usage denotes "freedom from death, continuance of life" (Collins 1982, 42–43). The two hymns at the beginning of the eighth chapter of *Atharva Veda* request that the life of a dying person be prolonged. The first verse of the first hymn, addressed to the Lord of Death, asks that this man remain in the world of nondying (AV VIII. 1). Subsequent verses (2–19) implore the dying man to recover his physical strength and the will to live a long and virtuous life. The second hymn also asks that a man be released from the snares of the Lord of Death to enjoy the full measure of nondying, a hundred autumns (AV VIII. 2). In *Atharva Veda* and in the commentarial literature of the *Brāhmaṇas*, the expression "nondying" when applied to human beings means a full life of one hundred years (ŚB IX.5.110; X.1.5.4).

Brahmin priests achieve power through their ability to recite ritual texts and manipulate divine power. They become like gods on earth, with the special privileges of teaching ritual texts, officiating at sacrifices, and accepting gifts as their religious duty. Brahmins control the rituals that make young upper-caste males "twice born." This second birth relegates to inferior status a women's labor and elevates in its place the ritual labor of male priests; it marks the beginning of the young man's study of Vedic texts. After the completion of his study, Brahmin priests perform the marriage rituals that enable him, with his wife, to perform the sacrificial duties required of upper-caste males. The rituals of sacrifice construct for this sacrificer a divine self (*ātman*), a divine world for it to inhabit, and the power to sustain that self in its world (Gonda 1985, 202–4; Smith 1989, 91–119).

Even if the married couple's proper performance of Vedic rituals postpone physical death for a hundred years, death cannot be postponed indefinitely. The dead, however, can live on in their children. Children who resemble their deceased parents and grandparents enable the dead to live on in their loved ones' memories. A fertile wife secures the "immortality" of her husband when she gives birth, as this passage from the *Aitreya Brāhmaṇa* states:

> The husband enters the wife;
> Becoming an embryo, he enters the mother.
> Becoming in her a new man again.
> He is born in the tenth month. (Olivelle 1992, 26)

Olivelle observes that the belief that a son constitutes the immortality of the father is already expressed in a *Rig Veda* prayer ("Through offspring, O Agni, may we attain immortality.") and frequently repeated in the later commentarial literature (1992, 26–27). The procreation of sons also is necessary because only sons can perform the rituals that prolong the lives of their deceased parents in the afterworld.[1]

One verse of a *Rig Veda* text on the creation of the world speculates on sexual desire as the primal seed of life (RV X.129.4). Both early and later Vedic texts offer instruction on how this seed of life is implanted. The act of procreation has religious significance because no successful conception occurs without the intervention of the creator god, Prajāpati. The *Rig Veda* contains a dialogue between a couple desirous of a son and a Brahmin priest who stands in for Prajāpati (X.183.1–3). These verses indicate that although the man and the woman prepare themselves through austerities (*tapas*) and meditation for sexual union and the desired conception of a son, Prajāpati plants the seed of life and sanctions their union.

Upaniṣadic Texts on Spiritual Immortality

A later Vedic text, the *Bṛhadāraṇyaka Upaniṣad* (BU VI.4.3) makes an explicit correlation between a divine sacrifice performed by Prajāpati in his creation of the first woman and the married couple's sexual union, performed with procreation in mind:

> Her vulva is the sacred ground; her pubic hair is the sacred grass;
> Her labia majora are the Soma press; and her labia minor are
> the fire blazing at the centre. A man who engages in sexual intercourse
> with this knowledge obtains as great a world as a man who performs
> a Soma sacrifice. (Olivelle 1996, 88)

The *Bṛhadāraṇyaka Upaniṣad* warns that Brahmins who engage in sexual intercourse without understanding the spiritual significance of the act depart this world in ignorance (BU VI.4.4).

"One kind of immortality ('above the navel'), spiritual immortality, is destroyed by the birth of a son and the consequent ties to the world of *saṃsāra*," Wendy Doniger O'Flaherty points out, but "the other kind of immortality ('below the navel'), physical immortality, is assured by the birth of a son to perform *śraddhā* rites" (1980a, 4). The *Bṛhadāraṇyaka Upaniṣad* and other early Upaniṣads (ca. 800–600 B.C.E.).concentrate on explaining how to achieve spiritual immortality. These texts cast doubt on the efficacy of the two central activities of the Vedic world—offering sacrifices and begetting male offspring—which provide only physical immortality. A man felled by death cannot take root and grow again from the seed that produces a son (BU III.9.28). The divine self forged in the performance of the Vedic sacrifices now becomes part of the cycle of death and rebirth (BU IV.4.6). These Upaniṣads speak of knowledge that is distinct from the ritual knowledge that is limited to Brahmin priests. This knowledge, acquired through meditation, reveals that each individual's soul (*ātman*) is identical in nature and substance with *Brahman*, the source of all life. Without this knowledge, the soul is reborn in an endless cycle of death and rebirth. The knowledge that an individual self (*ātman*) is identical in nature and substance with *Brahman* (BU IV.4.5), coupled with the relinquishing of all desire (BU IV.4.7), is the way that a mortal becomes immortal. The Upaniṣads promote what Patrick Olivelle describes as "an individualist ideology in which both the situation after death and final liberation are determined by what an individual does and knows and not by intermediaries, whether priests or heirs" (1993, 63).[2]

In the Upaniṣads we see a shift in religious activity from the outward performance of rituals to the inward practice of mediation and the rejection of the dominant role of Brahmin priests as ritual intermediaries. This changing focus of religious practice becomes even more apparent in Buddhist texts. Buddhist writers reinterpret the function of a sacrifice, the use of austerities, and the qualities of a true Brahmin.

Buddhist Critiques of Brahmanical Views

The *Kūṭadantasutta* criticizes the Brahmanical sacrificial tradition and redefines the nature and purpose of the sacrifice (D I 140–49). The Buddha responds to the Brahmin Kūṭadanta's questions about the most profitable sacrifice. He describes a series of sacrifices, beginning with sacrifices in which no animals are killed and no trees cut down to construct the sacrificial post. The series culminates in the most profitable of all sacrifices, the life of a monastic who is adept at meditation and has acquired insight into the truth. The goals of the Vedic sacrifice—a full life of one hundred years, accompanied by the pleasures of material wealth and strong, healthy sons—comes under direct attack in other Buddhist texts. The *Dhammapada* says that better than living for one hundred years and performing a fire sacrifice is honoring a person with self-control; better than living a hundred years without morals and mental concentration is a single day in the life of a person who has good morals and mental concentration, and better still than living for hundred years without perceiving the realm that is free of death, is one day in the life of someone who perceives the realm that is free of death (Dhp VIII.7–16).[3]

Buddhists differ with their Brahmin counterparts over how to realize this deathless realm. In the *Bṛhadāraṇyaka Upaniṣad*, the sage Yājñavalkya prepares to divide his property between his two wives and withdraw to the forest for a life of solitary meditation. His wife Maitreyī protests the property settlement and asks instead for Yājñavalkya to teach her about the immortal state (BU II.4, IV.5). He says:

> One holds a husband dear, you see, not out of love for the husband; rather, it is out of love for oneself (*ātman*) that one holds a husband dear. One holds a wife dear not out of love for the wife; rather it is out of love for oneself that one holds a wife dear. (Olivelle 1996, 28)

Yājñavalkya advises her that by concentrating on the self she will gain knowledge of the whole world. That is all the instruction needed to gain immortality (BU IV.5.15). In the following dialogue (S III.1.8) the Buddha offers very different advice to his royal patrons:

> King Pasenadi had gone to the upper terrace of the palace with Queen Mallikā. Then he said to her, "To you is there anyone dearer than self?" "Great king, to me there is no one dearer than self. How about you?" "To me too, Mallikā, there is no one dearer than self." (Gombrich 1996, 62)

When King Pasenadi tells the Buddha about their conversation, the Buddha responds that anyone who loves self should not harm others. The Buddha's response plays with the ambiguity of the word *ātman*, which is generally used as a reflexive pronoun, but in the *Upaniṣads* is used specifically to refer to a cosmic self that is identical with the essence of the world (*brahman*). The Buddha deliberately avoids speculation about the essential nature of the world and instead instructs the king in moral behavior (Gombrich 1996, 62–64).

In the *Bṛhadāraṇyaka Upaniṣad* passage that this discussion between King Pasenadi and his wife seems to assume, the sage Yājñavalkya prepares to divide his possessions among his wives before he enters the fourth and final stage of life. These stages mark the progression of an upper-caste male's transition from chaste Vedic student (stage one), to married householder (stage two), to retired married life in the forest (stage three), and finally to the chaste life of the renouncer (stage four). According to the classical literature on these stages of life (*āśrama*), a man can go the forest only after he has finished his Vedic studies, taken a wife, fulfilled his obligations to his ancestors by producing a son, and has seen the face of his grandson. Olivelle points out that in the earlier formulation of these stages each stage was a legitimate mode of life open to a young adult male after he completed his Vedic studies (1993, 113–39). Buddhist and later Brahmanical texts, such as the *Mānava Dharma Śāstra* (Laws of Manu), regard life in the forest as the prerogative of upper-class men who turn to spiritual practice in their old age. Buddhist texts use the concept of chaste religious practice (*brahmacarya*) to refer to the Buddhist monk's or nun's lifelong pursuit of religious truth, rather than the temporary chaste state of a student of Vedic religious texts before his marriage (Gonda 1985, 299–309).

Candrakīrti's Critique of Brahmanical Views on Family Life

Candrakīrti rejects the classical Brahmanical formulation of four stages of life. He shows contempt for the argument that men should not adopt a renunciant life before fulfilling all the obligations of a married householder. He puts the following words in the mouth of a family man: "First we become adults, get married, father sons, entrust the family responsibilities to them, and then we go" (§92). Candrakīrti questions why a man would bother to create a family, if in the end he is going to reject them and become an ascetic. He ridicules the notion of postponing religious practice until old age in the following anecdote: "A man picked up a mango that had fallen into the dirt. Someone else asked him, 'What are you going to do with it?' 'I'm going to wash it,' he replied, 'and throw it away'" (§94). Implicit in this anecdote is the idea that human life is precious. Why waste this rare opportunity by getting married? It is far better, Candrakīrti contends, to choose the pure unencumbered life of a monastic. This anecdote not only criticizes the Brahmanical support for the pleasures of family life but also mocks the Brahmanical concern with external purity. Brahmin householders can cleanse the dirt on their bodies through ritual bathing, Candrakīrti says, but they can never cleanse themselves of the errors that pollute their minds. By not cleansing their minds (§329), they fail to take full advantage of the potential innate in the human condition and throw away the chance for real freedom the Buddhist path offers.

Controlling Wives

Married life is depicted as far from ideal in Candrakīrti's commentary. The Brahmanical law books insist that a wife's role is to bear children; she is the field in which only her husband sows his seeds (Olivelle 1993, 185–86). Male guardianship of married women specifically involves their sexual lives. Men should govern their wives' behavior. The *Mānava Dharma Śāstra* states that a man should keep his wife busy at home, looking after his money and his household (MDŚ IX 9–13). Occupied with collecting (and spending) his money, cooking his food, cleaning the household utensils and furniture, and in the performance of her own religious obligations, she will have no opportunity to stray. The married householders in the stories and examples that Candrakīrti cites in his commentary have little control over their wives. He questions sexual fidelity of wives numerous times (§83, §256, §263, §276, §285, §439). He claims that wives want even greater control of the family money and will nag their husbands to spend more on jewelry and clothing (§326). A husband who expects his wife to attend to his needs may find the tables turned and face a wife who demands his services as her personal servant (§298). The expectation that four wives will provide more comfort than one proves unfounded when all four wives spend their time quarreling over how it should be done.[4] Candrakīrti describes each one of these wives negatively: the first wife is always arrogant, the others are always crying, getting angry, or acting crazy (§166).

The Pain of Having Children

Even the wife's role in producing a son comes under attack. Candrakīrti tells a story about a Brahmin woman who goes to the forest for the wrong reason. Instead of choosing permanent renunciation over conventional family life, she temporarily becomes an ascetic in the hope of persuading the gods to grant her a son:

> A Brahmin woman went to the forest to perform austerities so that she would become a mother. Some boys stopped her and she began to cry. They asked, "Are you crying because of the pain of losing someone?" "I'm not crying because of any loss," she replied, "I'm crying because I haven't experienced the pleasure of having sons." They asked her, "What's the point of this action?" (§272)

From the time of the *Rig Veda*, Brahmanical tradition has encouraged the performance of austerities for the purpose of producing sons. Like the boys in the story, Candrakīrti questions the value of the wife's actions. He rejects the high value that lay life places on the procreation of sons. Instead of joy, her desire for sons and the rigorous austerities she performs toward that end lead only to grief.

Candrakīrti argues at length against the position that the birth of a son is a joyous event. Sons are far more likely to give their parents' grief than joy. Sons may die long before their fathers (§§48–54). Although Candrakīrti acknowledges that a father will mourn the death of his son, he claims that this grief is misplaced. Instead of grieving for the dead, the father's concern should be with the living. In particular, he should bear in mind that his own death is imminent (§48). The father's ignorance will condemn him to death over and over again unless he makes a determined effort to eradicate it (§54).

Candrakīrti does not deny that fathers love their sons, but he stresses the inequality of the relationship. Sons do not love their fathers with the same intensity as their own fathers love them. He takes a hard look at the task of raising children to adulthood and finds it difficult and unrewarding. He rails against the ingratitude of sons who repeatedly fail to acknowledge the debt they owe to their fathers for raising them:

> Sons cause trouble hundreds of times and are remiss in acknowledging past favors. Because the greater share of their love is for their own sons, they forget the past and ignore their fathers at the same time, just as if their fathers were strangers! They become preoccupied with their own pleasures. (§59)

These sons' attachment to their own children will launch them on the same downward spiral that has already claimed their fathers. A mind guided by attachment will fall into undesirable rebirths, he warns fathers, just as naturally as water flows downhill (§60).

The Fragility of Family Ties

Candrakīrti casts his cynical eye on the bonds of paternal affection. He rejects these fathers' claim that the love they show their sons is unconditional. He doubts that their love extends to disagreeable and disobedient children. What these misguided fathers regard as love seems to him nothing more than a bad business deal. Fathers swap their love in exchange for their sons behaving in an acceptable manner. He tells this story to support his position:

> A king had a son whom he loved very much. When this son died, his ministers told him, "He has become rigid." When the king heard that, he became enraged and intended to beat his son because he had misunderstood them. Then his ministers told him, "He died." Relieved, the king instead beat a large drum for joy. (§67)

This story involves an initial play on words and becomes a black comedy of miscommunication. When the dimwitted king heard his ministers say that his son had become rigid, he thought they meant his son had become obstinate and noncompliant. What the ministers had intended to communicate was that rigor mortis had set in. The king's initial misunderstanding of the situation of his son's death and the muddled circumstances under which he received this news provoked two inappropriate emotional reactions: anger and then joy. First the king gets the words wrong. When he does get the words right, joy replaces his anger and he beats a drum instead of his son. Throughout this story, this foolish king continues to misinterpret the message of his son's death. He never realizes that the situation calls for abandoning the bonds of attachment.

Doubt about the firmness of these bonds of attachment between fathers and sons recurs in a second story that shares some of the features of the first:

> While the king was crossing the river, demons seized his boat. He had a minister whose name was Happy. This minister thought that he must protect his king. So after he had entrusted his sons into the care of the king, he jumped into the river. "Carry me away," he urged the demons. "Release your hold on the king." They released the king. When the minister's sons heard that their father had died, they became very upset. They became happy, however, when the king provided them with delightful things. The pain they felt because of being separated from their father vanished. (§70)

The opening of this story is largely irrelevant to the point Candrakīrti wants to make. The conditions that result in the father's death, while dramatic, are not the focus of attention. They merely set the stage for the sons' reaction to their father's death. The circumstances under which his sons hear of his demise and become the king's wards lead them first to react with pain and then with pleasure. In these two stories, the situations are reversed; in the first a son dies; in the second, a father. Both stories convey a single message. They undermine conventional wisdom about the love of one family member for another. Candrakīrti cites them as a warning to renounce family ties before death forces the separation.

The point of these stories is the same as a similar story about "the cruel transience of human bonds" that Rajasthani villagers told to the anthropologist Anne Grodzins Gold. A renouncer gives a merchant's son an herb that makes him appear dead but in fact allows him to experience his family's reactions. He heard them weeping loudly over his corpse. Then renouncer told them that they could bring him back to life if just one of them would agree to drink the water in which the corpse was washed and by doing so die in his place. In response to his suggestion:

> The father said, "But I have my business to attend and I must take care of it." The mother said, "I have my husband here and it would be sinful to leave him." The dead man's wife said, "If his own birth-givers won't sacrifice their lives for him, why should I who am the daughter of another house?" (Gold 1988, 107)

The renouncer volunteers to drink the water and revives the young man, who now chooses to renounce the world and follow his guru. This story shows that the bonds of familial attachment are doubly false because "they are not merely ephemeral in the face of time and mortality but also hypocritical façades even for their limited duration. The fact of death's parting loved ones, then, denotes not a painful severance of real bonds but an unmasking of false ones" (Gold 1988, 108). It is a story that Candrakīrti surely would have cited had he known it. He holds a similar view about the fragile bonds of family life and considers genuine only the bonds built among members of the religious community.

The fragility of familial ties is shown in another story that Candrakīrti tells that is much older. There are multiple versions of this story that must have been well known to his audience, because Candrakīrti provides us with few of the details. In the earliest version of this story, *Aitreya Brāhmaṇa* VII.13–18, translated by O'Flaherty (1988, 9–25), the childless King Harishchandra asks the god Varuṇa for a son. Varuṇa agrees on the condition that the son later be sacrificed to him. The king keeps postponing the sacrifice until his son, Prince Rohita, reaches adulthood and refuses to be sacrificed. Exiled to the wilderness, he sought to ransom himself with a substitute sacrificial victim.

> In the wilderness, he came upon Ajigarta Sauyavasi, a seer, who was overcome with hunger. He had three sons: Shunahpucha, Shunahshepa, and Shunolangula ("Dog-arse," "Dog-prick," and "Dog-tail"). (Rohita) said to (Ajigarta), "Seer, I will give you a hundred (cows); I want to ransom myself by means of one of these (sons)." The father held back his eldest son and said, "Not this one." "Not this one," said the mother, speaking of the youngest. But they agreed on the middle son, Shunahshepa. (O'Flaherty 1988, 22)

Varuṇa accepts this surrogate, Ajigarta agrees to wield the sacrificial knife, but the gods whom Śunaḥśepa had asked for assistance release him. Śunaḥśepa repudiates his Brahmin father for selling him and thus behaving like an outcaste. The story ends happily with his adoption by the officiating priest, Viśvamitra.

The version Candrakīrti quotes comes from the Vālmīki *Rāmāyaṇa*'s retelling of this story. In this version, King Ambarīṣa must atone for his carelessness in allowing the god Indra to steal the sacrificial victim by finding a human substitute. He offers the Brahmin Ṛcīka a thousand cows for one of his sons. Ṛcīka refuses to sell the oldest son; his wife refuses to sell the youngest. The middle son, Śunaḥśepa, agrees to be sold. While Ambarīṣa indulges himself in a midday nap, the miserable Śunaḥśepa finds the sage Viśvamitra and begs the sage to protect him as a father would a son. Viśvamitra teaches the boy the words he must use to invoke the gods when he is bound to the sacrificial altar. The gods, as requested, grant him the gift of longevity. Candrakīrti quotes the middle son's response (*Rāmayaṇa* I.60.20):

> The middle son told the prince, "Father will not sell the eldest. Mother will not sell the youngest. I understand that the middle one must be sold. Prince, lead me away." (§35)

Although Candrakīrti chooses this story to make the point that people should never place themselves in danger (he conspicuously fails to mention that the gods intervene), it scores other points, as well. The story casts doubt on the natural bonds of affection between fathers and sons and reinforces the beliefs of middle children everywhere about the inequities of parental love. The story also raises interesting questions about the caste system. Viśvamitra is of royal birth, but he behaves like a true Brahmin. Ajigarta, a Brahmin by birth, behaves like an outcaste. This state of affairs supports the Buddhist belief that moral behavior—not birth—defines Brahmin status.

The action of the Brahmin's middle son might seem praiseworthy, but Candrakīrti does not commend the son for his willingness to sacrifice his life. The son has sold himself into bondage, and Candrakīrti has no respect for people who "sell themselves and adapt themselves to society's customs" (§35). He criticizes conventional wisdom about the firmness of ties that bind parents and children and rulers and their subjects. The choice of bondage over freedom, the choice of societal obligation over individual responsibility—these are the critical decisions that Candrakīrti encourages his audience to consider carefully. The life choices that people make also affect their reaction to the inevitability of death.

The Inevitability of Death

Buddhist teachers past and present emphasize the importance of developing an awareness of the fact that we all are going to die. The main thrust of their teaching is threefold: death is certain, the time of death is uncertain, and only the merit acquired through religious practice will be of any value when death comes. The acts performed in this life, virtuous or not, will influence the direction the next life takes.

Why Fear of Death?

When asked "Why should I fear death?" Candrakīrti reminds the questioner that all human beings have mortal bodies. Each successive moment of life brings death closer. Because of birth, illness and old age occur, and these natural conditions inevitably lead people into the presence of death. He quotes the following verse from Ārya Śūra's *Jātakamālā* (XXXII.21):

> O king, beginning from that very first night,
> When a man takes up residence in the womb,
> Advancing with no delay,
> Every day he comes closer to Death. (§16)

In this verse the Bodhisattva responds to his father's questioning of his resolve to become a renouncer. No human being, the Bodhisattva argues, has the power to escape old age and death.

Despite the inevitability of death, people continue to avoid thinking about it. The human life span, the dissenter argues, is one hundred years (§18). If sixteen of these years pass by, there will still be eighty-four years remaining! So, there is plenty of time left to enjoy the delights of sexual pleasures.

There will be sufficient time to engage in religious activities in old age, when death's approach is closer. Candrakīrti responds that because the length of any individual's life span is uncertain, there is no way to know whether the time remaining will be long or short (§19). Even the wishful thinking that death will occur in the distant future communicates a fear of death.

The dissenter concedes that death is a public event, but modifies his argument and claims that because the exact time of death is unknown there is no need for anyone to become preoccupied with it (§30). That very uncertainty about the time of death, Candrakīrti insists, should make people fear death's approach even more (§31). At some point death will seize the unwary. Instead of waiting until the physical signs of the body's weakness reveal death's ruthless power, people should reflect right now on the concept of death. Uncertainty over the time of death, he says, is no excuse for people to imagine that they are immortal.

Medicines and life-prolonging elixirs can ease the pain that accompanies old age and illness, but Āryadeva reminds us that there is no cure for death (CŚ I.5). Death should remind all human beings of their impotence. The Buddha uses the analogy of cattle awaiting the butcher's knife to warn his disciples of the inevitability of death (A IV 138). Candrakīrti brings up this example in this debate about death, and goes even further in by suggesting that the inevitability of death should inspire fear:

> Take for example the death of cattle brought to be slaughtered. All have death in common. Each cow sees another one die. Because this is the same for human beings, why aren't you afraid? There are two reasons why death is not feared: either death has never been seen or it has been transcended. The second is impossible for you! The pariah Lord of Death stands right before you and blocks the path to life. So what's the point of being unconcerned? Of course, you become just like a cow by remaining unconcerned! (§28)

Death, which human beings have in common with other species, is not something that people should choose to ignore. Candrakīrti intends to create a fear of death in people who seem unconcerned about it. He doesn't hesitate to level the insult that anyone unconcerned about death is as dumb as a cow. He uses strong language and the vivid personification of death as a knife-wielding butcher to awaken people to the imminent threat that death poses.

Facing Death with Confidence

In the first verse of the *Catuḥśataka*, Āryadeva emphasizes how foolish it is for people to sleep comfortably while they remain under the control of the Lord of Death. Candrakīrti similarly stresses the importance of alert, careful behavior by telling the following story of a man asked to hold steady an oil lamp:

> The king invited a minister who had been selected for the honor to his palace. His royal attendants, with the exception of the oil lamp bearers, accompanied the king. The minister served as his honored attendant. The unhappy oil lamp bearers conspired to have the minister killed and they induced the king to believe lies. But the minister was unharmed because he had the confidence to control himself. (§12)

This minister understands the dangers of his situation, overcomes his fear, and with confidence successfully performs the required service. The story contrasts the opposed powers of fear and confidence. Confidence overcomes fear and enables the individual to confront death successfully. Candrakīrti interprets this story as warning that people should concentrate on acquiring the skills that will enable them to conquer death.

Candrakīrti tells us what conclusion we should draw from the story, but in his telling of it he leaves out many of the details that would make story's meaning clearer. The excerpt indicates that the king asked the minister to hold an oil lamp carefully. Perhaps the regular oil lamp bearers feared for their positions if he carried out this task without spilling any of the oil. This supposition would explain why they would conspire to have the king put this man to death should he fail in his duty. The minister escaped harm because he remained vigilant and exercised great care. Candrakīrti uses his story to illustrate the main point of Āryadeva's verse:

> Were someone whose master
> Is the ruler of the three worlds,
> Lord Death himself who has no master,
> To sleep peacefully, what else could be more wrong than that? (§7)

The king stands in for the Lord of Death. The minister is the counterexample to the fool who remains asleep and inattentive in the presence of a powerful master who can put him to death.

Geshe Ngawang Dhargyey, in his oral commentary on this *Catuḥśataka* verse, told a different story about a man asked to carry a bowl of oil down a narrow plank of wood, under the threat of death at the hands of the king should he spill a single drop.[5] A similar story occurs in the *Telapatta Jātaka* (Ja I 393–94, no. 96). The Buddha asks his audience to suppose that a young man was given a vessel of oil filled to the brim and asked to carry it down the road. On one side of road stands the most beautiful woman in the country and on the other side, a noisy crowd admiring her beauty. Right behind him another man follows, carrying an upraised sword, ready to cut off his head if he should spill a single drop. The Buddha turns to his audience and asks, "What do you think, monks, would this man under those circumstances be careless in carrying the bowl of oil?" The oil vessel, the Buddha explains, is a metaphor for a composed state of mind. The practice of mindfulness is the proper means of protection. Although this version is more complicated than the story Candrakīrti relates, similar structural elements exist in both. Both situations involve the threat of death; in the first story the threat is implicit, in the second it is explicit. Both require that the men recognize the threat and exert prompt action to avert the danger that surrounds them. Both stories conclude that control over the mind is the only means of avoiding certain death.

Personifying Death

These Buddhist stories that personify death as a powerful and fearsome figure have much in common with Brahmanical portraits of Yama. The *Rig Veda* 10.14 describes Yama as the Lord of the Dead who prepares a place for the dead in his world. In the later commentarial texts, we see a more sinister portrait emerge. The *Jaiminiya Brāhmaṇa* tells a story of a young Brahmin's journey to a world where he sees human beings devouring one another and a naked black figure with a club guarding a stream of blood (O'Flaherty 1985, 33–39).

Buddhist stories about Yama and his surrogate, Māra, place limits on their power. A story included in Nagnajit's *Citralakṣaṇa* illustrates this subordination of Yama's power to the principles of karmic action. A virtuous king has asked Yama to restore to life a young boy who fell ill and died unexpectedly. Yama responds: "My independence is limited and to return or free him is not within my power. All beings are subject to my power because of the reward that their own deeds merit." The god Brahmā backs up Yama's statement, "The King of men, the Master of Death is not to blame; the blame lies on the other hand with Karma. Because of the good and bad deeds that this boy had committed earlier, he was born in the form of a human being, and death has come to him early" (Day 1982, 9).

The Master or the Lord of Death is one of the epithets that the Buddhist tradition assigns to Māra. The railings of the monuments at Bhārhut and Sañci depict fierce battles with Māra described in the hagiographic accounts of the Buddha's life. The artists who carved the earliest of these monuments at Bhārhut (ca. 2nd century B.C.E.) show Māra accompanied by his three seductive daughters. At Sañci the artists also depict the fierce assault led by Māra's sons and an army of loathsome demons. Despite Māra's association with demons and the terrifying aspects of dying, these artists portray Māra as a handsome figure, resembling Kāma, the god of love (Karetsky 1982, 75). Aśvaghoṣa in the *Buddhacarita* says the world calls this enemy of liberation the god of love (BC XIII.2).

After his unsuccessful attack at Bodhgayā, Māra continues to pursue the Buddha in hope of catching him off guard. On one occasion, Māra comes upon the Buddha talking to his assembled disciples about the brevity of life, the certainty of death, and the necessity of living a chaste religious life (S I 107–8). Māra says:

> Human life is long.
> An intelligent person should not worry about that.

He should behave like a baby lulled to sleep with milk.
Death is not approaching.

The Buddha responds in kind.

Human life is short.
An intelligent person should worry about that
He should behave as if his hair were on fire.
Death is approaching.

Māra assumes different forms, animal and human, in his attempts to deter the Buddha from teaching. Each time the Buddha recognizes him and sends him away defeated and disappointed.

Māra's string of defeats continues when he comes up against the Buddha's enlightened disciples.[6] Several monks evoke images of war as they prepare themselves for the confrontation with Māra. "I am putting on my armor," one monk says, as he leaves to meditate alone in the forest (Thag. 543); another speaks of his intention to "thrust away the army of Lord Death" (Thag. 7). The use of these martial images suggests that each monk envisioned himself as replicating the paradigm battle of the Buddha with Māra. Talaputta wonders:

When will I be swift to grasp the teacher's sword,
Of fiery splendor, forged of insight?
When will I be on the lion's throne
And promptly destroy Māra and his army?
When will that be? (Thag. 1095)

The use of martial imagery is rare in the nuns' accounts of their triumph over Lord Death. Although they employ their knowledge of the Buddha's teachings as a means of defeating Māra, they do not see themselves as mirroring his actions because the circumstances of the encounter differ. Although Māra often sent his daughters and other women to tempt the men, he comes himself to seduce these women (S I 128–35). He seeks them out in the solitude of the forest, and tries to deter them from religious practice. Uppalavaṇṇā confidently rejects his advances:

Māra, even if 100,000 men like you
Were to come together,
I would not tremble or move a hair.
So, what can you alone do to me? (Thīg. 235)

Māra fails to frighten these women and impede their religious practice. Each nun recognizes him and sends him away defeated and disappointed. These enlightened disciples do not tremble before Māra because they have no fear of death.

Religious Practice Conquers Death

The Buddha and his enlightened disciples, Candrakīrti points out in his commentary on the first verse of the *Catuḥśataka* (§10), do not fear death because they have won the battle with the Lord of Death and are no longer under his control. Candrakīrti gives two reasons why unenlightened people should fear death: death is certain, and the time of death is uncertain. He gives two reasons also why people do not fear death: either they have never seen death occur or they have triumphed over death, like the Buddha and his resolute disciples (§28).

Ignorance Is No Excuse

Ignorance about death is the primary reason why people are not afraid. Much of Candrakīrti's commentary on the first chapter of the *Catuḥśataka* vigorously attacks the willful ignorance of people who fail to acknowledge the presence and power of death: "The pariah Lord of Death stands right before you and blocks the path to life. So what's the point of being unconcerned? Of course, you become just like a cow by remaining unconcerned" (§28). This comparison to cows evokes the image of placid cows being lead to slaughter unaware that the butcher awaits them. The lack of concern and indifference about the inevitable approach of death places ignorant people in the hands of death. Candrakīrti urges his audience to react to death with the same concern they would show if their hair or clothing had caught on fire (§11). Old age, illness, and pain are the signs that death is approaching (§15). Although illness and old age can be treated, it is impossible, he argues, to find a cure for death (§25). He warns the unwary: "In this world at some time—today or tomorrow—the Lord of Death will approach you, who are subject to death, and seize you. When you become weak, then you will understand" (§31). Because of the uncertainty of the time of death, it is better to prepare for death long before the physical signs of illness and old age appear.

Inappropriate Mourning

Since death is certain and the time of death is uncertain, Candrakīrti regards religious practice as the only effective means of preparing for death's arrival. Feeling sad over the death of others is appropriate (§48), but an obsessive preoccupation with mourning is an unhealthy practice. He condemns at length the excessive attention paid to mourning the deaths of family members (§§48–57, 69–72). He implies that this extreme concern with mourning prevents the mourners from adopting practices that will benefit them when they confront their own deaths.

In this staged debate on death, Candrakīrti's opponent claims that even if people do not torment themselves with grief because of their concern for the family member who has died, they perform the actions of mourning because of society's expectations (§71). Men, as Jonathan Parry observes, are the public mourners, while women are expected to mourn in the privacy of the family compound. The men of the family accompany the corpse to the funeral pyre and assist the priest in performing the proper rituals. The women's role is to grieve: "Some beat their breasts; others allowed their hair to become loosened and disheveled" (Parry 1994, 153). Candrakīrti reserves his harshest criticism for people who beat their breasts and tear out their hair when they know that these actions have no value. He may be directing his comments to men, and subtly suggesting that they are behaving like women. His explicit criticism, however, falls on people who flaunt their ostentatious grief to gain advantages for themselves and to impress others. These people he calls "hypocrites" and "unscrupulous fools" (§72). He warns people against going down the fool's path by following society's customs. He advises them to maintain their self-control and not succumb to grief.

For Candrakīrti, proper religious practice centers not the family but on the individual. Each mourner must focus on his or her own inevitable death and act appropriately. It is imperative, Candrakīrti urges, to "protect yourself from harmful actions and from hell, etc., since you do not know when or where you will go" (§178).

Death as a Sign Pointing to Renunciation

Candrakīrti regards death as a problem whose solution is clear: death is for all people, as it was for the Buddha, a sign directing them toward renunciation. Progress toward becoming a Buddha, the culmination of the Bodhisattva path set forth in Āryadeva's *Catuḥśataka* and Candrakīrti's commentary, begins with the physical act of moving the body outside the confines of household life. The separation anxiety that makes it hard for people to leave home comes under a heavy barrage of criticism. Only a fool would hesitate to leave home when confronted with the fact that death forces the separation of family members. Fear of death becomes the goad (like the rod the Lord of Death is imagined to wield) that drives people from their homes and sets them on the path to Buddhahood. Candrakīrti vehemently rejects the idea that the appropriate time for leaving home is the age of retirement. He finds it unacceptable that someone might refuse to leave home just because it is painful to leave family behind (§§89–90). In the quiet of the forest, "the noise of worldly affairs" has been left behind and proper reflection on death can take place (§96).

The forest, moreover, is the ideal location for "cultivating the applications of mindfulness" (Thag. 352). Mahāyāna texts also promote the forest as the ideal location for religious practice. In Ārya Śūra's *Jātakamālā* (XXXII.43), the Bodhisattva depicts the household life as a haven for carelessness, arrogance, lust, anger, and greed that offers no opportunity to engage in the spiritual life. Reginald Ray, in his study of Buddhist saints, finds that early Mahāyāna texts advocate that the renunciant Bodhisattva should live alone in the forest, practicing meditation, and not in a monastery, preoccupied with matters of monastic discipline (Ray 1994, 255–66). One of these scriptures, the *Ratnaśrī*, claims that solitary life in the forest is far less regulated than life in the monastery and thus more conducive to spiritual practice (Pagel 1995, 113–14).

Becoming Mindful of Death

The practice of becoming mindful of death takes as its object of observation the human body. Bodies are marked by the effects of age and illness. The signs of death's approach are visible on the body as its parts break down with age and it can no longer perform the functions of walking with ease. The sight of bodies damaged by the effects of age and illness contributed to the Buddha's decision to leave home. In its account of the Buddha's life story, the *Lalitavistara* describes the deterioration of an aging body:

> Age makes attractive bodies unattractive.
> Age takes away one's dignity, strength, and power.
> Age takes away pleasures and makes one an object of contempt.
> Age deprives one of vitality and age kills. (XIII.75)

Disease similarly affects the body toward the end of life, as the *Lalitavistara* explains:

> At winter's end wind and great snow storms
> Deprive even the grasses, shrubs, trees, and herbs of their vitality.
> In the same way disease deprives people of their vitality:
> Their faculties, physical appearance, and strength deteriorate. (XIII.77)

These physical signs of aging and illness change the body and make its impermanence evident to the attentive observer.

The method of observation that the Buddha advocates extends beyond the more obvious signs of physical deterioration. The application of mindfulness to the body makes a monk aware of each breath that animates the body and of each bite of food that nourishes it. It is not sufficient, the Buddha says, to cultivate mindfulness of death by reflecting that life may last a single day and night (A III 303–6). Even the thought that life may last no longer than the time it takes to eat a meal, or swallow four or five times, shows a lax cultivation of mindfulness. Only the monk who cultivates mindfulness as he swallows a single time or as he takes a single breath practices in the proper way. People who remain attentive and mindful of death will triumph over all fear.

Candrakīrti's final comments on this first chapter of Āryadeva's *Catuḥśataka* advocate meditation on death as the right means for eradicating all fear of death. When he advises the intelligent person to cultivate the thought "I am subject to the law of death" in the manner prescribed by scripture, he has in mind the Buddha's teachings on the proper way to cultivate mindfulness of death (§96). The death of the body is an observable event that Candrakīrti uses to force people to overcome the ignorance that makes them want to believe in the illusion of its immortality. He encourages people to fear death because this fear can persuade them to begin traveling on the Buddha's path. Fear can become a starting point in a gradual process of human transformation, which culminates in enlightenment and freedom from all fears. Once this point is reached, the body can be easily abandoned. The elder monk Ajita describes his own enlightened perspective: "I have no fear of death, I have no longing for life; attentive and mindful, I will give up the body" (Thag. 20).

3

THE BODY IN PAIN

Candrakīrti's comments on the first chapter of the *Catuḥśataka* emphasize the importance of understanding that impermanence indelibly marks the human body. Painful feelings that arise in the body often signal the onset of illness, and illness and old age are the messengers that warn of death's approach. Although our inclination to avoid pain and suffering is as natural as the desire to escape death, it is just as misguided. Like death, pain is unavoidable. "Even though people flee pain," Candrakīrti says, "pain follows these people, just as their shadow does" (§116). Buddhist scriptures indicate that physical pain interferes even in the Buddha's affairs.[1] The Buddha authorizes his disciple Sariputra to teach in his place, while he stretches his aching back and lies down to rest (D III 209). On another occasion, when a splinter of stone pierces his foot, he experiences sharp and intense pain (S I 27). The people who come to visit him remark on how patiently he endures physical pain without the slightest mental discomfort. He is aware of the pain, but it does not trouble him because he has trained his mind through meditation. In the second chapter, of the *Catuḥśatakaṭīkā*, Candrakīrti concentrates first on making his audience aware of physical pain and suffering, since it is the easiest to recognize.

Types of Suffering

The word that is often translated as suffering (Pāli *dukkha*, Sanskrit *duḥkha*) encompasses far more than physical pain to include the daily stress of working for a living, as well as the mental anguish of a beloved child's death. The Buddha identifies three types of suffering: (1) ordinary physical and mental suffering, (2) the suffering brought on by the change of pleasure into pain, and (3) the suffering inherent in the very nature of constructed things (S V 56).

Buddhists maintain that suffering includes not only the physical pain of hunger and illness but also the mental frustration that comes from the relentless pursuit of pleasure. Pain appears disguised as pleasure and reveals its true nature only when fleeting pleasures are transformed into painful feelings. The most pervasive aspect of suffering permeates all the mental and physical constructs (*saṃskāra*) that build an individual's body and the world in which it travels. Candrakīrti quotes this passage from the Buddha's first discourse, which indicates the extensive nature of suffering (S V 421).

> Birth is suffering. Old age is suffering.
> Parting from what is pleasant is suffering.
> Meeting with what is unpleasant is suffering.
> Wanting and not getting what one wants is suffering.
> In short, the five aggregates of attachment are suffering. (§204)

The range of human suffering includes the physical pain of birth and aging, the mental pain of losing beloved relatives and encountering unwelcome tax collectors, the frustration of unfulfilled expectations, and the daily discomforts of being human.

The Body as Vehicle for Pain

Candrakīrti acknowledges that the first chapter's discussion of the body's impermanent nature might have left his audience feeling depressed and discouraged. A body so susceptible to injury and disease might seem more like an enemy than an ally. When asked what purpose the human body serves, he responds that people who take good care of their bodies live long and virtuous lives (§103). This advice follows the moderate path expressed in Buddha's first discourse, which avoids both the tortuous austerities of the renouncer and the sensual indulgences of the libertine. Candrakīrti similarly condemns ascetics who pull out their hair and expose themselves to the elements.[2] He is even more interested in condemning the libertine's mistaken belief that body provides an endless source of pleasure.

Growing Pains

The experience of physical pain even precedes our entrance into the world. "While we tend vaguely to picture the foetus as luxuriously floating in the secure and balmy bliss of its own custom-built swimming pool," Jonathan Parry tells us that his Indian informants speak of it as "bound in an excruciatingly constricting confinement, suspended in filth and pollution" (1994, 168). Buddhist texts share this dark vision of the fetus painfully confined in its mother's womb. The *Garbhāvakrāntinirdeśa* (Discourse on Entering the Womb) describes the filthy world the fetus inhabits in lurid detail:

> It is nourished every month by its mother's uterine blood. The bits of food its mother has eaten are ground by her two rows of teeth and swallowed. As it is swallowed, the food is moistened from below by saliva and the oozing of mouth sores, while it is polluted from above by thick saliva. The remains of that vomit-like food enters from above through the umbilical cord's opening and generates growth. Through the thickening, quivering, elongated, and globular stages, the embryo is completely transformed into a fetus with arms and legs. The placenta encloses its arms, legs and cheeks. Reeking like an old rag used for mucus, the stench is unbearable. Enshrouded in pitch darkness, it moves up and down. The bitter, sour, pungent, salty, spicy and astringent taste of its food affect it like hot coals. Like an intestinal worm, it feeds on filthy fluids; it finds itself in a swamp that oozes rotting filth. (Tsong kha pa 2000, 274)

At the end of this agonizing and unpleasant period of gestation, the fetus painfully navigates down a narrow birth channel and emerges squalling and naked into a new world. Candrakīrti also envisions the mother's womb as an outhouse and compares the fetus trapped inside it to a dung worm that feeds off manure (§325).

Physical pain continues unabated throughout the body's growth and maturity. Even the good intentions of parents, who want nothing more than to bring pleasure to their children, can have the opposite unintended effect. When parents provide their children with the greatest comforts, that very overindulgence makes their children more vulnerable to pain. The children's bodies are delicate and easily wounded, unlike their parents' bodies, which are accustomed to pain's effects. "Just as the flame of a blazing fire sears a young tender leaf, contact with even a small amount of pain will injure them," Candrakīrti says. "But it will not injure their mothers and fathers" (§126). He argues that pain will prevail despite the best efforts we make to prevent it. To underscore this point, he tells an Indian equivalent of the Western fairy tale about the delicate princess and the annoying pea:

> During the hot season, in the middle of the day, a man slept comfortably in a chariot. The king saw him by chance and took pity on him. Later, when this man was reclining on soft cushions, he could not sleep because a single mustard seed had touched him. (§129)

In this rare instance of a royal display of compassion, the king's well-meaning but misguided action makes the situation much worse. The king bungles his attempt at cushioning the pain of his impoverished subject. A poor man, once so thick-skinned that he could sleep soundly in a uncomfortable chariot under the scorching midday sun, now recoils from the touch of a single mustard seed.

Working Hard for a Living

Although few people suffer the intense suffering of chronic physical pain, Candrakīrti contends that the more modest suffering of work afflicts men and women on a daily basis. This discomfort goes unnoticed because few people recognize the pain that underlies all their daily activities. Delusion clouds their perception. He cites the following example of a deluded husband whose wife controls his discomfort:

> His own wife gave orders to this fool: "Fetch the water for my bath!" And he obeyed. She ordered him to perform other services in the same way: "Get the wood! Heat the water! Massage me and rub me with oil!" There was no part of her body that he did not massage and he even enjoyed doing it! (§298)

Candrakīrti sets up a sensual scene few women could resist. The pleasures of a warm bath drawn by a compliant husband and an invigorating oil massage could easily relieve the pain of a hard day's work. As difficult as it may be for a modern woman to imagine such pleasure, this scenario was even less likely in Candrakīrti's time. The unusualness of the situation follows from two inversions of normal behavior. First, as the Brahmanical law books dictate, women should cater to men.[3] Second, the lengthy list of tiring chores the man's wife orders him to carry out should make him exhausted. Instead, an incredulous Candrakīrti remarks, "He even enjoyed doing it!" People begin working in the morning soon after they arise. They undertake this daily drudgery, Candrakīrti argues, not because they expect to receive any pleasure from their labor but because working enables them "to keep the body alive." Work, he insists, is a painful activity. He tells this story of equal-opportunity discomfort: "'I suffer hundreds of times,' a husband complained to his wife,' while you remain in the house with no troubles at all.' His wife replied, 'First, you do all the housework for twenty-four hours and then you'll understand!" (§370). This brief narrative concludes with the husband taking up his clever wife's suggestion and Candrakīrti's wry comment, "he came to regret what he had said." Candrakīrti uses this story and the previous one about the wife who puts her husband to work illustrate his point about the prevalence of unacknowledged pain. The two stories illustrate also what Stephanie Jamison has called "the Smart Woman/Feckless Man syndrome." Despite the abundance of Hindu and Buddhist texts that attest to the inherent fickleness, stupidity, and incompetence of women, she finds an equally persistent and contradictory pattern of resourceful, energetic women coupled with weak, dilatory men (Jamison 1996, 15).

The Pains of Old Age

While in the prime of life, most people remain unaware of the prevalence and persistence of physical pain. Once they become old, the chronic nature of pain is far easier to recognize. Numerous Buddhist texts speak about the painful results of aging. The *Lalitavistara* says:

> Age thins the multitude of men and women,
> Just as a wind storm thins out a grove of sal trees.
> Age steals one's vigor, skill, and strength.
> An old person is like someone stuck in mud. (XIII.74)

Candrakīrti also addresses this issue. He condemns the obtuseness of young and able-bodied people who cannot even imagine the suffering of those less fortunate: "When someone becomes weak, he cannot lift even his own arms and legs without effort and someone else must carry him. When someone is able-bodied, he does not understand the pain involved in such activities as sleeping, stretching out, and contracting arms and legs" (§173). The young and able-bodied foolishly imagine that the pleasures of sound sleep and a good stretch will last throughout their lives. He sharply criticizes the ironic behavior of the young men who mock the frailty and aged appearance of an old man but expect that their own youthful vigor will last forever:

> You delight in living for a long time without becoming feeble, but you dislike old age, which you associate with wrinkles and white hair. That will not happen if you do not live very long! Alas! This perverse conduct of yours seems right only to a foolish ordinary person who is just as stupid as you are! But not to anyone else! (§45)

Candrakīrti points out that as the body matures during childhood, adolescence, adulthood, and old age, pain increases (§§143–44). Every day as people grow older, they acquire the aches and pains of illness and old age and come closer to death.

The Permeable Boundaries of Physical and Mental Pain

Establishing the boundary between physical and mental pain is difficult when both are associated with the body. The boundary appears permeable because body metaphors are often used to describe mental pain. Candrakīrti speaks of the intense anguish that parents feel when a beloved child dies: "This pain is bone-crushing and heart-breaking because of love" (§111). The complex nexus of causes and conditions that lead to a child's birth in this world and to his death and rebirth in another are beyond the ability of unenlightened parents to understand. It is the nature of the body to become ill, grow old, and die. Birth inevitably leads to death. People, Candrakīrti says, "exert themselves to produce sons and then grieve when they encounter the result of birth" (§57). Protracted grief over a family member's death is never appropriate. In particular, Candrakīrti ridicules as vain and hypocritical the mourning customs that prevail in society. The mourners' loud wailing and the beating of breasts is just an outward show, a keeping up of appearances before nosy neighbors (§72).

The Pain of Parting

Death makes parting from family and friends inevitable. Candrakīrti doubts whether it is ever good to love at all, given the brutal pain that parting from loved ones inflicts. Although he acknowledges the pleasure that comes from being together with loved ones, his focus remains fixed on the intense pain of parting. In making his case against attachment to beloved family members, he reminds his audience of the familiar story of Rāvaṇa's theft of Sītā. The *Rāmāyaṇa* describes in powerful and poignant language how the fierce love that Rāma felt for his beloved wife drove him mad when the demon king Rāvaṇa abducted her:[4]

> He hunted through the forest tirelessly but could not find his beloved. Grief turned his eyes blood red, grief gave him the look of a madman. Rāma dashed from tree to tree, from river to river, up and down the mountain, lost in lamentation and sinking ever deeper into the muddy waters of grief. (Pollock 1991, 213)

Rosalind Lefeber comments that the love that ensured Sītā's fidelity through her long imprisonment in Rāvaṇa's island kingdom is admirable but not surprising. What is extraordinary, given the tradition of multiple wives among the ancient kings and the three wives of his own father, she says, "is Rāma's absolute faithfulness to Sītā throughout the epic" (Lefeber 1994, 42 n. 142). The image of a man as strong as Rāma struck down by grief convincingly conveys the overwhelming power of pain to intrude upon pleasure. Seen in this light, both love and its object seem more conducive to pain than to pleasure. Candrakīrti applies the case of Rāma's particular grief to the plight of all human beings. The pain of parting from loved ones increases many times over for people caught up in the vicious cycle of death and rebirth. People who suffer now because of the death of close relatives will suffer the same experience over and over repeatedly. "The suffering that separation produces increases for the multitude of human beings who become fathers, mothers, and other relatives," Candrakīrti says, "as they wander around in the cycle of death and rebirth" (§75). Ignorant behavior keeps people stuck in this vicious cycle as they take on and discard one body after another.

Even the Rich Suffer

The pain of meeting with unpleasant people occurs frequently and is as unavoidable as the pain of parting from loved ones. Bandits, thieves, and tax collectors infest the roads and the towns of the world that Candrakīrti's stories and examples evoke. The encounter between beggars and the moneyed class proves unpleasant for both parties. The suffering of the poor during a famine, tormented by the pain of hunger and thirst, becomes prolonged when they beseech the rich in vain for assistance. "Despite the gestures and entreaties the poor direct toward the rich," Candrakīrti says, "the rich have no compassion and treat them with contempt" (§305). The pain of the poor in this example is both physical and mental, since they suffer from the pangs of hunger and the pain from unfulfilled hopes of relief.

Both physical and mental pain torment people throughout their lives. The poor disproportionally suffer the effects of physical pain. Physical pain more often afflicts poor families, whose food, shelter, and clothing are inferior because of their poverty. The privileged rich, a dissenting voice says, seem immune from pain. Candrakīrti replies that their pain is primarily in their minds: "They come from the best families and have great wealth. But they have many desires and they suffer constant mental pain from not getting what they want" (§135). The Buddha's description of suffering as wanting and not getting what one wants characterizes the rich as well the poor. Envy plagues their lives when the high-status positions they covet cannot be obtained. Even when they do obtain high positions, their uncontrollable desires for even more power can bring them down. Candrakīrti reminds his audience of the well-known story of King Māndhātā who, when he was given half of Indra's divine kingdom to rule, wanted to rule the entire kingdom (§151). As a result of his plot to assassinate Indra, he plummeted from heaven to earth, where he died in disgrace.[5]

Money, prestige, and women are the perennial objects of male desire, even though anxiety about keeping them soon surfaces. Candrakīrti argues that this anxiety destroys what little pleasure there is in having them. One anxious man fears losing the king's favor and his coveted position as the royal elephant trainer when the king rewards an inexperienced man who is temporarily successful in riding a wild elephant (§136). A nervous king fears he has lost his peoples' favor and ends up losing both his sanity and his kingdom:

> Fortune-tellers told a king that it was going to rain and that anyone who drank that rainwater would become insane. The king covered his well for his own safety. The rain fell and one of his relatives drank the rainwater and became insane. Even though the king was sane, people thought he was insane because his nature was the same as his relative's. The king heard about this matter and he thought, "If they already think that I am insane, they will ridicule me and destroy me." Then he drank the rainwater. (§335)

Although this story of the king's stupidity supports arguments against hereditary rulers, Candrakīrti uses it to show how fear can undermine and destroy lives. The superstitious king's initial fear comes from the fortune-teller's appalling prediction. He takes rational precautions to safeguard his sanity, but his obsessive fear of what his people will think compels him to act in a seemingly irrational way. The king and his subjects both believe that insanity is contagious, since close relatives share particles of the same body.

The contagion of insanity will pass through the particles that connect this unfortunate king with his crazy relative.[6]

The Torment of Sexual Desire

Candrakīrti regards women as prime objects of male anxiety. He claims that a man's sexual appetite builds up throughout the day and reaches its peak of intensity at night. The short-lived pleasure of the act itself must be a letdown, compared with this prolonged period of anticipation. He questions why men don't give up sex, since the pleasure of orgasm "just lasts for a moment" and the effort required to reach it makes them exhausted (§288). Moreover, he argues, taking a different line of attack, it is impossible to have sex with a woman without jealousy interfering (§289). The possessive attitude men take toward women ("She's mine; she doesn't belong to anyone else") reveals the pain of jealousy. Candrakīrti's sardonic condemnation of a husband's jealous refusal to share his wife with others when he can't enjoy her indicates his contempt for men who argue that sex is a pleasurable activity.

Candrakīrti takes the position that it is impossible for a man whose mind is tormented by sexual desire to experience any pleasure at all. He tells the story of a foolish student who fantasizes for a year about having sex with the queen:

> The fool saw the queen; and after he saw her, he desired her. He bribed her maidservant with gifts. He asked, "Is it possible to meet with her?" "It's possible," she replied. Then she discussed this matter with the queen. "The king's palace is well guarded," the maidservant said, "nevertheless, when your majesty goes for a walk, this affair will be possible." The maidservant told the fool about this. At the end of one year, he had stockpiled perfume, incense, flowers, garlands, and cosmetics for the queen. "Tomorrow when the queen goes for a walk," the fool thought, "I'll meet with her." He made elaborate preparations in his own room. On that day, his teacher had lost a cow and sent him out to find it. After he had gone out, the queen came to his room. When he returned, she had gone. (§285)

This improbable story about a student who had sexual aspirations well above his station illustrates how the best of plans can go astray. The requisite bribes for the go-between and the high cost of setting the stage for the act of seduction undoubtedly undermined the student's finances. More important to Candrakīrti is the waste of a good mind distracted for an entire year on a scheme so easily sabotaged by the wanderlust of a cow. He takes for granted the wanton nature of cows and women, and he finds fault with the student for allowing his mind to become aroused by sexual desire. Instead of the rare pleasure of royal sex, this foolish student experiences the common pain of frustrated desire.

There is nothing at all about sex that Candrakīrti finds pleasurable. Neither the physically tiring act itself nor the foreplay that leads up to it is worth the effort. In yet another attempt to quash sexual desire, he tells of a would-be lover's eagerness to embrace the woman he desires. Enslaved by his passion, this fool subjects himself to a dominatrix's abuse: "She smacks his head with a stick, spits on him, and beats him with a whip" (§305). Physical pain and the suffering of insatiable sexual desire torment men who cannot control their sexual appetites.

Candrakīrti quotes an unidentified verse on the insatiable desire for sexual pleasures:

> Just as fuel makes flames flare up,
> Just as people crossing makes the river rise,
> In the same way, by indulging their sexual pleasures,
> People increase their longings for sexual pleasures. (§251)

This poet draws upon the usual metaphor of sexual desires as flames raging out of control. The whole world, as the Buddha once explained, is on fire (Vin I.21). The eyes, the shapes and colors they perceive, the mental impressions and sensations that ensue are all ablaze, he says, with the fire of desire, anger, and delusion. Just as fire can blaze out of control and become destructive, so can the water of a flooding river. The unknown poet suggests that as the crowd of people crossing the river raises its level to dangerous heights, the swelling water may well engulf them all. People who surrender to the ravenous demands of sexual pleasures put themselves at risk of destruction as surely as if they had encountered the dangerous forces of fires or floods.[7]

The Transformation of Pleasure

The suffering brought on by the change of pleasure into pain is the second of the three types of suffering. Although the initial feeling of the body's contact with heat or cold may be pleasant, Candrakīrti argues that the prolongation of that contact transforms a pleasant feeling into a painful one (§150). Contact with something painful always produces painful feelings. When that contact is increased, the agony of even greater pain tortures both mind and body. The fact that pain does not change prompts Candrakīrti to conclude that it is normal for the body to experience pain (§154). Conditions both inside the body and outside it frequently trigger painful feelings. Over time, as elements that form the body deteriorate, experiences that once produced pleasure no longer have the same effect. Even sex, which held a powerful attraction for men in the prime of life, cannot get a rise out of old men (§279).

The Painful Consequences of Sensual Indulgence

Not only desires that go unfulfilled but also desires that are indulged can approach the threshold of pain. Candrakīrti warns people against following the dictates of their appetite for sensual pleasures. The glutton who indulges his appetite for food and drink suffers the physical pains of his overindulgence and the scornful reproach of his doctor:

> A man thought, "I will eat even though that last meal is not yet digested." He asked some Brahmins, "Should I please myself and eat?" They replied, "Eat." In the same way, they gave their consent to drinking water and sleeping, and all the other actions he asked about. He experienced pain after he had done all this. His physician asked him, "Why did you act like that?" (§391)

This story pokes fun at overindulgent fools and the indifferent advice of Brahmins. Only his physician (a surrogate for the Buddha) questions his behavior.

Even without overindulgence, pain can quickly override the enjoyment of sensual pleasures. Candrakīrti creates the scene of a rich man enjoying all the sensual pleasures that wealth brings. He envisions Devadatta reclining on cushions spread out on a soft carpet and enjoying all sorts of things that captivate his senses of vision, hearing, smell, taste, and touch (§111). Suddenly a swarm of annoying insects sting his flesh, and that singular experience of pain swiftly replaces all his previous pleasure. Pleasure arises, Candrakīrti asserts, when people use their imaginations to construct desirable identities for themselves: "I am a donor. I am a lord. I enjoy desirable objects" (§139). This pleasure is not real because it can be so easily lost. The imagined loss of desirable objects destroys in an instant any pleasure derived from having them. Candrakīrti uses the example of Devadatta to demonstrate how quickly feelings change; and change is itself painful.

Candrakīrti frequently reminds his audience that they should consider the future results of actions that they undertake. Actions that bring momentary pleasure may well have more lasting painful results. He singles out for special mention people who place themselves in jeopardy because of their excessive thirst for alcohol. Two stories he cites speak of the painful consequences that ensue for men whose drinking landed them in trouble (§38). The first story tells of a prostitute who took revenge on an insolvent client who had spent all his money on beer. She waits patiently for the right opportunity and executes a clever plan that exacts payment from him several times over. After they sell their two sons to a merchant, she persuades him to remain behind in the merchant's residence while she steals the children away. Instead of the children, the merchant takes home the foolish man as his servant. The prostitute not only reaps an immediate monetary reward after she sells the scoundrel but she also gets back two sons to provide for her future. By taking that first drink, the foolish man sets in motion of chain of events that ends with his sale into bondage. In the second story, a man walked into a tavern, claimed he would pay, and began to drink heavily. When the time came for him to pay up, he couldn't. He was then seized and beaten. The ramifications of both stories go beyond the obvious lesson: pay now or pay later. In both cases a thirst for sensual pleasures (sex and/or alcohol) sets in motion the actions that will bring painful consequences. The refusal of both men to acknowledge their debts makes it inevitable that others will demand payment. Candrakīrti uses these two stories to stress the inexorable force of karmic action. Why gamble with your future, he asks, when you could wind up in hell (§37)?

Temporary Relief

Candrakīrti concedes that people can relieve their pain, but only temporarily. This temporary relief of pain should not be mistaken for pleasure. He provides several examples to prove his point. After becoming tired of walking, people may find relief in the pleasure of riding on horseback. Candrakīrti claims that this relief of pain is short-lived, since pain inevitably comes back (§181). The location of the pain may shift, as it does in the example of the horseback rider, whose sore backside is now more painful than his formerly aching feet. Candrakīrti gives a similar response to the example of shifting a burden from one shoulder to the other. Compared with the intense pain of the shoulder that first held the burden, the insignificant amount of pain felt when shifting it to the other shoulder seems pleasant. A careful analysis of this situation, however, reveals that there is no pleasure at all, since it is pain alone that arises (§§188–89). A nauseated man might feel relief after emptying the contents of his upset stomach into a pot (and a rich man might feel pleased that he can afford a gold one), but there is nothing at all pleasant about vomiting. Candrakīrti concedes that people do relieve pain when they change their modes of transportation, shift a burden, or purge themselves when ill. The pleasure that these unenlightened people imagine they feel he attributes (§§185–86) to their inability to understand that they wrongly perceive pleasure in situations that enlightened people recognize as painful.

Even the pleasure acquired from watching the seasons changes is suspect. When the winter comes, people wrap themselves in warm clothes and blankets to ward off the cold. When summer comes, they apply cooling lotions to their bodies. These are only temporary remedies for discomfort, which people use when they fear the cold or the heat. Fear motivates their actions, Candrakīrti concludes, not pleasure (§169). The beauty of spring is deceptively beautiful because it makes people forget that death is present at every moment. Behind the splendor of the seasons lurks death. Each moment that passes brings death closer. The seasons' cyclical changes, Candrakīrti observes, should bring to mind the cyclical changes of death and rebirth (§85).

The Transitory Delights of Divinity

Death followed by rebirth in a divine world is not a change for the better. The *Vimānavatthu* and other Buddhist texts that encourage lay people to donate their money speak of the rewards of heaven in sensuous language. In the worlds of the gods, the shimmer of gold radiates from trees and houses, from clothing and ornaments that divine beings wear, and from their luminous faces. The commentaries to these tales, however, recognize the seductive nature of these descriptions and compare life in these divine realms unfavorably with the experience of Nirvana.[8] Even divine pleasures, which seem everlasting, eventually fade and yield to pain. Human pleasures are fleeting, but so too are the pleasures of deities. Although in the *Suhṛllekha* (SL 9–11) Nāgārjuna speaks of divine rewards for moral behavior, he later warns (SL 70–72) that the pleasures of heaven give way to the pains of hell.

> After experiencing for a long time the pleasures
> Of caressing the breasts and waists of divine women,
> Once again in hell you will suffer the unbearable touch
> Of devices that grind, cut, and tear.
> After dwelling for a long time on the peak of Mt. Meru,
> Enjoying the pleasures of your feet touching pliant ground,
> Reflect that once again you will experience the unbearable pain
> Of walking over hot coals and rotting corpses.
> After coming to beautiful groves and having fun
> With divine women who delight and serve you,
> You will once again dwell in forests whose leaves are like swords
> That slice off your ears, nose, hands, and feet.

Divine women, as Nanda discovered, far surpass the beauty of any woman on earth. Greater than the pleasure gods once felt embracing divine women, Nāgārjuna says, is the pain that arises from seeing the signs that indicate they will soon die. When the cushions dying gods sit on become uncomfortable, their flower garlands wilt, their complexions become repulsive, and their bodies and clothing stink of sweat, they know that death is imminent (SL 98–100). The force of immoral actions committed in the past will propel these gods down to the lower realms of hell.

The Pervasive Nature of Pain

All beings caught up in the cycle of birth, death, and rebirth experience mental and physical pain. Beings in hell experience most often the physical suffering of painful feelings. Deities experience more intensely the mental suffering brought about by change. The suffering present in the very nature of constructed things applies to all beings equally. P. S. Jaini notes that this third type of suffering is associated specifically with neutral feelings. This type of suffering is not a feeling as we ordinarily understand it, and it is not the consequence of any past action. Only exceptional practitioners recognize that this third type of suffering pervades the entire cycle of death and rebirth (Jaini 1977, 53–57). Because this type of suffering is so subtle, it is the most difficult to recognize and eradicate. Candrakīrti explains that although ordinary people do not notice an eyelash landing on the palm of their hands, they feel pain when that eyelash lands in their eye (MKV 476). Ordinary people do not notice the pain of constructed things, while exceptional practitioners experience severe pain from their knowledge about the transience of constructed things.

Lethal Body Parts

Ordinary people and exceptional people differ markedly in their ability to recognize the painful nature of the five aggregates. The Buddha tells his disciples a story to illustrate these aggregates' insidious nature (S III 112–14). A murderer disguises himself and seeks employment in the house of the man he intends to kill. He maneuvers himself into a position of trust. Since he is now considered a friend by his victim, he has no trouble finding an opportunity to cut him down with his sword. Disciples who consider the body and the four mental aggregates to be a self and who fail to recognize their impermanent and painful nature do not understand that these five aggregates are murderers. Candrakīrti similarly describes the deadly nature of the aggregates when he says that ordinary people "suffer continually because they must act in cooperation with the five aggregates, which are like a thief's executioner" (§174). Like the executioner, these aggregates hold people captive and put them to death.

The Buddha describes the five aggregates and the four elements that make up the material aggregate of the human body in lethal terms when he compares them to five murderers and four poisonous snakes (S IV 173–75). In the Mahāyāna text, the *Vimalakīrtinirdeśasūtra* (The Teaching of Vimalakīrti), the layman Vimalakīrti speaks at length about the body and its illnesses. Since the body's five aggregates are like five murderers and its four elements like four poisonous snakes, he urges his companions to develop disgust for the body and turn their attention instead toward the body of the Buddha (Lamotte 1976, 33–38).[9] Candrakīrti explains how these four elements—earth, air, water, and fire—combine to form the human body (§165). The element of earth provides the physical support for the other three; without it, the fetus would abort in its first stage of development. The water element binds all the elements together; and the fire element and wind element enable the fetus to mature and grow. Despite their cooperation in producing the body, the elements themselves are mutually antagonistic. Earth impedes the motion of the air; air scatters earth; water quenches fire; and fire dries up water.

Physical pain does not require any outside force or object to set it in motion, since these antagonistic elements that form the body engage constantly in mutual conflict. This ancient scientific explanation of the body's composition and its susceptibility to illness may have been as difficult for Candrakīrti's audience to grasp as it is for us.[10] To make body's hostile combination of elements easier to understand, he uses the analogy of a polygamous man's dysfunctional household:

> One of four mutually antagonistic wives was always acting in an arrogant way. The second one was always crying. The third was always angry; and the fourth was always acting crazy. They were unable to agree on how to provide the proper care for their husband's body when he requested their services. Because of their mutual antagonism, they did not attend to him properly. They also performed other actions improperly. (§166)

Each of the four elements that construct the human body is as hostile to the others as these four disagreeable wives. The resultant conflict inside the human body is just as severe as the discord in the polygamist's household. Exceptional people, who apprehend the nature of the body as it really is, Candrakīrti concludes, see the human body as an enemy because it is so susceptible to pain and injury (§101).

Vasubandhu's Views on Pleasure and Pain

The sharp distinction Candrakīrti draws between intelligent people who perceive accurately the painful nature of the human body and misguided fools who do not simmers beneath his exposition of another Buddhist philosopher's views. In a lengthy section at the end of his commentary on the second chapter of the *Catuḥśataka*, he criticizes the position that Vasubandhu takes on the nature of pain and pleasure in his *Abhidharmakośa*, the classic treatment of Sarvāstivādin Abhidharma thought that is still studied in modern Tibetan monasteries. Candrakīrti had access to a copy of Vasubandhu's text from which he quotes. Although his criticism is caustic and occasionally personal, he presents Vasubandhu's views without deliberate distortion.

Vasubandhu begins his discussion on pleasure and pain in the *Abhidharmakośa* with a rhetorical question.[11] Why, he asks, should all constructed things be considered painful (AKB 875)? When Vasubandhu answers his own question, he brings in an additional qualification: these constructed things must also be contaminated.[12] In the verse (AK VI.3) that Candrakīrti quotes, he says:

> Pleasant, unpleasant, and neutral—
> Contaminated things are without exception suffering,
> Each according to its circumstances,
> Because of their connection to the three types of suffering. (§205)

Vasubandhu explains that all contaminated things should be classified as painful because all three types of suffering apply to them (AKB 875–77). The suffering of pain characterizes a feeling that is painful when it arises and while it lasts. The suffering of change characterizes a feeling that is pleasant when it arises and while it lasts, but later transforms into a painful feeling. The suffering of constructed things characterizes neutral feelings as being painful, since all constructed things are impermanent. This third aspect of suffering is so subtle that only exceptional practitioners comprehend it. Vasubandhu uses the same analogy as Candrakīrti in explaining this third type of suffering. Ordinary people are like the palm of the hand that does not feel the pain of an eyelash; the exceptional practitioners are like the eye tormented by an intrusive eyelash. These exceptional people, moreover, are so sensitive that the pain they experience in the highest heavens far exceeds that felt by fools in the lowest hells. Vasubandhu implies that their recognition of the impermanence of pleasant feelings in the highest heavens brings them intense pain. He does not deny that other less sensitive beings do experience pleasant feelings.

Vasubandhu challenges the opinions of "certain teachers" who deny that any pleasant feelings exist and attempt to prove that all feelings are painful. "Now how," he asks, "do they perceive feeling which is pleasant by virtue of its inherent nature as painful?" He answers this rhetorical question with his own summary of their main arguments (AKB 879–80). They argue that causes of pleasure, such as food and drink, heat and cold, do not invariably produce pleasure. Excessive use of these things, or the use of them at the wrong time, will produce pain. They conclude that these are causes of pain from the very beginning, since it is not logical that an increase of something that causes pleasure should produce pain, either simultaneously or at a later time. These critics of pleasure further argue that the awareness of pleasure is based on the relief of pain or on the adjustment of pain. They claim that there is no awareness of pleasure as long as there are no painful feelings of hunger, thirst, cold, heat, fatigue, and so on. Moreover, only ignorant people believe that a minor adjustment in the feeling of pain, for example shifting a heavy burden from one shoulder to another, is felt as pleasure.

Vasubandhu's rebuttal of these arguments uses cause and condition as equivalent terms (AKB 885–86). He argues first that the critic of pleasure does not understand what causes pleasure. There are many conditions necessary for pleasure to occur, and no single one of them is sufficient. Pleasure depends upon the physical state of person who experiences it and the particular circumstances under which that pleasurable experience takes place. He uses an example to prove his point. The same cooking fire produces different results according to the state of the rice. The inherent nature of the fire remains unchanged despite the different properties of the raw rice. Given suitable rice, the fire will invariably produce a good meal. Vasubandhu implies that the inherent nature of pleasure similarly remains unchanged. Under suitable conditions, a person will invariably experience pleasure. He then argues against the position that pleasure is the alleviation of pain. People experience pleasurable smells and tastes without any awareness of a pain that is being relieved. In meditation, the pleasure felt does not relieve pain because there is no pain in meditation states.[13] He explains the example of the shifted burden in regard to the momentary duration of physical and mental states. When someone shifts a burden from one shoulder to the other, pleasure arises in association with that new physical state and it lasts as long as that physical state lasts. Pain arises due to the particular circumstances of change occurring in the body, just as sweet wine changes and becomes sour over time.

Candrakīrti's Criticism of Vasubandhu's Views

Vasubandhu does not identify the "critics of pleasure," but his arguments resemble those Āryadeva presents in the second chapter of the *Catuḥśataka* (vv. 12–13, 17, 20–22), and Candrakīrti rises to Āryadeva's defense. Candrakīrti points out in his commentary on verses 12 and 13 that conditions for pleasure, such as contact with heat and cold, with increased use or when used at the wrong time, will produce pain (§§150, 154). Āryadeva raises the argument that the idea of pleasure is based on the alleviation of pain only to dismiss it. There are not always remedies for pain (v. 17, §168). Even when remedies do exist, such as riding on horseback to ease the pain of walking (v. 20, §180), vomiting into a golden pot (v. 21, §184) or shifting a burden from one shoulder to another (v.22, §187), pain is present from the very beginning and pain prevails in the end. Candrakīrti comments that that people afraid of the cold wrap themselves in blankets and put on warm clothes to relieve their fear (§169). If these remedies produced pleasure by virtue of their nature, they would produce pleasure at all times. He claims that people have pain all the time, even when they are unaware of its presence. "If pain, subtle in nature, were not present from the very beginning," Candrakīrti argues "then later on it would not be recognized as pain after it has increased" (§181). In shifting the burden, the intense pain felt in one shoulder ceases and a lesser degree of pain now arises in the other shoulder. Candrakīrti concludes that pain is felt under those circumstances; the idea of any pleasure is erroneous (§189).

Candrakīrti refers to the opening line of Vasubandhu's attack ("First of all, this critic of pleasure should be questioned") before he launches his own vigorous defense of Āryadeva's position (§216). Vasubandhu begins his criticism with a rhetorical question (AKB 878–79) ("How do they perceive feeling which is pleasant by virtue of its inherent nature as painful?"), and Candrakīrti responds with a rhetorical question of his own ("How can a thing said to have an inherent nature exist?"). He asserts that Vasubandhu's advocacy of things that have "a substantially existent inherent nature" is nonsense, and he attributes it to Vasubandhu's failure to understand the profound teaching of nonduality, "which repudiates belief in existent things and nonexistent things." Candrakīrti argues here from the perspective of ultimate truth, in which there are no dualities. Ultimately, there are no things that are self-caused and existent because of their inherent nature, and there are no things caused by others and existent because of causes and conditions distinct from themselves. Even from the perspective of conventional truth, Candrakīrti denies that there are things that exist by virtue of their inherent nature. The production of something that already exists because of its inherent nature, he argues, serves no purpose and its purported production is no different from the magical illusions that a conjurer produces (§220).

Candrakīrti convincingly defends Āryadeva against the charge that his critique applies to all discussion of pleasure (§235). The criticism applies only to people (like Vasubandhu) who maintain that pleasure exists because of its inherent nature. The poison of desire should be rejected, Candrakīrti explains, but not pleasure because pleasure itself is faultless (§293). For Candrakīrti and Āryadeva, discussion of pleasure has practical value as the means for showing ordinary people the first stages of the Buddha's path. Discussion about the pleasures to be found in the next life can motivate people to act virtuously in this life (§450). Neither Āryadeva nor Candrakīrti denies the conventional reality of pleasure as a feeling that arises and ceases in dependence on various causes and conditions.

Vasubandhu defines pain as harmful and undesirable and pleasure as beneficial and desirable (AKB 881). He claims that a pleasant feeling which is desirable because of its own characteristic (*svalakṣaṇa*) never becomes undesirable. He acknowledges that exceptional practitioners find fault with pleasant feelings, since they perceive the impermanent aspect of these feelings and associate them with careless behavior. Since perception of these defects, and not the unique characteristic of pleasant feeling, motivates their pursuit of detachment, Vasubandhu concludes that a pleasant feeling exists by virtue of its own characteristic. Candrakīrti responds that if pleasant and painful feelings exist because of their own unique and distinct characteristics, they would forever exist independently of one another (§222). This position contradicts the Buddha's teaching of the dependent existence of things, which Āryadeva clearly supports: "There is no independent existence for anything anywhere at any time" (CŚ IX.9ab).

Candrakīrti aims a parting blow at Vasubandhu by accusing him of misrepresenting Āryadeva's views and also of misunderstanding the difference between the Buddha's definitive and interpretable statements (§242). The vast quantity of the Buddha's discourses led later generations of his disciples to distinguish between discourses whose meanings are definitive and can be taken literally (*nītārtha*) and interpretable discourses whose meanings require further interpretation (*neyārtha*). Most Buddhist schools accept as definitive the discourses that speak about suffering, impermanence, and the absence of a self.[14]

Vasubandhu claims that the Buddha's statement that pain is present in feelings is definitive (*nītārtha*) because he is speaking about the second type of suffering, the suffering of change (AKB 881). Vasubandhu argues further that the statement that it is an illusion to regard what is painful as pleasant expresses a specific intention (*ābhiprāyika*) that requires further interpretation (AKV 882). Ordinary people associate the idea of pleasure with pleasant feelings, desirable sense objects, and good rebirths. It is incorrect to regard these things as entirely pleasant, Vasubandhu says, and not regard them as being painful in some ways. It is wrong to claim that pleasant sensations do not exist, since the Buddha speaks about pleasant, neutral, and painful feelings as real. Vasubandhu rejects the assertion that the Buddha speaks of the existence of pleasant things in conformity with the views of ordinary people.

Āryadeva and Candrakīrti associate interpretable discourse with conventional truths that enable teachers to introduce people to the Buddhist path. Candrakīrti claims that only discourses that speak about emptiness are definitive (MĀ VI.97).[15] Since Vasubandhu fails to understand that things are empty of any inherent nature, he misunderstands the Buddha's teachings and Āryadeva's teachings.

Candrakīrti emphasizes the importance of being mindful of painful feelings because this awareness of pain can lead people to adopt the Buddha's path, with its goal of bringing suffering to an end. In his commentary on the second chapter of Āryadeva's *Catuḥśataka*, he speaks briefly about the illusion that people have about the purity of the human body (§§229–31). In his commentary on the third chapter of the *Catuḥśataka*, he explains in graphic detail why the body (especially the female body) should be regarded as impure.

4

THE DANGERS OF CORPOREAL PASSION

Buddhist monastics deny that corporeal passions provide any pleasure at all and contrast their fleeting and painful nature with lasting pleasures of a chaste, contemplative life. They share the view of their Christian counterparts, who thought that "to have intercourse was to open the human body to the firestorm that raged through the universe" (Brown 1988, 116). Abstinence quenches the fire of sexual passion and marks the beginning of the monastic's path to the cool and tranquil state of Nirvana.

Candrakīrti refutes the conventional wisdom of his day that married men should pursue the pleasures of intercourse while they are still young and turn their attention to abstinence only in old age. He uses the human body to illustrate two illusions that trap the ignorant in the firestorm: mistaking pleasure for pain and mistaking purity for impurity. His comments stress that only fools believe that human bodies are sources of pleasure; the wise recognize that passion produces both physical and mental pain. Spent passion leaves men physically exhausted, while unsatisfied passion continues to torture their minds. After exposing the painful nature of the body, he directs his attention to a vigorous attack on the illusions people have about the pure nature of the human body. Although he aims pointed comments against Brahmins who take pride in their own purity, his main target is the man who perceives a woman's body as pure and alluring.

A Buddhist Critique of Brahmin Views on Purity

Buddhist scriptures condemn Brahmin priests for their involvement in rituals that require the death of animals. These mercenary priests lust after the wealth that the rituals' sponsors give them for carrying out these bloody sacrifices. The sponsors solicit Brahmins for this work because the alleged superior purity of Brahmins uniquely empowers them to communicate with the gods in these rituals. Brahmins claim that the *Rig Veda* (X.90) sanctions their superior social status and purity with its foundational myth of the gods' sacrifice and dismemberment of a divine person (*puruṣa*). This text legitimizes the division of society into four classes: the Brahmins come from the divinity's mouth; his arms, thighs, and feet become, in a sequence of diminishing purity, warriors/rulers, farmers/merchants and servants. The *Mānava Dharma Śāstra* (I.92–93) states that Brahmins are legally entitled to their superior status because the god's mouth was his purest part.

The False Purity of Superior Birth

The Buddha criticizes the Brahmins' claim to inherent superiority based on the purity of their birth. The *Agaññasuttanta* begins with the Buddha asking the ex-Brahmin Vāseṭṭha what kind of abuse he has had to suffer from Brahmins because of his decision to become a monk (D III 81–82).[1] Vāseṭṭha responds that Brahmins abuse him by flaunting the purity of their superior birth. They denounce him for deserting his own kind and taking up with people of the lowest class, born from the god's feet. The Buddha rejects the Brahmins' claim of birth from the creator god Brahmā's mouth. He reminds Vāseṭṭha that the evidence of ordinary perception shows that Brahmins emerge from their mothers filthy wombs in the same way as human beings from other social classes.

Candrakīrti further ridicules the Brahmins' belief that their birth could be considered pure. "How could people who are not mentally impaired," he asks, "think that the perpetually impure matrix out of which they emerged is pure?" (§317). The child who develops in the mother's filthy womb feeds off the fluid of her waste products. These proud Brahmins who spent nine or ten months in their mother's womb are no purer than a worm that fattens itself up on a pile of dung. "Out of ignorance," he concludes, "they develop pride in their wealth, in their purity, and in their power" (§326).

Several times Candrakīrti delights in telling stories that mock the Brahmins' concern with physical purity. One of these stories involves a young man who seduced another's man's wife:

> A young man who had become involved with the wife of rich man arrived at that man's house. He was then seized and thrown into a sewer. There he was nourished by the sewage. One day because of a heavy rainfall one side of the sewer collapsed and he emerged from it. His relatives led him away and brought him into their house. They summoned a skilled physician. After several days much of his strength and color had been restored. On another occasion he had his body washed and oiled. When he went out into the middle of the main road, a poor man accidentally brushed against him with his clothes. The young man, inflated with pride, reviled him: "Shame on you! I am unclean because of this filthy clothing of yours!" (§326)

Like the developing child in the womb, this young adulterer remains confined in a filthy prison with no sustenance other than raw filth. He too emerges from his foul prison into the welcoming embrace of his relatives. The rains make possible his fortuitous rebirth, and the application of water and fragrant oils to his body restore his body's pristine appearance. His pride in his appearance and in his social class surfaces when he angrily rebukes a poor man for accidentally touching him. He believes that the contagion of that brief physical contact makes him unclean. The story ridicules the rigid notion that external contact, a single brief and accidental brush with a poor man's clothing, can make someone impure. The real impurity resides in the polluted mind of that indignant fool. Candrakīrti uses this story also to illustrate his disdain for the Brahmins' claim that their social class and obsessive concern with physical purity makes them superior to all others. From a Buddhist perspective, the intentional contamination of the mind through the poisons of anger and pride makes someone unclean and defiled.

Polluted Bodies

The body that emerges from the foul enclosure of the maternal womb is itself a container of filth. The concept of the person as a container of filth, which is implicit in the association of the Sanskrit word "person" with words that signify enclosure as well as earth and excrement, is made explicit in Buddhist writings.[2] Candrakīrti tells another story that mocks Brahmanical concern with physical purity:

> An itinerant trader spent the night in a room of a village inn. He defecated in various spots and left very early the next morning. Among the travelers there were Brahmins who were left behind because they were asleep. The inn's watchman came in, seized them, and shouted angrily: "You idiots! Shame on you! Clean up the shit down there before I beat you!" Then all the Brahmins each cleaned up his own excrement but not anyone else's.[3] (§20)

For Candrakīrti's Indian audience, the humor of this story involves high-caste Brahmins being forced to perform the actions of outcaste sweepers. The story turns the ordered world envisioned by the writers of the legal codes upside down. In a role reversal these writers did not sanction, even in the worst of times, highborn Brahmins carry out the unclean work of lowborn sweepers and scavengers. The threat of corporal punishment inflicted on a Brahmin also conflicts with the class-conscious world of the legalists. The legal codes did not permit even high-caste kings to beat Brahmins.[4] The very idea that a low-caste watchman would put his hands on his social superiors, insult them, and threaten them with a beating if they did not clean up their own dirt would amuse Candrakīrti's audience by its audacity.

Polluted Minds

The "dirt" that defiles the place in which it is left and those who clean it up is matter transposed across boundaries: from in the body to outside and from one caste to another; but, as Glucklich points out, the crossing of physical and/or social boundaries is not as fundamentally important to the experience of bodily pollution as is the experience of the body as "ours" (Glucklich 1994, 19). In the story that Candrakīrti narrates, physical and social boundaries are crossed when the excrement passes outside the boundaries of the high-caste Brahmins' bodies and they are then forced to take on the low-caste duties of a sweeper. For Candrakīrti as well, what is fundamentally important is the identification of the body as "mine."

The Brahmins' experience of physical impurity is closely tied to their belief in personal identity or, more literally translated, their belief in a real body (*satkāyadṛṣṭi*). In this context, body does not refer just to the physical body but instead to the entire body of the five aggregates that form the basis for an ordinary person's belief in his or her personal identity (Collins 1982, 93). The appropriation of the body (and its expelled contents) as "mine" provokes the incisive criticism of Candrakīrti's interpretation of this story:

> They are known as Brahmins who hold the heterodox belief in a real person because they seize as "mine" even what is impure. The expedient threat "you will be beaten" makes these Brahmins who hold the view of a real person clean up their excrement. Although the excrement is equally impure, they say, "This is mine, that is not," and see it as unequal. (§20)

Candrakīrti ridicules the Brahmins' attachment toward what they perceive as '"I" and "mine" by showing that their feelings of pride and ownership extend even beyond the boundaries of the body to the excrement it discharges.

In the *Madhyamakāvatāra*, Candrakīrti employs logical reasoning instead of ridicule as a strategy for shattering belief in a personal identity. He argues that the self cannot be identified with the physical and mental aggregates of a human being, since it would follow that the self, like these components, must be multiple and impermanent in nature. It is equally wrong to believe that the self and the physical and mental aggregates are totally different, since things that are totally different can never enter into any kind of relationship. The self, Candrakīrti claims, should be regarded as a convenient label for its parts (MĀ VI.150–65). It depends on them in the same way that a chariot depends upon the assembly of constituent parts, such the wheels, the axle, and so forth. The expression "self" is meaningful in ordinary language, but logical analysis shows that it has no actual referent. In his commentary on the *Catuḥśataka*, Candrakīrti rejects belief in the self on psychological grounds. The attachment Brahmins feel toward what they consider "I" and "mine" not only makes these Brahmins arrogant and conceited but also perpetuates their fear of death and their fear of contagion from contact with people they consider less pure.

Semen and the Power of Chastity

Arrogant fools associate both purity and power with physical control of the body in the following verse, which Candrakīrti quotes:

> Fools, arrogant about their purity,
> And deluded by desire, say that the body
> Should not be repudiated because of its nature
> And because of the power acquired from chastity. (§319)

These arrogant fools, of course, are Brahmins convinced of their own purity and proud of their Vedic learning and their tradition of chaste behavior. Brahmanical texts assert that the power of chastity comes from controlling the flow of semen. These texts advocate abstention from sexual intercourse because it involves the loss of a powerful but impure substance (Gonda 1985, 284–314). Brahmins, like early Christian ascetics, believed in "a powerful fantasy" about the male body: that the most virile man "lost little or no seed" (Brown 1988, 19).

Although Buddhists advocate chaste behavior, they reject the idea that unspilt semen provides a reservoir of untapped virility. The exhaustive and explicit code of conduct recorded in the *Vinaya* details many violations of chaste behavior that will get a monk expelled or suspended from the community. Masturbation and the intentional spilling of semen results in temporary exclusion from the monastic community. The *Vinaya* tells the story of the young monk Seyyasaka, whose haggard and lackluster appearance reveals his unhappiness with his chaste life (Vin 3.110). He has his strength and bright complexion restored after he takes up the daily practice of masturbation on the advice of an elder monk who enthusiastically recommends it as a way of releasing sexual tension. When other monks bring his behavior to the attention of the Buddha, the Buddha rebukes him for failing to understand that Buddhist teachings are intended to control sexual desires. Seyyasaka's loss of his mental control over his sexual feelings, rather than his physical loss of semen, brings him the censure of the Buddha and his fellow monks.[5] In what seems a parody of the Brahmanical notion that a man's physical health is dependent upon retention of his semen, in this example, a young monk regains his vitality after he begins to masturbate daily (Faure 1998, 86).

Sex and the Married Man

This belief in the power of unspilt seed and the virility of the chaste ascetic conflicts with the Vedic injunction that a man must fulfill his debt to his ancestors by producing sons. A man must have sons and grandsons to ensure that his lineage continues. His male descendants are responsible for performing the rituals that will ensure his own continuance in heaven.[6]

Reluctant Husbands

In *Rig Veda* I.179 Lopamudrā seeks to divert her husband Agastya from his vow of chastity so that she can have his child. She eventually persuades him. The Vedic poet concludes that the reluctant Agastya achieves the best of both worlds: immortality in the world of the gods through his practice of asceticism and the perpetuity of his lineage in the human world through the birth of children. The ideal situation for a man who has conflicting religious goals of asceticism and the continuance the family life is to pursue asceticism actively as an individual and private matter and acquire sons from sexual activity in which he is a passive and reluctant participant (Jamison 1996, 16).

Brahmanical law books regulate sexual relations between these reluctant husbands and wives. These works require men to have sexual intercourse with their wives during the time in their menstrual cycles when conception is most likely to occur. The reluctant husband engages in sexual intercourse only during his wife's most fertile period, not for pleasure but for the sole purpose of procreation. There are rules concerning the importance of making love at the proper time, and penalties or atonements for both men and women if they fail to take advantage of this opportunity for conceiving a child. According to the *Āpastamba*: "A man who fails in his duty to his wife should put on the skin of a donkey with the hair turned outwards and go to seven houses calling (out to each in turn): '(Give) alms to a man who has failed in his duty to his wife!'"[7] The *Āpastamba* permits a man to have sex with his wife if she wants it, even outside of the brief period when she is most fertile (II.1.18–19). Olivelle suggests that the Vedic text that permits this behavior is *Taittīrya Saṃhitā* (II.5.1.5), which says that Indra gave women the gift of becoming pregnant after their period and of enjoying sex right up to the time of delivery. "The intent appears to be that a good man should eschew such intercourse," Olivelle writes, "but if the woman wants it (women being viewed as unable to control their passions), he should oblige because of this vedic text" (1999, 367). This gift of enjoying sex that the god Indra gave women makes their less eager husbands decidedly uneasy.

Unfaithful Wives

The law books' injunctions about guarding women specifically address male anxieties about female sexuality. These works take the position that women need to be protected from damaging outside influences and from their own dishonorable inclinations. The *Mānava Dharma Śāstra* states that men must understand their obligation to protect their wives so that these women have no opportunity of bringing dishonor upon their families (IX.5–6). A man who guards his wife secures his family's honor, gains legitimate sons, and protects his own future (IX.8–9). Because of unbridled lust and a fickle temperament, a woman will give herself to any man regardless of whether he is handsome or ugly (IX.11).

Buddhist moral arbiters share a similarly dour opinion of the fickle nature of women. *Cullapaduma Jātaka* (Ja II 116–21, no. 193) claims that a woman will give herself to any man, no matter how ugly he is. In this story, the Bodhisattva saves the life of a thief whose hands, feet, nose, ears were sliced off. While the Bodhisattva is away, his wife's earlier revulsion for this thief turns into passion. Now that she no longer loves her husband, she tricks him into climbing a mountain and pushes him over the edge. She then masquerades as a devoted wife who carries her disfigured lover from village to village. For her performance, she receives abundant praise and an ample supply of food from the villagers. The Bodhisattva survives her attempt on his life and exposes her deceit. Other stories similarly expose the deceitful nature of women who entertain their lovers as soon as they can get their unsuspecting husbands out of the house (Jones 1979, 94–99).

Āryadeva warns men about the dangers of unguarded female sexuality: "As long as she does not know someone else, she is yours" (CŚ III.8ab). Candrakīrti comments that a wife will continue to love and remain faithful to her husband as long as a she does not "experience the taste of another man" (§275). Once she has that opportunity, and has sex with another man, her love for her husband vanishes. Women are quick to change their minds, quick to quarrel with their husbands, and quite susceptible to temptation from other men. Candrakīrti encourages men to be suspicious of their wives' fidelity when he complains about their mysterious ways: "Women are hard to fathom; their way of doing things is difficult to comprehend" (§275). Since women are so difficult to understand, they cannot be trusted.

Candrakīrti adds to these suspicious husbands' fear with his tales of unfaithful wives:

> A man desired a certain Brahmin woman. She told her husband, "A man came into my presence and I was afraid of him. When he comes again, I'll tell you." After she said that, she waited. When the man appeared again, she had changed her mind and was now attracted to him. She did not tell her husband that the man had come. (§276)

This story illustrates his point that women frequently change their minds. Their promises of fidelity cannot be trusted. Their deceitful actions speak louder than their soothing words.

The Male Fantasy of Adultery

Although the law books provide little evidence to support the idea that unfaithful wives were as common as Candrakīrti would have us believe, the male fantasy of adultery occurs often in folklore, in epic romances, and in texts on the merits of sensual pleasure (Doniger 1995). Wendy Doniger says that the *Kāmasūtra*'s inventory of the wife's reasons for committing adultery presents us indirectly, through a male scribe's point of view, with a sympathetic image of a very long list of unhappily married women "who can be gotten without any trouble":

> a woman who stands at the door, a woman who looks out from her porch onto the main street; who hangs about the house of the young man who is her neighbor; who is always staring (at you); a woman who is sent as a messenger but throws sideways glances at you; one whose husband has taken a co-wife for no good reason; who hates her husband or is hated by him; who has no one to look after her; who has no children; who is always in the house of her relatives; whose children have died; who is fond of society; who is addicted to pleasure; the wife of an actor; a young woman whose husband has died; a poor woman fond of enjoying herself; the wife of the oldest of several brothers; a woman who is very proud; a woman whose husband is inadequate; a woman who is proud of her skills; a woman who is distressed by her husband's foolishness or his lack of distinction or by his greediness; a woman who was chosen as a bride when she was still a young girl, but somehow was not obtained by that man, and now has been married to someone else; a woman who longs for a man whose intelligence, nature, and wisdom are compatible to her and not contrary to her own personality; a woman who by nature is given to taking sides; a woman who has been dishonoured (by her husband) when she has done nothing wrong; one who is put down by women whose beauty and so forth as the same as hers; whose husband travels a lot; the wife of a man who is jealous, foul-smelling, too clean, impotent, a slow-poke, unmanly, a hunchback, a dwarf, a jeweler, vulgar, sick or old. (Doniger 1994, 171)

These images speak of lonely women without children or husbands to care for, and of dissatisfied women whose husbands are incompatible intellectually and/or sexually. The *Kāmasūtra* cites far fewer reasons for a wife not to commit adultery. These include affection for her husband and her children, the fact that she is past her prime, is unable to find an opportunity to get away from her husband, or has respect for proper behavior (Doniger 1994, 171–73).

Candrakīrti supplies a bizarre example of two faithless marriage partners who pursue an adulterous liaison and wind up in bed with each other.

> A man saw another man's wife, lusted after her, and thought: "Someday I will have sex with her." Later, his friend told him, "She is the very one you're seeking but don't say anything to her. She is a modest woman from a good family." Then, in the dark, that man had sex with a woman who was his own wife. He was quite happy and said, "There is no woman like her!" (§256)

The man set up by his devious friend knew so little of his wife's ways that he was unable to recognize her in the dark. His immodest wife was similarly ill-informed about her philandering husband. Candrakīrti uses these stories about adulterous liaisons to undermine his audience's belief in the sanctity of marriage. The stories suggest that, despite a façade of modesty and wifely devotion, women will seize any opportunity to cuckold their husbands.

The *Kāmasūtra* cautions would-be adulterers to distinguish between women that are easily procured and those that are not. Despite these injunctions that place the wives of kings and Brahmins off limits to the prudent man, Candrakīrti's stories imply limitless availability. Even queens (§285.) and Brahmin women (§276) are quite willing to engage in adulterous behavior with younger and more attractive partners. The *Kāmasūtra* argues that adultery was once common because "Women are alike, just like cooked rice" (Doniger 1994, 170). Candrakīrti supports this view with a story he tells:

> "You are ugly," her husband told an ugly woman. "A man obsessed with sex doesn't discriminate between beautiful and ugly women," she retorted. He did not understand her, so she put lentil soup in several bowls and called him when it was time to eat. "What is this?" he asked her. "It's lentil soup," she replied. "Now you see that I have put it in several bowls." "How are they different?" "It's just the same with having sex!" (§256)

The analogies used in the *Kāmasūtra* and in this story make sex seem as ordinary as a simple meal of cooked rice and lentils. There is nothing special about the lentil soup poured into the various bowls, and nothing to differentiate one bowl from another. Candrakīrti argues further that the sexual act is the same regardless of whether a man has sex with beautiful women or ugly ones. The point he wants to advance is that women are common commodities. They are easily procured: "like goods sold on the street" (§263)."

Rare Examples of Chaste Wives

Despite the dissimilarity of their contents, the law books and the *Kāmasūtra* entertain similar suspicions about the willingness of wives to pursue extramarital affairs. The epics have a slightly less prejudiced view of women's chastity. Sītā willingly follows her husband into exile and remains faithful even when the demon Rāvaṇa threatens her with death. Disguised as a Brahmin ascetic, Rāvaṇa takes advantage of the unguarded Sītā's hospitality and abducts her. Vālmiki's version of the *Rāmāyaṇa* implies that her own willful action of persuading her male relatives to leave her unguarded leads to the damaging consequences of her abduction and of her exile. After Rāma slays Rāvaṇa and rescues Sītā, he asks her to prove her sexual purity by undergoing a trial by fire. She emerges unscathed, and they return together to the capital city. Public doubt about her chastity, however, forces him to banish her to the forest, where she finds refuge and gives birth to twin sons. When Rāma later recognizes them as his and invites her back, Sītā refuses. She calls upon Mother Earth to swallow her up in act suggestive of ritual suicide (*satī*).

The *Rāmāyaṇa* mentions the practice of ritual suicide in speaking of a Brahmin women who was molested by Rāvaṇa. *The Mahābhārata* reports that after the death of King Pāṇḍu, one of his wives chooses to die with him on his funeral pyre, while another wife and her two daughters-in-law choose to live as ascetics. None of the Vedic texts mentions this practice, nor does it receive any support in the legal literature (Kane 1968–77, 2/1: 625–36; Altekar 1956, 114–25; Sharma et al. 1988, 31–38). References to the custom of a virtuous woman committing suicide after the death of her husband are also rare in Buddhist literature. Aśvaghoṣa, in a section of his *Saundarananda* (VIII.42) devoted to scurrilous attacks on women, seems to doubt the sincerity of the wives who follow their husbands in death.

> Though women mount the funeral pyre,
> Though they follow and give up their lives,
> Though they do so without coercion,
> Still, they do not really display devotion.[8]

In framing his discussion about the dubious virtue of women, Candrakīrti has a dissenter raise this extreme case of wifely devotion: "A woman will kill herself after her husband has died. A man won't do the same thing for a woman" (§274). He does not doubt these women's devotion to their husbands, although he agrees with Āryadeva that "a virtuous woman who remains faithful to her husband is very rare" (§275).

Jealous Husbands

Fear of their wives' infidelity plagues husbands and arouses their jealousy. Candrakīrti fans the fires of jealousy when he tells a man rejoicing over his acquisition of an exceptionally beautiful wife: "Since it is doubtful that she is solely yours, it must be possible for every man to have her" (§263). He adds that it should come as no surprise that other men also find her attractive. He concludes that for the right price men can have any woman they want (§265).

Candrakīrti responds to the claim that having sex is pleasurable by arguing that a man's enjoyment of sexual activity cannot keep pace with his insatiable desire (§289). Since it is impossible to have sex day and night without interruption, he slyly suggests that a generous man should be willing to share his wife with others when he tires. Men should be able to enjoy sex without the pain of jealousy and the fear of losing their prized possession. His comments resemble the Christian monk Jerome's similarly sarcastic remarks: "What harm does it do me if another man lies with my wife? . . . If it was intended that the organs of generation should always be performing their office, when my vigor is spent, let another take my place and, if I may so speak, let my wife quench her burning lust where she can" (Clark and Richardson 1977, 53). The physical act of sex is exhausting and disappointingly brief, but Candrakīrti is more concerned with condemning the mental attitude that underlies sexual activity. The possessive attitude men adopt toward their wives ("She is mine; she doesn't belong to anyone else") arises from their self-serving attitudes and their ignorance of proper behavior. He tells the story of a king who has so many wives he doesn't know what to do with them all. A monk's persuasive talk on virtuous behavior finally persuades the king to release these superfluous wives (§290).

Sex and the Backsliding Monk

Leaving home provides the solution to the pain of jealousy and the hard work that supporting a family requires. For many monks the difficulty of overcoming attraction to women still remains. The renunciation of lay life does not remove them completely from the temptation of sexual desire.[9]

The Seduction of Ascetics

The adversarial relation between women and men on the sexual battleground has a long history in the religious texts of Brahmins and Buddhists. Popular stories in the Hindu epics and in Buddhist collections of *Jātaka* tales pit women experienced in the art of seduction against naive young ascetics. The *Mahābhārata*, the *Rāmāyaṇa*, and two Jātaka stories, the *Alambusā Jātaka* (Ja V 152–60, no. 523) and the *Naḷinikā Jātaka* (Ja V 193–209, no. 526) tell the story of how a devious woman successfully seduces an innocent ascetic.[10] In the *Naḷinikā Jātaka* version, the young Isisiṅga is so innocent that he does not know the difference between men and women. Naḷinikā, disguised as an ascetic, comes to the secluded hermitage where Isisiṅga lives with his father. Isisiṅga, who had never seen a woman before, asks Naḷinikā if his "best member" has disappeared.[11] She explains that a wild animal attacked her and ripped it off. Ever since then the wound has been itching, she says, and she invites him to relieve this itch: "I need you to rub against it and give me the greatest pleasure." When his father returns and finds his feverish son, Isisiṅga tells him about this beardless youth who "embraced me with soft arms and gave me pleasure." His not-so-innocent father informs him this was a female demon; and Isisiṅga, now thoroughly frightened, resumes the chaste life of an ascetic meditator.

This view of women expressed by Isisiṅga's father does not focus on the deficient and wounded nature of female bodies. The dangerous and destructive power of sexual desire concerns him far more. Sexual desire is dangerous because it places men under the control of deceitful women. He uses strong language and the powerful image of this women as a demon to pull his son back from her arms and return him to the safety of a chaste life.

The characterization of seductive women as demonic also occurs in the stories that Candrakīrti uses to warn men about dangerous women in disguise. In the first of these stories (§109), a beautiful women captures a man's attention while he rides in his chariot through the forest. This demon's successful impersonation of a beautiful woman gains her a place in his chariot. But when an ugly female demon pops up in front of him, he slices her in two with his sharp sword. Two ugly female demons now confront him. These flesh-eating female demons, out of control, continue to multiply every time he wields his sword. Finally, a knowledgeable god intervenes and instructs him to kill the beautiful woman riding in his chariot; only then will they all vanish. In the second story (§348), the flesh-eating female demon masquerades as a man's wife. Once he catches a glimpse of her real form, he becomes frightened and no longer desires her. Candrakīrti explains that he fears her real nature because it is painful, disgusting, changeable, and completely beyond his control. All these stories of disguised demonic women are meant to frighten men about the uncontrollable nature of sexual desire. Women whose appetites for sex incite them to bring men under their control are compared to female demons with an appetite for devouring male flesh. The sword is an ineffective weapon in this battle; the wise man arms himself with knowledge.

Candrakīrti argues that sex diminishes a man's physical power and places him in the hands of domineering women. The loss of physical control, however, is less significant than the loss of mental control. Sexual desire exercises so much such control over the mind that "men deluded by desire, overwhelmed by attachment, and lacking in shame and modesty" pursue women at all costs, even the loss of their virtue (§271). He argues that sex attracts only those men whose minds are held captive by the illusions that "what is impure is pure and what is painful is pleasant" (§297). An active imagination creates the illusion of a beautiful woman who then becomes the object of male desire. She is no more real, he claims (§284), than the woman a magician creates to play tricks on a gullible audience.

Candrakīrti directs his efforts to curbing the male appetite for sex. Men who succumb to sexual desire are no better than animals, dogs, asses, elephants, and pigs that copulate with females of their own kind (§259). Intelligent men should recognize the debased nature of sexual attraction. The *Manual of the Christian Soldier* takes a similar line of attack in urging Christian ascetics to fight against sexual desire: "First of all, think how foul, how unworthy of any man is this pleasure which reduces us from an image of divinity to the level, not merely of animals, but even to that of swine, he goats, dogs, and the most brutish of brutes" (Miles [1989] 1991, 163). Men who lack all shame and modesty succumb to the intoxicating wine of sexual desire, Candrakīrti says, behave in ways that destroy their virtue and claim their lives (§278). For these men the battle is over.

Monks and the Lures of Former Wives

Former wives who fought to retain their husband's affections posed a significant problem to the monastic community. The frame story that introduces and concludes *Naḷinikā Jātaka* depicts the Buddha counseling an audience of monks. His specific target is a monk whose ex-wife had tried to seduce him and force his return to lay life. The Buddha explains that this monk's wife had attempted to seduce him in the past. She was the disguised ascetic and the monk was Isisiṅga.

In the commentary to the *Dhammapada*, the Buddha tells the story of a wavering monk who left the monastery seven times to return to the embrace of his wife. Cittahattha initially joins the community because he thinks that monks eat well and don't have to work for their living. When he is put to work serving senior monks, he decides to return home. He sees the consequence of their sexual activity on his seventh trip home. As his wife lies sleeping, her swollen pregnant body curbs his sexual appetite:

> Her outer garment had fallen off, saliva was flowing from her mouth, snores resonated in her nasal passages, and her mouth was wide open. She looked like a bloated corpse. . . . Grabbing his yellow robe by the hem, he ran out of the house, tying the robe about his belly as he ran. (Wilson 1996, 80–81)

The sight of her bloated body makes him shed his illusions about her appearance. "That it was sleep that transformed Cittahattha's wife in this way," Wilson writes, "suggests an analogy between her and demonic shape-shifting women who are said to lose their disguises and assume their true forms when asleep or dead (1996, 219 n. 12). Like the man who recognizes the true nature of the shape-shifting demon who impersonated his wife, Cittahattha now sees that his wife's real nature is impermanent, painful, and disgusting.

The use of sleeping women's bodies to illustrate the dangers of the world and the temptation of sexual desire follows the example set in the Buddha's biography. The event that turns his mind away from sexual pleasures and toward the religious life is the sight of female musicians and dancers, provided for his amusement by his doting father. Their attempts at entertainment put him to sleep. When he later awakens, he finds these beautiful women distinctly unattractive. They slobber, snore, grind their teeth; and their clothes in disarray reveal their "disgusting" naked bodies. Their bodies remind him of a cemetery strewn with putrid corpses awaiting cremation (Wilson 1996, 65–70; Faure 1998, 15–16).

The initial prohibition in the *Vinaya* against sexual intercourse occurs after the Buddha is confronted with the case of another young monk who has sex with his former wife. Sudinna is a spoiled only child whose parents reluctantly consent to his ordination. They give in to his demands only after he prepares to make good on his threat to starve himself to death if he does not receive their permission. His determined and resourceful parents successfully persuade him to engage in sexual intercourse (three times) with his willing ex-wife to provide themselves with an heir. The Buddha severely criticizes Sudinna. It would have been better for him to thrust his penis into the mouth of a poisonous snake or into a pit of blazing charcoal than into his ex-wife, since by breaking his commitment to chastity, he will die and be reborn in hell (Horner 1938, 1: 21–38; Wilson 1996, 20–24; Faure 1998, 75–76).

This story indicates that the blood ties and generational links that bind families together no longer hold for monastics. Instead of fulfilling his social obligations to his birth family and acquiescing to his father's desire for immortality, Sudinna should have been more concerned with his obligations to his monastic family and with his own mortality. Mohan Wijayaratna explains that sexual offenses involve "defeat" in the battle against the enemy of sensual desire. Those members of the religious community who recognize their inability to maintain control over their sensual desires and formally leave the community to return to lay life before committing a sexual offense are not defeated, since they have withdrawn from the battlefield before the enemy can defeat them (Wijayaratna 1990, 93).

Māra battled unsuccessfully for control over the Buddha. His sexual surrogates, his three dancing daughters, could not deflect the Buddha's mind away from meditation and his goal of enlightenment. Unsuccessful in his attack on the Buddha, the Lord of Death turned his attention to the Buddha's disciples and enlisted their ex-wives on his side.[12]

The monk Candana describes his former wife:

> Covered with gold ornaments,
> Attended by maidservants,
> And bearing our son on her hip,
> My wife approached me.
> I saw her coming,
> The mother of my child,
> Adorned, well-dressed,
> Like a snare of Lord Death laid out. (Thag. 299–300)

He says that this sight of his wife led him to develop the proper perspective. The dangers of sensual pleasure suddenly become clear and his disgust with the world is now firmly established. Death cannot defeat him.

Monks Accosted by Harlots

Because of the possibility that frequent contact with women might lure monks back into the profane world, disciplinary rules were formulated to keep this contact to a minimum. The daily necessity of begging for alms brings monks into contact with women. The laywomen who provide for the care of monks by donations of food and wealth are singled out for praise, but there are other women out on the streets whose motives for engaging monks are not so benign. While out on the morning begging rounds, Nāgasamāla sees a woman dancing in the street:

> Adorned, well-dressed, garlanded,
> And anointed with sandalwood paste,
> A woman danced to music in the middle of the road.
> And while I came, I saw her,
> Adorned, well-dressed,
> Like a snare of Lord Death laid out. (Thag. 267–69)

Sundarasamudda describes in similar terms his encounter with a harlot who had attempted to seduce him:

> I saw that harlot,
> Appealing to me,
> With her palms pressed together,
> Adorned, well-dressed,
> Like a snare of Lord Death laid out. (Thag. 463)

These monks' verses share the same cluster of images: man as the hunted prey, Lord Death as the hunter, and a woman as the baited snare. Each of these monks' descriptions of women concentrates on their illusory external appearance. The bait appears even more attractive because of the gold ornaments, fine clothing, and scented garlands that adorn these women's bodies. In each case, the proper perspective arises, the danger of sensual pleasures becomes clear, and disgust with the world is established. These negative images of women as temptresses suggest that some of these monks saw women's sexuality as threats both to their individual spiritual growth and to the stability of the monastic community as a whole.

The Body's Deceptive Appearance

The poems written and collected by Buddhist monks acknowledge the disturbing effect that a woman's gaze has on a man. Ārya Śūra's *Jātakamālā* describes the Buddha's past life as a virtuous king. The virtue of the Bodhisattva is tempted by the beauty of his minister's young wife: "the graceful movements of her body, her smile, her glance" (XIII.15 a). Another poet, whose verse the monk Vidyākara collected in his anthology of poems, speaks about the potent force that a woman's glance exerts:

> It brings paralysis and dizziness of mind,
> it rouses fever, and at the last
> it even drives out consciousness:—
> her glance holds mortal poison. (Ingalls 1965, 184)

Candrakīrti warns his audience that women are "poisonous adversaries" who assist sexual desire in conquering imprudent men (§293). He uses the language of erotic poetry in describing the position of a libertine opponent who wonders how a man can turn his mind away from "shapely women, pleasant to embrace, whose limbs are alluring, who enchant both his eyes and his mind, and who melt the hearts of impassioned men with sidelong glances that reveal their hearts' desire, just as the touch of fire melts fresh butter" (§252).

Candrakīrti intends to quench this burning desire by attacking the deceptive appearance of feminine beauty. He argues that a woman's beauty is just on the surface, and beneath this beguiling surface "a woman is filthy, like a rotting heap of excrement" (§254). The fragrant scent of flowers braided in her hair and sandalwood paste on her skin all camouflage the real stench and impurity of her body. Even the skin that covers her shapely limbs assists in this deception.

Turning the Female Body Inside Out

Buddhist monks often share the same prejudices about women's bodies as their Brahmin counterparts. Male bodies are impure but women's bodies are even more impure. Only women's bodies release the impure bodily fluids associated with menstruation and the act of giving birth. The traditional medical and legal texts say that the blood flow of a menstruating woman makes her impure for three days. These texts stress the danger of sexual contact with women during their menstrual periods with the warning that if a man has sex with a menstruating woman during these crucial three days, the child that results from this union will be considered an outcaste or cursed. Menstruating women themselves are treated during this time as if they were outcastes and are physically separated from the rest of family. They are reintegrated back into the life of the household only after taking a purifying bath (Leslie 1989, 283–85, Olivelle 1999, 264). The pollution associated with giving birth similarly segregates women (Babb 1975, 71–76; Olivelle 1999, 262).

Sexual intercourse and its anticipated result, the birth of children, are women's domains. "Women die insatiable and inexhaustible in respect to two things, Monks," the venerable Kaccāna says. "Which two? Sexual intercourse and giving birth" (A I 78). Monks' misogynist remarks about women, whose bodies represent the polluted realm of sexual desire, are associated with their fear of losing physical and mental control. The remarkable statement about the insatiable and inexhaustible character of women reflects the belief that sexual intercourse is dangerous for men because it causes fatigue, releases impure bodily fluids, and results in the birth of children. Children hinder their parents from making progress on Buddha's path.

Monks' verses in the *Theragāthā* warn of the polluting substances that female bodies contain. Mogallāna, one of the most distinguished of the

Buddha's early followers, harps on this theme of the foulness of women's bodies in his harsh denunciation of a harlot who had attempted to seduce him:

> You skin-covered bag of dung!
> You ogress with swollen tumors on your chest!
> In your body nine foul streams ceaselessly flow. (Thag. 1,151)

Any monk concerned with preserving his purity should avoid her, he says, just as he would a pool of excrement. Nandaka similarly reviles a woman who accosted him—according to the traditional commentary it was his ex-wife—with the same harsh words. Her body is vile, evil-smelling, and the source of nine foul streams (Thag. 279).[13]

These intemperate attacks on the impurity of women's bodies persist in the works of Mahāyāna monks. Candrakīrti quotes at length a section from Nāgārjuna's *Ratnāvalī* (II.48–51) that similarly describes a woman's body as a container of filth:

> Desire for a woman primarily arises
> From thinking that a woman's body is pure.
> In reality there is nothing pure
> In a woman's body.
> Her mouth is a vessel of impurities:
> Foul saliva and scum are on her teeth.
> Her nose is a vessel for snot and mucus,
> And her eyes are vessels for tears and filth.
> The interior of her body is a vessel for
> Excrement, urine, sputum, and bile.
> Someone who does not see a woman in this way
> Because of delusion, desires her body.
> If people are very much attached
> Even to the body, that stinking object,
> Which should be a reason for detachment,
> How can they be led to escape from desire? (§230)

Candrakīrti regards sexual desire as an ignorant and base reaction to the visual stimulus of a woman's body. The beauty of a woman's body is "an object of enjoyment even for dogs and vultures!" (§255). He compares the deluded lover's sexual appetite to the sordid cravings of scavenger dogs and vultures who would feast on her flesh. He implies that these carnivores, dogs and vultures, crave her body for the pleasure of ripping it to pieces and devouring the remains. Candrakīrti then proceeds to rip apart the female body and lay bare its entrails in his effort to dissuade ignorant men from pursuing women's deceptive attractions. The purity with which men invest women's bodies comes from the dazzling and blinding effect of gold ornaments, silk garments, and fragrant perfumes that mask their true nature. By stripping way all the coverings, even her skin, the true impure nature of the female body is revealed.

Candrakīrti uses graphic language to emphasize the impure nature of women's bodies:

> They naturally have a foul odor and their continually oozing bodies resemble the city's filthy sewers. Many men are obsessed with acquiring that impure thing, which is filled up just like an outhouse. Like the hole of an outhouse, it is dark, filthy, stinking, and attractive to a swarm of insects! Inside a woman is filthy, like a rotting heap of excrement, and outside only her skin encloses that filth. (§254)

His language is particularly graphic in portraying that part men want to penetrate as the hole of an outhouse: "dark, filthy, stinking, and attractive to a swarm of insects."[14] Several times (§254, §268, §309, §311, §325) Candrakīrti uses this memorable metaphor for women and their bodies when he stresses the need for men to reject sexual desire. By turning the female body inside out and focusing attention on the most repulsive of its contents, he intends to evoke strong feelings of disgust. He repeatedly emphasizes the repulsive nature of the female body to expose and counteract the misguided mentality that instigates male sexual activity.

Meditation on the Cremation Ground

Women's live bodies arouse unenlightened monks' lust because they fail to see these bodies' true foul nature. Meditation on the unpleasant sight of a woman's dead body while it decomposes makes the recognition of its foul inner nature much easier. The story of the monk Upagupta's encounter with a famous prostitute indicates how a monk should focus his mind on a woman's body. After the prostitute Vāsvadattā is judged guilty on trumped-up charges, her mutilated body, with its hands, feet, nose, and ears cut off, is discarded on the cremation ground, where Upagupta encounters her. Vāsavadattā's maid, "with the blinders of one who has served too long in a house of prostitution and seen too many skewed forms of sexuality," thinks that Upagupta has come there for sex" (Strong 1992, 77). Upagupta has come instead to meditate on the impermanence of her body and the impurity of her decaying corpse.[15]

Kulla's verses describe this traditional practice:

> I went to the cremation ground
> And saw a women discarded,
> Left behind on the cremation ground,
> Food for maggots.
> See the diseased, impure, putrid body,
> Which once beguiled fools.
> Now it swells and festers. (Thag. 393–94)

Although this meditation practice successfully eliminates most monks' lustful thoughts, one monk found that even the sight of a maggot-eaten female corpse aroused his lust. He quickly fled from the cremation ground, sat down, concentrated his mind until the proper perspective arose, the dangers of sensual pleasures became clear, and his disgust for the world was established (Thag. 315). Aversion is the proper response for a monk whose mind is properly focused on a woman's body—live or dead.[16] The gruesome practice of meditating on a decaying corpse enables unenlightened monks to see through the camouflage of clothes and flesh and properly regard the human body as though it were a living skeleton.

Developing Disgust for the Body

Candrakīrti wants to grab his audience by the nose. His frequent comparisons of the human body to an outhouse focus attention on unpleasant realities that most people would rather ignore. He underscores this point with the following story of a woman lovely on the outside but filthy inside:

> A rich man had in his possession a very beautiful woman who carried a copper pot. Men desired her, courted her, and sought her out. Then one day she went outside and vomited into that copper pot. After they saw that, they considered her damaged goods, plugged their noses, and went away. (§318)

Candrakīrti mocks the behavior of the men who plug their noses and walk away oblivious of the fact that this disgusting filth resides in all their bodies. Although people can wash the outside of their bodies, there is no way for them to clean up the filth inside their bodies:

> The king employed the friend of a villager to build an outhouse. At one point, the villager's friend whitewashed it. The villager observed him purifying it with incense, etc. His friend laughed and said to him, "Right now it is clean!" (§330)

The actions of the villager's friend who whitewashes the outhouse and uses incense to make it smell good are no different from actions of ignorant people who use cosmetics, flowers, and perfumes to make their bodies seem more attractive. These are only temporary remedies: "wearing flowers, etc., is not enough to make the body continually fragrant with the finest scents, just as garlic doesn't continue to make it smell bad!" (§338). Perfumes, flower garlands, and clothes conceal the "open sores of this body" (§340) and make it seem attractive; eventually even these flowers wither and decay.

Observant people recognize that impermanence and impurity indelibly mark human bodies. They find the body as disgusting as "a piece of excrement" (§343). Candrakīrti uses these repellent descriptions of bodies with the intention of provoking disgust. These descriptions of the body's impurity function much like meditation practices on the body's foul composition, which evoke "strong sensations of revulsion through the technique of taking note of excrement and all the other polluting substances that reside inside the body" (Trainor 1993, 70–71). Sue Hamilton contends that the intent behind such negative passages is not to encourage disgust toward impure bodies but to discourage people from seeking anything permanent in or identifying with their bodies.[17] Negative statements about the body ultimately lead the practitioner of mindfulness to the understanding that the body is impermanent, painful, devoid of a self. This understanding is the culmination of the practice of meditation on the body, but its beginning is more modest. The gripping character of these detailed descriptions of the body both in texts on meditation and in Candrakīrti's commentary persuades me that their initial focus is on generating disgust for the body's impure constituents.

The deliberate development of disgust for the human body is the starting point in the difficult task of eliminating sexual desire, which is the real target of these harsh statements. Similar descriptions occur in Christian monastic writings. About the Christian monk "who dipped his cloak into the putrefying flesh of a dead woman so that the smell might banish thoughts about her," Brown remarks that "the sheer physicality of such stories bruise the modern sensibility" (1988, 242). In the Buddhist process of mental training, however, the focus does not remain fixed on the revulsion created by putrefying flesh. The gradual development of mental training starts by developing disenchantment with the body; and from that point, the training moves forward to developing disenchantment with the world of the senses. Candrakīrti takes the common fear of pollution and disgust for the impure substances inside the body as a means of directing unenlightened people onto the path that leads to the pure state of enlightenment.

5

THE KING AS THE EMBODIMENT OF EGOTISM

In the first three chapters of his commentary on Āryadeva's *Catuḥśataka*, Candrakīrti uses the body to explain how people's belief in immortality, their pursuit of pleasure, and their obsession with purity is founded on illusion. In the fourth chapter, he undermines popular belief in the immortal nature of the king, his ability to enjoy the pleasures of his office, and the purity of his royal lineage. The king also comes under sharp scrutiny because he embodies the arrogance and egotism associated with the illusion of a self. Candrakīrti demonstrates his familiarity with the literature of epics and the law books on the king's role as the embodiment of virtuous behavior (*dharma*). He believes that a Buddhist king shares with his people the same obligation to observe the ethical guidelines for virtuous behavior set forth by the Buddha. The hierarchical perspective of Buddhist discourse places the king, like the people he governs, in the position of an ordinary person who is subordinate to his superiors, the monastics who follow the Buddha's path. The powerful and privileged place the king occupies as a reward for the merit accumulated over his past lives can be easily lost if he fails to exemplify virtuous behavior.

The King's Role: God on Earth?

In the fourth chapter of the *Catuḥśataka*, Āryadeva questions the king's role as the protector of his people and the privileges he enjoys as a result of his status. Candrakīrti puts this discussion in the form of a dialogue between Āryadeva and an unnamed Indian king. Candrakīrti regards a king as the human being who best personifies the concepts of egotism and selfishness. He explains, "Egotism arises from the imagination of one's own superior characteristics: 'I am the lord'" (§353). Selfishness, however, arises in regard to notion of power over things that are appropriated as one's own:

"These are my things." The king claims that the authority of ancient beliefs and treatises sanctions his right to use force to reap taxes from his own people and material rewards from his conquests over other people. He contends that he has every right to be proud of his powerful position as lord of the people and delight in the advantages that his sovereign power provides. Candrakīrti counters the king's claims with arguments designed to destroy his egotistical and selfish attitude.

The King Is a God in Human Form

Brahmanical literature identifies Indra with sovereign power and characterizes him as superior to all other gods in physical strength and virility. Other deities, including various solar gods, the "emperor" god Varuṇa, and Yama, the god of death, also become associated with sovereign power and glory (Smith 1994, 93–95). Human kings who share sovereign power and glory with these gods are considered the gods' representatives on earth. The functions of kings are equated with those of the gods. Like Indra who nourishes people on earth with showers of water, the king showers benefits on his kingdom. Like the sun god who draws the water from the earth, the king draws tax revenues. Like the wind god moving in all directions, the king moves everywhere throughout the kingdom aided by his ubiquitous spies. Like Yama, who controls all human beings, and Varuṇa, who binds the wicked with his ropes, the king controls and punishes his subjects. In his destruction of the wicked, the king has the brilliant energy of Agni, god of fire; and like the earth, he supports his subjects and should be "welcomed with great joy like the moon" (Gonda 1969: 31, 34, 103–9).

Belief in the king's divinity is well attested in the *Mahābhārata*, the *Rāmāyaṇa*, and in the law books. In the *Mahābhārata* (XII.68.1), the sage Bhīṣma responds to Yudhiṣṭhira's question about the reasons that Brahmins say that the king is a god among human beings. Bhīṣma informs him (XII.68.40–7) that no one should ever show disrespect for the king by considering him to be a mere human being, for he is a great divinity present in the form of a man. He can assume any of five different divine forms at the appropriate time. He assumes the form of Agni when he scorches with his anger those who deceive him, the form of the omnipresent sun when he sends out his spies, the form of Death (*Mṛtyu*) when he destroys the wicked, the form of Yama when he punishes the wicked, and the form of Vaiśravaṇa, god of wealth, when he grants prosperity to the righteous. "The power of kings is infinite," a similar passage in the *Rāmāyaṇa* (III.38.12) asserts, "they are able to take on any of five different forms: They can be hot like Agni, god of fire, bold like Indra, or mild like the Moon; they can exact punishment like Yama, or be gracious like Varuṇa" (Pollock 1991, 166). Passages like these grant kings the status, the powers, and the significance of gods. These are not simply descriptions of shared characteristics or figures of speech. They should be considered substantial identities because the terrestrial king "literally *becomes* the one or the other god" under the right circumstances (Pollock 1991, 64).

The King Is Not a God nor Does He Act Like One

The divinity of the king is not a belief that Candrakīrti holds. We know from the references he makes throughout his commentary to the stories that these epics tell and from his quotations of verses from the *Bhagavad Gītā* and Vālmīki's *Rāmāyaṇa* that he must have been cognizant of their views on the divinity of the king. He does not address the issue directly, although he appears to satirize the king's polymorphous forms in the following passage:

> Consider the example of a royal dancer. A royal dancer one minute assumes the role of a king; one minute he assumes the role of a minister; one minute, the role of a Brahmin priest; then, the role of a householder; and, finally, the role of a servant. In the same way, the king's role is temporary, since he dances on a stage made up of the five places of rebirth. (§354)

The dancer, through the artifice of cosmetics and costumes, deftly conveys the illusion that he has become a king, a minister, a priest, a householder, and a servant. There is no substantial identity here: each of the roles the dancer plays is temporary. Candrakīrti warns the king that his role of king is temporary and the stage he dances on is the cosmos, with its five potential places of rebirth among gods, humans, animals, ghosts, and hell-beings. Not only is the king not at present a god in the form of a man but also he is unlikely to become a god in future because of the perilous nature of his royal role.

At the beginning of the wilderness episode in Rāma's story (III.1.17–18), the seers tell him that a king, a fourth part of Indra, who protects his people as a guardian of righteousness, is worthy of their reverence and esteem. The poet states his own view that kings, gods who walk the earth in the form of men, should never be criticized or insulted. Candrakīrti puts into the mouth of his royal opponent the similar opinion that people who depend on the king for their protection should not criticize him. In response, he says that even if all the people, householders together with wandering ascetics, depend on the king, he should still be criticized. "Even though the king is the father of his people, he is still criticized because he is associated with violent actions, which have as their result many bad rebirths" (§398). He further cautions that a king who has no teacher to guide his behavior will be unable to reject the kind of behavior that leads to a painful rebirth. Although Candrakīrti implicitly rejects the claim that the king is "existentially or ontologically a god" because he incorporates the divine essence, he directs explicit and pointed criticism at the related claim that the king is "functionally a god" because, like a god, he saves and protects.[1] The king's role as protector is not a divine function but a human function, developed and maintained by his fellow human beings.

Buddhist Explanations of Social Classes

Shulman's observation about Hindu kings, "In a sense, every king has fallen to earth from heaven" (1985, 245), concerns the Brahmin-lead sacrificial rituals that establish the king's legitimacy. Through his participation in the sacrifice, the king ascends to heaven and returns back to earth. The Hindu king, considered partly human and partly divine, occupies a precarious throne and must navigate with care the potential pitfalls his lust for power may create. When the Buddhists write about the king's fall from heaven (and the possibility of return) they have in mind something quite different. The Buddhist king places himself in a precarious position by his willing participation in violent actions that threaten his life now and in the future. The king has no chance of making it back to heaven if his violent actions lead him straight to hell.

The Aggaññasuttanta *on the Origins of the Four Classes*

The *Aggaññasuttanta* (D III 85–97) explains how the present corrupt social order came about from a series of morally suspect actions that precipitated the downfall of humanity. The Buddhist story satirizes Brahmanical values in its clever attack on the preeminence of the Brahmin class and the divine origins of the four social classes (*varṇa*).[2] According to the *Aggaññasuttanta*, as the creation of the world began and a solid scum formed on the surface of the waters, the bodies of luminous beings who ate it lost their luster and became corporeal. Greed prompted these beings to grab handfuls of food and stuff it into their own mouths. Arrogance made some proud of their good looks and contemptuous of others they derided as ugly. Sexual distinctions appeared, and with them came lust and sexual intercourse. Lust seduced the good-looking men and women into copulating out in the open (the housing industry developed to hid their indiscretions). Indolence lead some to steal and lie and lead others, who had been wronged, to angry recriminations. Eventually, different social classes arose from these behavioral differences.

The *Aggaññasuttanta*'s description of social classes parallels Buddhist moral teachings. The lowest class engages in actions that violate the injunction against taking life; the highest class engages in actions that characterize the chaste practice of a renunciant. The royal class emerged from the necessity of appointing a person to protect the fields from thieves who would steal the grain. The Brahmin class arose as certain people retreated from an immoral society and took refuge in forest hermitages where they devoted themselves to meditation. The negative emotions—greed, arrogance, lust, indolence, anger—that plagued this devolving community are the same emotions that continue to bring about the downfall of human beings in general and kings in particular.

The King's Contract with His People

The *Mahābhārata* (XII.67.20.32) describes how the gods created the first king to avoid the pitfalls of anarchy, the "law of the fishes" in which the strong overpower and consume the weak. The people agree to pay into this king's treasury a share of their harvested grain in exchange for protection. Kauṭilya, who refers to this story in his treatise on political theory (*Arthaśāstra* I.13.5–7), indicates that kings receive a sixth of their subjects' harvest. The law books also make this correlation between the subjects' payment of taxes to the king and his duty of protecting their interests (Lingat 1973, 207–13; Kane 1968–77, 3: 57–63).

The taxes the people pay are the king's wages, and he has an obligation to the people who have put him in power. Āryadeva attacks the king's pride in his royal position by reminding him that his job is an appointive one and his subjects pay his wages:

> Supported by one-sixth of your subjects' harvest
> What pride do you have?
> On every occasion your work
> Depends upon your being appointed. (CŚ IV.2)

Āryadeva's reminder to the king that he has been appointed by his people alludes to the description of the first king the "great appointee."[3] Candrakīrti retells the traditional story of the king's origins and provides his own moral commentary (§357). He explains that when people of the first eon began to take what had not been given to them, the majority of them paid a man who was strong enough to protect the fields with wages amounting to one-sixth of their harvested grain.[4] This man came to be called a "king" because he made the people happy with his work of protecting the fields.[5] From that time on, the people supported every king with wages amounting to one-sixth of the harvested grain. Candrakīrti emphasizes the king's dependence on his own subjects' labor. Even though he exercises control over his servants' labor, he should not be arrogant in his treatment of them. Moreover, it is wrong for him to be proud and think of himself as generous after he has given back to them in wages the money he has received from them in taxes (§361).

Candrakīrti interprets this story of the king's origins as an ongoing social contract between a king and his people. This contract is morally, not legally, enforceable. If the king abuses his position through his greed for wealth, women, and alcohol, he will pay for the consequences of his ignorant and immoral behavior later when he is reborn in a far less exalted state (§365).

Candrakīrti is less concerned about the political consequences of the contract than with the moral consequences. Intelligent people consider the king to be in a precarious position because of the temptation power places upon him, and because his job requires that he protect his subjects by inflicting harm on thieves and other lawbreakers.

Although Candrakīrti's arguments primarily attack the king's unwarranted pride in his position, he implies that the people have the moral right to overthrow an immoral king:

> If he thinks "the protection of my people depends on me" and becomes proud, why, then, since his own protection depends on his people, does he not lose that pride when he understands that he himself must be protected? A king who is not supported by his people cannot govern his people. (§369)

He uses the metaphor of a good marriage to describe the proper relationship between a king and his people: "Just as each one of a married couple supports the other, so the king protects his people and his people protect their king" (§370). Kings who govern with compassion and win their people's trust have legitimate moral authority; the people have the authority to overthrow an immoral king. A king who has no popular support cannot govern (Gonda 1966, 33–34).

Later, in commenting on Āryadeva's statement (CŚ IV.21ab), "All methods of livelihood are designated in society as caste (*jāti*)," Candrakīrti retells the entire story:

> Now in the first eon all beings that arose were self-generating because their birth did not depend on external factors, such as semen. Because they were generated only from mind, they had their own luminosity that arose from mind. They had magical powers, flew through the sky, and were nourished by bliss. They had all the marks of happiness and were lacking male and female sexual organs. It was impossible for caste to differentiate them because they all arose from a self-generated source. Later, these beings began to eat coarse food. When they became accustomed to very coarse food, channels for urine and excrement developed as a result so that the food could be expelled. When they saw the different physiques created by male and female sexual organs, beings who had the desire for sexual pleasures set about doing together what was wrong because they had been accustomed to it in their past lives. For this reason, birth from the womb developed. Then, when others were at fault in hoarding grain, some among their society began to take what was not given to them. Different classes came about because of the acceptance of different livelihoods. A large group of people commissioned a capable man to protect the fields. By accepting that work, he became known as a person of the royal class. Those people who sought to restrain their senses in order to perform austerities and turned their backs on the villages

became known as Brahmins. Those who served the kings became known as the class of commoners. Those who engaged in harmful actions such as plowing were known as the lower classes. (§435)

He uses the story to make his point that the title of king is a only job description. The king should not take pride in his social class, since class is only a label for people based upon the type of work they do. Class or caste classifies people based on their occupations in the same way that people classify a pot as "a pot of grain" or "a pot of butter" on the basis of the function it performs (§436).

Actions and Class Mobility

In the *Aggaññasuttanta*, the Buddha addresses two young Brahmins who want to become monks. These two, who bear the names of two famous old Brahmanical families, Vāseṭṭha (Sanskrit Vāsiṣṭha) and Bhāradvāja, appear in two other well-known texts critical of Brahmins, the *Tevijjasutta* (Discourse on the Three Knowledges D I 187–252) and the *Vāseṭṭhasutta* (Discourse to Vāseṭṭha, SN III 115–23). In response to their queries concerning whether one becomes a Brahmin by actions or by birth, the Buddha responds that class differences are just a matter of conventional designations. He defines as a Brahmin the person whose actions reflect the practice of a chaste religious life. The commentaries on both of these discourses connect them with the *Aggaññasuttanta* in a continuous narrative. After they hear the *Vāseṭṭhasutta*, the young Brahmins declare themselves to be lay followers of the Buddha; after they hear the *Tevijjasutta*, they take the novice ordination; and, at the culmination of *Aggaññasuttanta*, they are ordained as full-fledged monks (Collins 1993, 318–19).

Candrakīrti likewise rejects birth as a basis for class designations. He aims a particularly low blow at the king's pride in the purity of his royal lineage when he implies that king cannot be certain about his royal birth. Since women often deceive their husbands, the king might in fact be a bastard. If the queen had an adulterous liaison with a lower-class lover, her son would not be a member of the royal class. "The kings of today," he concludes, "mainly have their origins in the lower class (*śūdra*)" (§439).

Candrakīrti notes with evident sarcasm the limitations that society places upon upper-class mobility. Although his royal opponent concedes that birth alone does not make a person a king, he now claims that actions—especially the action of protecting the people—make a man a king (§442). This is a claim that Candrakīrti considers unworthy of a full-fledged rebuttal. If actions determine a man's class status, he says sarcastically, "then, of course, even a member of the lower classes who performs the actions of a Brahmin will become a member of the Brahmin class and he will accept gifts and recite texts!" (§443).[6] The consequence that a class of people who were prohibited by the law books from studying the Vedas should recite them and receive gifts in payment for doing so was so absurd that no further argument was required. There was widespread abhorrence among Brahmin priests at the idea of members of the lower classes even hearing the Vedas by accident, let alone studying them. The law books prohibit the recitation of the Vedas within the earshot of the lower classes. One of these law books, the *Gautama Dharmasūtra*, even recommends that molten lead should be poured into the ears of any member of the lower classes who listens to the Vedas (Olivelle 1993, 193). In contrast to the rigid limitations Brahmins place on the lower classes' acquisition of religious learning, the Buddha taught Upāli, a low-class barber's son, who became celebrated for his knowledge of the monastic code (A I 25). Candrakīrti concludes this section of his commentary by pointing out that class distinctions depend upon the viewer's mutable perspective. He cites the example of people facing each other across a river; each group designates the opposite bank as "the other shore" (§444).

Actions, not inherited class status, also determine who is worthy of respect. Candrakīrti compares the situation of the king, who takes pleasure in the respect his people pay him when they bow before him, to that of a old monk in the monastic community whose pleasure comes from the prostrations made to him (§424). Although Candrakīrti describes this old monk as an ordinary person, even an ordinary monk deserves some respect. The old monk is the object of the respect not because of his own qualities but because of his monastic status and role. As the monk Nāgasena explains to King Milinda, the two outward signs that a monk has been ordained—the yellow robe and the shaven head—indicate that the monk deserves respect (Miln 162–63). This custom supports the critique that "Buddhists worship the robe and not the wearer" (Seneviratne 1999, 278). The similar customary respect that his people exhibit toward the king is also due to his office. For this reason, Candrakīrti asserts that the king should not be proud or pleased when his subjects pay tribute to his status. His critique implies that, despite the outward show of respect, neither man embodies the righteous qualities that command true respect.

Nāgārjuna makes the point that merit determines who has access to sovereign power (RĀ IV. 43). Candrakīrti similarly explains that people become kings not through an accident of birth but through the deliberate cultivation of meritorious actions. There is nothing remarkable about how someone becomes a king, since the accumulation of merit from the past performance of good deeds gives equal access to all. He compares acquiring a kingdom to learning a trade. The proper training provides those who pursue it with a trade; in the same way, the proper moral training makes certain individuals fit to rule a kingdom (§432).

Righteous Kings and Royal Thieves

The Brahmin law books do not concern themselves with the manner in which a king comes to the throne. No law prescribes why or how a particular individual is fit to rule. The exception is *Nārada* (XVIII.25), which says that the austerities that a king has performed are responsible for his assuming sovereignty over his subjects; this statement however, "has a Buddhist sound" (Lingat 1973, 208–9).

Righteous and Unrighteous Kings in the Past

In the *Aggaññasuttanta*, the people chose a capable and charismatic individual to become their king. In other Buddhist works as well, capable and virtuous behavior plays the dominant role in determining who is fit to rule. The *Cakkvattisihanādasutta* (Lion's Roar on the Universal Monarch Discourse, D III 58–79)[7] describes a time in the distant past when all beings lived for thousands of years in peace and prosperity. King Daḷanemi rules in accordance with moral law; and, as a consequence, poverty, violence, and all other forms of immoral behavior are unknown in his kingdom. When the wheel (or comet) that signifies that he is a righteous universal monarch starts to move through the sky toward the earth, he understands the time has come for him to entrust his kingdom to his son and retire to the seclusion of a forest hermitage.[8] Many generations later, a king does not govern according to the wise advice of previous royal sages. He rules the people according to his own ideas, with disastrous results. Poverty increases because of his ungenerous nature. Poverty, in turn, causes theft and other forms of immoral behavior (lying, murder, disrespect for parents, and so on). After generations of increasing immorality pass by, the situation becomes so bad that people have a life expectancy of only ten years. Some of these people, in the course of a single week, mistake one another for wild beasts and take each other's lives with sharpened swords. Only a few that flee to the forest unwilling to kill or be killed survive the mass slaughter. At this point, the cycle shifts: "so glad are the survivors to see one another that they resolve to take up morality once again and their life span and comeliness begin to increase" (Nattier 1991, 14). The free choice of this moral minority makes it possible, many generations later, for the next Buddha Maitreya to teach during the reign of Saṅkha, a future righteous universal monarch.[9]

The righteous king's court, with the king at its center, represents a model that the entire kingdom should follow. This model reflects also the ideal expressed in the *Aggaññasuttanta* that virtuous behavior is not distributed equally among the people. Renunciants and royalty are allotted a larger share and are expected to live up to a higher standard of moral behavior. Buddhist teachings on generosity and nonviolence provide the legitimizing ethic for the rise of a righteous king and the rationale for his continued rule. Past acts of generosity account for sovereignty in the present life, according to such Buddhist texts as the *Kummāsapiṇḍa Jātaka* (Ja III 405–14, no. 415). In the *Kurudhamma Jātaka* (Ja II 365–81, no. 276), King Dhanañjaya refrains from killing, stealing, sexual misconduct, lying, and the use of intoxicants. He sets the example for his family, his court officials, and all his subjects, including servants and prostitutes, to observe these five precepts.[10]

Candrakīrti constructs his image of the righteous king from the legends of King Aśoka and from Vālmīki's description of King Rāma in the *Rāmāyaṇa*. The righteous king represents an ideal standard upon which the entire kingdom should model itself. As the *Rāmāyaṇa* represents it, the welfare of the kingdom depends exclusively on the king. The king's central position in the life of community was steadily enhanced; by the end of the epic period, his power encompassed every sphere of social activity (Pollock 1986, 11). The *Rāmāyaṇa* and other works present an idealized portrait of the king whose compassion extends to all his people, who relieves the poor and oppressed, and guards them from all dangers, internal and external (Gonda 1966, 69).

Rāma receives the following advice from sages, who urge him to rule his kingdom with the benevolence that a father reserves for beloved sons:

> But he who strives constantly and energetically to protect all who live in his realm as though they were his very own life, or sons dearer to him than life, secures long-lasting fame, Rāma, for many years to come. (Pollock 1991, 96)

Āryadeva draws on a similarly idealized image of the righteous king as a protective father when he describes the kings of the past:

> Previously the virtuous kings protected society
> Just as they protected a son.
> Now those who rely on the law of an age of discord
> Have made it into a hunting ground. (CŚ IV.15)

Candrakīrti explains that in the past righteous kings investigated what was proper and improper and took as authoritative only those treatises that advocated virtuous behavior. These kings, who loved their people, protected society just as they would protect a beloved son. In contrast, present-day "kings born in the age of discord (*kali yuga*) rely on the evil nature of their own opinions and are obsessed by their desire for wealth" (§410). These merciless kings become predators and make the entire world their hunting ground. The *Mahābhārata* (III.37.186) similarly describes this age as a time of devastation when barbarian kings will rule with evil policies and the land will be overrun by game and predators.

Royal Thieves and Tax Collectors

Candrakīrti draws attention to the discrepancy between the righteous kings of the past and contemporary kings, who levy taxes and fail to provide any services in exchange. The king who takes money by force from his people, without giving them security in return, is a thief in disguise: "If he takes wages without protecting his people," Candrakīrti argues, "then, surely, he is a thief who lives in cites and towns without being recognized as a thief!" (§385). He may have in mind the advice a senior monk gave to another king: if a member of the royal class were to break into houses and steal or rob people on the highway, he would lose his previous designation as member of the royal class and now be called a thief (M II 88). Candrakīrti extends the category of thief to cover a king who takes taxes from his people unjustly. The comparison of kings and thieves is apt, for both take money by force, as the following story indicates:

> King Ugradatta's minister could not make the king's subjects pay their taxes. The king asked him: "Why couldn't you?" The king then became angry with his minister. The minister had a close friend and he told him about this. His friend advised him, "You must force them to pay." The minister then inflicted severe pain on them so that they would pay. (§403)

The king forcibly separates his own people from their property through oppressive taxes. He also seizes the property of other kings' subjects through his attacks on their poorly defended kingdoms. Candrakīrti compares his actions to those of a thief who takes advantage of a poorly guarded house and steals its contents. His caustic comments imply that the thieves who take advantage of this opportunity to steal are not doing anything wrong because they have followed the royal thief's example. Moreover, they are even more proficient at stealing than he is (§414)!

The distinction Dirks makes between legitimate and illegitimate exercise of force in his study of south Indian kings is not so straightforward for Candrakīrti.

> However close the position and activities of bandit and king, the nature of violence and coercion effected by the two differs fundamentally. The violence of the bandit is illegitimate; it represents and causes disorder. Banditry is defined as such because it is exercised from outside the central institutions of rule and culturally mandated positions of authority. Kingship, of course, is just the opposite. Kings are not only legitimate, they define the realm of the legitimate. (Quoted in Collins 1998, 26).

The righteous king defines the realm of the legitimate, but few kings, in Candrakīrti's opinion, are righteous. When unrighteous kings permit their tax collectors to use violent means to force their people to pay taxes, they are no better than thieves and murderers. Their immoral actions invalidate their authority. When the king fails to set the proper moral example, as *Cakkavattisīhanādasutta* indicates, his actions bring disorder to the entire society.

Foolish Kings and Their Brahman Advisors

Candrakīrti's vision of a righteous king who embodies the Buddhist principles of nonviolence and compassion finds little support in Brahmanical treatises on law and politics. These treatises all advocate the king's use of force in preserving and protecting the vested interests of the Brahmins who authored these works. When Brahmanical texts refer to the king's generous use of money, these donations are frequently connected with sacrifices and are gifts to Brahmins. As interpreters of the Vedas and morality, Brahmins place themselves on top of the hierarchical social system that the king was obliged to support and defend. Although the royal class had power, the Brahmin authors of these treatises claim for themselves the right of legitimating this power.

The King Tied to His Ministers

Brahmins once rode in the kings' chariots to keep a close eye on them and prevent them from wrongdoing (Heesterman 1985, 151). According to the *Mānava Dharma Śāstra* (VII. 57–59), the king should act only after he has first consulted the opinions of his ministers, especially the Brahmin, who is his "front man" (*purohita*) and who is consulted on all religious and secular matters. By his powerful presence and his ritual knowledge, the Brahmin shields the king from danger. The Brahmins, who receive donations from the king, through their ritual intervention help him avert the harmful consequences of this use of force. The relation of interdependence and the metaphor of marriage that Candrakīrti applies to the righteous king and his subjects (§370) is used differently in the literature about south Indian kings. In Shulman's study of this literature, the king and his Brahmin priest became an inseparable pair so closely intertwined that the metaphor of marriage applies. The unstable foundation of this marriage rests upon the ritual transfer of the evil consequences of the king's violent actions to the Brahmin priest who presides over these rituals and receives the king's gold as payment (Shulman 1985, 30–31, 87–88, 304).

Candrakīrti regards this coupling of the king and his Brahmin minister as foolhardy and dangerous. The story he tells of Ugradatta's reign is an extreme example of an unrighteous king in collusion with evil ministers. Cynicism about the motives of government officials and the low esteem in which these officials were held abounds in Candrakīrti's text. He criticizes the necessary dependence of the king on Brahmin power brokers. He points out that the fact that the king acts only after others advise him invalidates any claim of his independence. No one else in the world depends on the advice of others to the same extent as the king. Instead of helping him to make decisions, all this advice makes him appear indecisive and foolish (§377). In a particularly savage analogy, Candrakīrti reduces the king to the level of trained monkeys and dogs who must look to their masters for instruction before they act (§378).

The Conflicting Messages of the Sages

When the king attempts to legitimize his violent actions through an appeal to the authority of Brahmin sages, Candrakīrti attacks their credibility. Inferior sages advocate the king's use of violence; superior ones do not. He draws attention to three Brahmin sages whose conduct violates Buddhist moral precepts against taking property, sexual misconduct, and taking life. These sages' advice should not be relied upon (§406–7).

He refers first to the story of Viśvamitra, who took dog's meat from the hut of an outcaste.[11] At the time of a great famine, the starving Viśvamitra sees the flesh of dog hanging inside the hut of an outcaste. Despite his reservations about stealing and eating forbidden food, he enters the hut. Confronted by the angry outcaste, who heard him enter, Viśvamitra admits what he was about to do, and the two begin to argue. The outcaste takes the position of a literal interpretation of the law books' restrictions on a Brahmin's behavior. Viśvamitra cites the extenuating circumstances of the famine as the justification for his conduct. Viśvamitra wins the debate and the dog meat, which he ritually prepares and consumes. Candrakīrti, not an advocate of situational ethics, condemns the theft.

Another Brahmin sage, Vaiśiṣṭha, marries an outcaste woman, who gives birth to his sons.[12] Candrakīrti, unconcerned with this exception to the law books' strictures against marrying outside one's caste, condemns this forest-dwelling sage for his failure to remain chaste. Vaiśiṣṭha fails to uphold the high moral standards set by the first Brahmins, who regarded life in the forest as a retreat from the sexual excesses of village life.

The third sage, Jāmadagnya, annihilates the entire royal class. According to the version in the *Mahābhārata*, King Kārtavīrya spurns the hospitality of the sage Jamadagni's wife and abducts his calf (III.116.43–62). His son, Jāmadagnya, becomes infuriated when he hears the mournful cries of his father's cow, and kills King Kārtavīrya in a fierce fight. Kārtavīrya's sons then kill Jāmadagnya's father in revenge. After performing his father's funeral rites, Jāmadagnya carries out his vow to annihilate the entire royal class.[13] The poison of anger infiltrates Jāmadagnya's mind and, urged to violence by his mother ("Be a hero, take revenge!"), he takes his bow and aims to kill. Candrakīrti considers him an inferior sage because of his willingness to inflict lethal punishment on a thief. Any king who emulates the immoral behavior of these Brahmin sages or justifies his violent behavior on their authority, Candrakīrti warns, will face the painful consequences of a bad rebirth (§408).

The Dangerous Consequences of Wielding Power

Treatises on law and politics indicate that the king must compel his subjects to follow their respective duties. Kauṭilya says that it is the force of the king's rod that ensures that the people from the four social classes will carry out their respective duties and stay on the right path (*AŚ* I.4.16). The *Mānava Dharma Śāstra* states that the institution of kingship was created for the protection of the different social classes and stages (MDŚ VII.35). The law books grant the king the right to impose taxes and to punish criminals. These rights, seen from Candrakīrti's perspective, involve the king in harmful actions that imperil his future.

The King as Recipient of His People's Merit

The king, who makes certain each class performs their appropriate duties, receives one-sixth of the merit that his subjects accumulate from the proper performance of their caste duties, which will increase his life span and wealth.[14] A king who fails to supervise his subjects properly will receive a share of their demerit. According to the *Mānava Dharma Śāstra*: "One-sixth of the merit from all belongs to the king who protects his people. Also one-sixth of the demerit belongs to the king who does not protect them" (MDŚ VIII 304). The *Mahābhārata* similarly allots the good king a quarter of their merit and allots the bad king a quarter of their demerit (Mbh XII. 66.26, 73.20, 76.6–8).

In the debate set out in Candrakīrti's commentary, the king argues that a king who protects all his people in the same way as he does his son will receive one-sixth of the merit that results from his subjects' proper performance of their duties (§372). Candrakīrti emphasizes that the added burden of his subjects' demerit jeopardizes the king's chances for a good rebirth. Although a king may try to control his subjects' behavior, he has little control over his own fate once he dies. Āryadeva reminds the king of this when he says:

> It is difficult to find among all the castes
> People who are satisfied with their own work.
> If you incur their demerit,
> It will hard for you to have a good rebirth. (CŚ IV.6)

Candrakīrti adds that in this degenerate age it is rare to find people who perform their duties well. Most people seem unreliable and shiftless, and their actions are nonmeritorious. With a portion of their demerit added onto his own accumulation, the king has no hope of a good rebirth (§373). This bears out Shulman's comments: "at no point is the king safely beyond the sorrows of his subjects. In effect, he is one with them, but far more constrained than any other member of the kingdom by the accumulated burden of their ills and their demands" (1985, 92). According to Candrakīrti, this accumulated burden troubles him in this life and in the next.

The King's Use of Harsh Punishments

According to the law books, the king "appears to owe his authority neither to divine will, nor to his birth, nor to any social compact, but solely to the force at his disposal" (Lingat 1973, 215). The *Nāradasmṛti* (XVIII.14–16) warns of dire consequences if the king were not to punish deviations from the proper path: "Brahmins will neglect their priestly functions, Kṣatriyas will give up governing, Vaiśyas will abandon their work, and Śūdras will excel them all. If there were no kings to wield the rod on earth, the strong will roast the weak, like fish on a spit" (Olivelle 1993, 202). Brahmin legal theorists argue that the king's duty of protecting his subjects from internal threats to their security requires his use of harsh punishments to restrain the wicked and maintain proper order.[15]

Candrakīrti's royal opponent argues that if he does not punish criminals, all his people will then become degenerate (§384). His argument is in line with the position expressed in the legal treatises and the *Mahābhārata*: If the king does not wield the rod, the strong would steal from the weak, murderers would go unpunished, elders would receive no respect, and all of civilized society would in ruins (Mbh XII.68.10). This sums up the advice given to Yudhiṣṭhira, who is reluctant to assume the throne after the bloody battle that guaranteed his right to rule. His younger brother had earlier come to recognize the violent nature of the world: "I do not see anyone living in this world without violence. Beings live off other beings, the strong survive on the weak" (XII.15.20). Arjuna prides himself on taking what could be called a realistic view; his initial statements on punishment as the necessary guarantee of morality give way to a more general, somewhat cynical view of violence as the law of life (Shulman 1985, 29).

Candrakīrti argues against the king's use of violence (§385–87). If people who do wrong do not become the object of the king's compassion, then no one will ever become an object of his compassion. Compassion that extends even to those who do wrong benefits all of society. He claims that the violence that the king inflicts on criminals has negative consequences not only for those he punishes but also on his own future. He ridicules the claim that the king is only doing his duty when he punishes criminals, and that such actions lead him to heaven. "How," Candrakīrti asks, "can there be an opportunity for a future high position for inferior people here on earth who have cruel and merciless minds and behave like demons toward others" (§390).

The king attempts to justify the violent methods of punishment with the argument that the reputation of the king who uses force survives his death, while the reputation of a king who does not fades over time. Candrakīrti caustically remarks that such a reputation will not benefit that king, who will experience a painful rebirth as the consequence of using lethal force. A merciless king and outcastes who kill and cook dogs both enjoy notorious reputations, but in neither case is that reputation of any value in canceling out the effects of their violent behavior (§427). He tells the following story to make his point about the folly of pursuing renown after death:

> A rich man's daughter had died. She was carried away with great expense. Another girl saw this and after she had seen it, she thought, "I will also have such riches." She strangled herself and hung by a rope. She lost her life. (§428)

Candrakīrti concludes that the king who employs lethal force so that his edicts will indeed be remembered after he dies will achieve his objective. But his actions are just as misguided as those of the foolish woman who hanged herself.

The King at War

The king's use of lethal force and his quest for an enduring reputation comes into play most importantly in the exercise of war. The king's duty of protecting his subjects requires the use of military force against rival kings. Against the opinion that it is right to attack the weak points of an enemy's defense, Candrakīrti argues that if it is not wrong for a king to attack his enemies and reap the spoils of war, then thieves and other people who engage in this kind of activity do not do anything wrong either. He takes this argument to an absurd conclusion. The thieves the king has pledged to punish are not doing anything wrong when they follow his example and take advantage of the ineffective watchmen and steal rich men's property (§414).

War involves the king in competition with his rivals for scarce resources, such as land, livestock, and the labor of the conquered people. Scarce and valued resources are not exclusively material, "prestige being a crucially important example of a non-material resource that is highly desired and that figures prominently in warfare" (Lincoln 1991, 38). The king stakes his prestige on the battlefield. The king and his royal warriors seek fame and honor that heroes on the battlefield reap. Only cowards fear death on the battlefield. The *Mānava Dharma Śāstra* (VII.89) and other law books testify to the glorious end of the king who dies on the battlefield (Lingat 1973, 223; Kane 1968–77, 3: 57–58).

Candrakīrti acknowledges that even though kings face danger on the battlefield from being stuck down by sharp swords, they slaughter their enemies "with an assurance based upon their own scriptures" (§33). The scriptures he has in mind no doubt include the *Mahābhārata* and the text embedded within it, the *Bhagavad Gītā*. The *Mahābhārata* extols warfare as the principal duty of members of the royal classes. Its core story describes at length and in bloody detail the fierce battle between two rival camps of cousins competing for the throne. The code of conduct that a warrior must follow on the field of battlefield is explicit and unequivocal: a warrior's duty demands that he live by the sword and die by the sword (Mbh XII.22.5). Candrakīrti responds that no intelligent person would put his own life at risk for the sake of fame (§34).

From death in battle, warriors win fame and residence in heaven after death, where divine women, expert in music and dance, greet them (Mbh XIII.61.82–83). When Yudhiṣṭhira asks about the divine worlds attained by heroes who die in battle, Bhīṣma relates the conversation in which Indra explains that the space between the two opposing forces is the sacrificer's altar and the three Vedas are the three sacrificial fires (Mbh XII.99.38).

Heroes who have "poured out their bodies into the sacrificial fire of battle" should obtain heaven (Mbh XVIII.2.2). The king in battle who offers as an oblation his own body obtains by that sacrificial act the world of the gods (Mbh XVIII.114). In the *Bhagavad Gītā* Smith notes, "this conception of sacrifice is also used to redeem the function of kings and warriors whose professions otherwise contravene the newly-emergent Hindu doctrine of *ahiṃsā*" (1989, 214).

Even this revised conception of sacrifice would not convince Candrakīrti that violent actions committed on the battlefield have any redeeming function. He puts the following words in the mouth of the king: "After a king in the jaws of battle has triumphed over his enemies, he takes great satisfaction in seeing the abundance of wealth acquired through his heroism. If he dies in battle, he surely will go to heaven because he has sacrificed himself" (§417). Candrakīrti then provides scriptural support for his opponent's argument by quoting *Bhagavad Gītā* II.37: "If you are killed, you will gain heaven. Or if you conquer, you will enjoy the earth." In the verses preceding this one (II.31–36), Kṛṣṇa urges the reluctant Arjuna not to fear his own duty, for nothing suits a warrior better than to wage a righteous war. If he fails to wage such a war, instead of fame he reaps infamy and the contempt of friends and foes alike for his cowardice. In response, Candrakīrti questions why warriors who sacrifice their lives in battle are respected and people who sacrifice their wealth through obsessive gambling, drinking, and sexual activity are not (§419–21). He regards the warrior's pursuit of honor on the battlefield as a dangerous obsession, which places him in harm's way. The harm (*hiṃsā*) a warrior faces comes not only from the blows of his enemies' swords but also from his own deliberate use of weapons. "Surely, how can it be right for someone who has no mercy, who has cruel intentions toward his enemy, who enthusiastically attacks in order to kill, and raises up his sword with a view toward bringing it down on his enemy's head," Candrakīrti asks, "to go to heaven when his enemy kills him?" (§419). He emphatically denies the king's claim that going to heaven is certain for the warrior who dies in battle.

Candrakīrti may have in mind the story of a warrior who asks the Buddha what he thinks about the report that warriors who die in battle will be reborn in heaven (S IV 308–9). The Buddha informs him that any warrior who intends to kill others and then proceeds to do so will be reborn either in hell or in the animal kingdom. Convinced that his previous teachers had deceived him about the rewards of sacrificing himself on the battlefield, the warrior repudiates his violent past and adopts the nonviolent life of an ordained monk.

Candrakīrti criticizes the warrior who goes into battle without fear for himself and without mercy for his enemies. The spoils of war and even the promised sojourn in heaven he considers to be transient and not worth pursuing. The violent and ruthless behavior warfare calls for has no place in the Buddhist system of values. Like Scarry, he defines war as a "form of violence" whose activity consists in injuring others (1985, 63). The nonviolent and compassionate behavior that characterize the best of human beings has no place on the battlefield. Waging war requires not only that a warrior dehumanize his enemies in order to employ force against them but also that he "dehumanize himself before he can become an instrument of slaughter, effectively eradicating such human tendencies as guilt, fear, and compassion" (Lincoln 1991, 145). Candrakīrti similarly regards warriors who wage war as "dehumanizing themselves." People who harm others behave like demons in this life and will become denizens of hell in the next.

Candrakīrti satirizes the warrior's belief that "of all kinds of gifts, that of giving the body in battle is the highest" (Gonda 1966, 14) by telling the story of a cowherd's wife who attempts to give her father-in-law the highest of a woman's gifts, her body in bed:

> A certain cowherd's wife treated her father-in-law very disrespectfully while her husband was away from home. When his son returned, the old cowherd told him what had happened. He said, "If your wife ever again treats me disrespectfully, I will not stay in your house!" The cowherd was unafraid of his wife and devoted to his father. Consequently, he reprimanded his wife and told her, "If you ever again treat my father with contempt, you will not live in my house. You should do for him even what is very difficult to do, and you should give to him even what is very difficult to give." "Yes, yes," she promised him. The next time her husband was away from home, she very timidly and with great respect attended her father-in-law. During the day, she washed and anointed his body, presented him with flower garlands, and offered him food and drink. At night, after she had washed his feet with warm water and rubbed them with oil, she took off her clothes, and naked she proceeded to enter into an illicit union. She began to climb into his bed. The old cowherd exclaimed: "You evil woman! What have you begun to do?" She replied, "My husband told me that I should do for you what is very difficult to do and give you what is very difficult to give. There is nothing more difficult to do and nothing is more difficult to give." The old cowherd angrily retorted: "This is a good strategy to make me leave! You should be pleased! I will never again stay in this house!" After he said that, he left. His son returned and when he did not see his father, he questioned his wife, "What did you do?" She replied: "Husband, I deprived your father of nothing. With great respect and with pleasure, I bathed him, rubbed him with oil, and gave him food. I offered him everything!" Her husband sharply rebuked her and drove her from his house. After he had appeased his father, he brought the old man back into the house. (§420)

This amusing story about a foolish woman who is willing to sacrifice her body and the dishonorable result that comes of it illustrates the contempt in which Candrakīrti holds the notion of sacrificial death on the battlefield. This wife's misguided effort to serve her lord ends in dishonor and exile.

In much the same way, Candrakīrti implies that the warrior's misguided efforts to serve his lord on the battlefield will only bring him dishonor and death.

Kings and Renouncers

The fourth chapter of the *Catuḥśataka* concludes with Āryadeva's observation (CŚ IV.25) that the king's pride in his sovereignty will vanish once he has seen others with equal or superior power. How can he be proud, Candrakīrti asks, when another king is equal or superior (§454)? Candrakīrti may have in mind a king like Rāma or Aśoka. Unlike the royal warriors of the *Mahābhārata*, Rāma does not seek fame in battle, and the path toward heaven does not run through the battlefield. He is said to seek the fame that is acquired through righteousness on behalf of which "force is useless" (Pollock 1986, 66–68, 71). Candrakīrti is familiar also with the legends of King Aśoka and refers to his infamous prison, which appeared beautiful outside while inside its inmates experienced the tortures of hell (§155).[16] Buddhist legends emphasize Aśoka's merciless cruelty toward his court and his people before his conversion to Buddhism. After his conversion, he becomes the model of the righteous king, whose wealth is used for the benefit of his people and for the support of Buddhist religious institutions. Aśoka's own edicts indicate his remorse for the violence and suffering caused in the victorious war against the Kaliṅga people and his hope that his successors will renounce the use of force and conquer by righteousness, since righteousness is of value in both this world and the next.[17]

At the end of life, the righteous king's attention turns toward the full-time pursuit of religious practice. The tradition of an old king retiring to the wilderness to pursue a quiet life of contemplation is found in both Hindu and Buddhist literature. According to the *Mahābhārata*, death with honor comes to king in two ways: death on the battlefield or death in the forest for king who has become a renouncer (Mbh XV.8.12). The *Rāmāyaṇa* states that ancient royal sages established the custom of a king abdicating in old age in favor of his son and retiring to the wilderness (II.20.21).[18] Similar accounts of kings who retire to the forest in their old age occur in the Buddhist scriptures. In the *Cakkavattisihanādasutta*, the Buddha speaks of King Daḷhanemi's retirement to the forest. In the *Makhādevasutta*, he describes his own conduct in a past life as King Makhādeva (M II 75–82). Makhādeva perceives the gray hairs on his head as a sign of old age and death. He recognizes that he has spent enough time in the palace enjoying sensual pleasures. The time has now come for him to retire to the forest and pursue the pleasures of meditation.

In several of the stories of the Buddha's past lives, the renunciation of sovereign power takes place well before the onset of old age. These stories tell of young kings who renounce the world and of crown princes who chose the life of a renunciant over inheriting their father's duties. In one of these stories, the *Kuddāla Jātaka* a king proud of his victories has the pride deflated by an ascetic who convinces him that the only victory worth proclaiming is victory over his own desires (Ja I 313–15, no. 70). In the *Mūgapakka Jātaka*, the crown prince fears inheriting the kingdom because he remembers from his past lives that the result of a brutal reign is thousands of years in hell. He becomes an ascetic, and through a persuasive talk on the power of death he convinces his father and all others who hear him to become renunciants (Ja VI 1–29, no. 538).[19]

The crown prince in *Ayoghara Jātaka* similarly renounces the throne and explains to his father that he intends to live a renunciant life (Ja IV 491–99, no. 510). Candrakīrti quotes a verse (XXX.21) from Ārya Śura's retelling of this story in the *Jātakamālā*:

> O king, beginning from that very first night,
> When a man takes up residence in the womb,
> Advancing with no delay,
> Every day he comes closer to Death (§16)

The Lord of Death is far more powerful than any king on earth. Even kings who use their power to subjugate and punish their people are powerless before the Lord of Death. Human kings can be persuaded to be merciful, but not the Lord of Death. To emphasize this point, Candrakīrti tells the story of the poor washerman who damaged the king's clothes beyond repair. The washerman's defense that the mud stains on kings' clothes are not his fault persuades the king to withhold the rod of punishment. Candrakīrti comments at the end of the story that no pleas can ever appease the Lord of Death (§26). The king himself is responsible for stains of his unrighteous reign.

Buddhists regard the position of the king with ambivalence. A righteous king can rule with compassion and generosity and benefit all his people. But he may also find it difficult to control his sensual appetites and difficult to restrain his use of power. Candrakīrti's king claims that he is proud of his status because he can enjoy whatever objects he desires. Candrakīrti reminds him that intelligent people do not share the king's delight in his position. The king may indulge himself with the pleasures of fine jewels, fine women, and fine wines, but sovereignty is a precarious position to be in and will lead to disaster in the future because he has no control over his senses. Moreover, the king's subjects avoid wrong actions because they fear his punishment. When a king has no one to advise him against nonmeritorious actions, he will experience disastrous consequences of those actions in future lives (§365). Even universal monarchs may experience the unpleasant consequences connected with the exercise of sovereign power. The great emperor Kaniṣka is said to have been reborn as a fish with a thousand heads; because of his evil actions during his reign, a wheel of knives continually cut off these heads. In each of his successive rebirths, he was decapitated; the wheel of the universal monarch continues to turn after his death and his heads filled the vast ocean (Shulman 1985, 93).

When Nāgārjuna corresponds with the king, he advises him to become a righteous and compassionate ruler, one who bears some resemblance to the idealized image of King Aśoka. But if the king cannot rule the world in a righteous manner, Nāgārjuna recommends that he renounce his kingdom and become a monk:

> If because of the unrighteousness of the world,
> The kingdom is difficult to rule with righteousness,
> Then it is right for you to become a renouncer
> For the sake of righteousness and honor. (RĀ IV.100)

Unlike kings, Bodhisattvas control the direction of their future births. In the fifth and final chapter of the *Ratnāvalī*, Nāgārjuna explains to the king how to cultivate the qualities that characterize a Bodhisattva. He emphasizes the importance of repudiating pride (V.6–12). Candrakīrti similarly concludes his commentary on the first four chapters of Āryadeva's *Catuḥśataka* by advising the king to give up his unwarranted pride in his position. Āryadeva's last verse and Candrakīrti's commentary on it indicate that seeing others with "superior power" should quell any pride the king might have. The superior power they have in mind is the power of the Bodhisattvas whose career is examined in the fifth chapter of the *Catuḥśataka*.

According to Candrakīrti's summation of the *Catuḥśataka* (§1), the first four chapters explain how to repudiate distorted beliefs about permanence, pleasure, purity, and self, since they make mundane things seem more attractive than they really are. Āryadeva takes the human body as a prime example of a mundane thing that is often disguised to make it seem much more attractive than it really is. He strips away the illusions people have about the body and uses it to make them recognize the impermanence, pain, and impurity that characterize all existing things. In the fourth chapter, Āryadeva chooses the king to embody the selfish and egotistical attitudes that keep people imprisoned in the cycle of death and rebirth. Candrakīrti says that Āryadeva's intention in writing the *Catuḥśataka* was to make people born into this world disenchanted with the cycle of death and rebirth, and to guide them "toward a pure realm, unsurpassed perfect enlightenment, which has great compassion as its cause" (§203). The fifth chapter shows how the great compassion of Bodhisattvas enables them to choose to be reborn in the world and plunge themselves into an ocean of pain, "so that they may help all beings who have no guide cross over in the boat of the Mahāyāna" (§207). Disenchantment breaks the involuntary process of rebirth, while great compassion enables Bodhisattvas, the heroic warriors of the Mahāyāna tradition, to be reborn voluntarily so that they can lead others on the path out of bondage.

II

Translation

6

REJECTING THE ILLUSION OF PERMANENCE

Homage to the noble youthful Mañjuśrī.[1]

Introduction to the Text

§1. Here I intend to explain in detail in a single commentary the meaning of the verses in the sixteen chapters of the *Bodhisattvayogācāracatuḥśataka* written by Āryadeva. To communicate its main purpose it is said:

> After first analyzing how ordinary things really exist,
> Gradually, ultimate reality will be explained.

The first four chapters in the text explain how ordinary things really exist. The five aggregates, beginning with form, originate in dependence upon causes and conditions. Since they have an origin, they are impermanent. Whatever is impermanent is certainly painful because impermanence injures its nature. Whatever is painful is always impure because it produces disgust. Whatever is impure is not a self because it is wrong to generate "I" and "mine" toward a thing that must be rejected, and wrong to embrace egotism and selfishness. Since an ordinary thing appears different from what it is due to such a illusion, it is only after understanding that it must be repudiated that Buddhahood will be attained. The fifth chapter explains the Bodhisattva's actions because proper explanations about the Bodhisattva's actions lead to attaining Buddhahood. The sixth chapter investigates the afflictions because domination by the afflictions impedes a Bodhisattva's actions.[2] The seventh chapter examines sensual pleasures because they are the reason that the afflictions arise, persist, and increase. Sensual pleasures are also the reason that the afflictions arise in human beings whose perspective is fundamentally wrong about sense objects and who misunderstand the inherent nature of things. Since the mental stream of a student who wants to receive these instructions on the inherent nature of things must be prepared, this treatise's eighth chapter is the preparation for the instructions on ultimate reality. The eight subsequent chapters explain that things do not have a nature of their own. This is the summary of the *Catuḥśataka*.

§2. A contemporary writer of verse has divided this text into two parts. The verse writer, the venerable Dharmapāla, has taken the *Catuḥśataka* as it was written and divided it into two parts. The first part has a hundred verses on teaching meritorious practices. The second part has a hundred verses on philosophical disputes. Now I will put it back together in one part. After I have reunified the *Catuḥśataka*, I will explain it. In this way I will restore the earlier arrangement and help those who need assistance. Taking treatise as a whole, as it was meant to be, benefits both myself and others.

> §3. Since Āryadeva is considered to be Nāgārjuna's disciple,
> His philosophical system does not differ from his teacher's.

§4. Āryadeva was born on the island of Siṃhala as the son of the Siṃhala king. In the end he renounced his status as crown prince and entered the religious life. He then traveled to southern India and became Nāgārjuna's disciple. Since he followed Nāgārjuna's philosophical doctrine, the truth of the *Catuḥśataka* is not different in character from the truth taught in the *Mūlamadhyamakakārikāḥ*. Someone who comments on a difference in character and explains that Āryadeva's philosophical system is different is very confused because he has erroneously understood his teaching.

> §5. Because the word "four" (*catuḥ*) is omitted
> And because it explains concepts,
> This *Catuḥśataka* is called "The Hundred (*śataka*)."[3]
> It is called a "treatise" because it treats beliefs.

§6. Because the first word "four" was omitted and because it explains [a hundred] concepts, it is called "The Hundred." It is called a "treatise" because it treats various beliefs. The beliefs that it treats are four; and it has one hundred stanzas.

§7. In this context, because impermanence coincides with disgust and because suffering, etc., is easily recognized once impermanence is understood, Āryadeva first teaches about impermanence in order to explain how things really exist. He says:

> Were someone whose master
> Is the ruler of the three worlds,
> Lord Death himself who has no master,
> To sleep peacefully, what else could be more wrong than that? (CŚ I.1)

§8. Objection: Surely, Āryadeva in the *Catuḥśataka* must have relied on the Buddha and should pay homage to the Teacher at the beginning of the treatise to show his respect. Response: That is true, but his former teacher has already paid homage to the Buddha in the beginning of his *Mūlamadhyamakakārikāḥ*. Nāgārjuna says:

> I pay homage to the Fully Enlightened Buddha, the best of teachers
> Who taught peace, the calming of conceptual proliferation.
> Whatever has originated in dependence
> Is unceasing, unborn, not annihilated, not eternal,
> Not identical, not differentiated, not coming, not going.[4]

Since this *Catuḥśataka* is in accord with that treatise, Āryadeva does not need to pay homage to the Buddha. In my treatise, the examples Dharmadāsa used are given along with a commentary on each of the stanzas in the first eight chapters.

The Lord of Death's Power

§9. Because the person imputed on the basis of the five aggregates is injured and destroyed in this and that place of rebirth, it is a world of destruction.[5] The "three worlds" mean the three worlds of destruction because they destroy one's well-being. The "three worlds" refer either to the three realms, namely, the desire realm, the form realm, and the formless realm, or to the worlds of serpents, humans, and gods.[6] Now, the Lord of Death is the ruler of these three worlds because he freely exercises his control over their activity.

§10. The Buddha, who has triumphed over the demon of death, does not fear the Lord of Death.[7] Those whose mental streams have been refined with the radiance of the supraordinary path that has arisen from the Buddha's teaching have put an end to old age and are liberated. They also do not fear the Lord of Death. But the "someone" [in the verse] refers to someone in whose mental stream the noble path has not arisen. He is under the Lord of Death's control. He is not liberated from the bonds of the three worlds because he is attached to things and thinks that they are real. The Lord of Death himself, the ruler of the three worlds, who is not under the control of any other ruler and is not subject to anyone else, personally inflicts punishment on such a person.

§11. The human efforts of others cannot turn the Lord of Death away. He proceeds to destroy life, just as if he had raised up a sharp sword. Someone whose life is under Lord Death's control must act just as he would if the signs of death had taken hold of him or if his hair or clothing had caught on fire![8] Consequently, he must strive to correct himself by behaving carefully. If someone were to sleep peacefully and behave as if what should be done had already been done effortlessly, what else could be more wrong than that?[9] There is no one else who is more wrong than that person mentioned above who remains unconcerned! While he inhabits the realm of the Lord of Death's punitive control, he sleeps peacefully! As regards his objectionable behavior, he is wrong when he does not respect the noble path that has arisen. Thus, whoever inhabits the realm of the Lord of Death, who has a reputation for harsh[10] punishment, must take great care.

§12. Take for example the story about the king who made a man hold steady an oil lamp and the story of the man who died of fear.

§12 (1). The king invited a minister who had been selected for the honor to his palace. His royal attendants, with the exception of the oil lamp bearers, accompanied the king. The minister served as his honored attendant. The unhappy oil lamp bearers conspired to have the minister killed, and they induced the king to believe lies. But the minister was unharmed because he had the confidence to control himself. It became well known that he had behaved in that manner. Other people also should exercise care just like that. You must concentrate so that the Lord of Death can do no harm.

§12 (2). A man had strayed from the main road and reached a desolate wilderness. He was convinced that he would die because he had not been careful about observing the signs of the road. He was overcome and perished. Similarly, someone who is not concerned about the punishment of Death, the Lord of the three realms, will be defeated by the Lord of Death. For this reason, you must be aware of your [mortal] nature and always take care.

§13. It is said that:[11]

> Carefulness is the realm of the deathless.
> Carelessness is the realm of death.

Death Is Mandatory

§14. Objection: Even if the Lord of Death is the ruler of the three worlds, life comes before death and prevents it. As long as there is life, there is no fear of death because death is impossible for one just born. Response: Life does not prevent fear of death because even life exists for death's sake. Thus, Āryadeva says:

> Birth exists for the sake of death.
> For someone who proceeds under another's control
> It seems as if death is mandatory
> And life is not. (CŚ I.2)

§15. Because "old age and death have birth as their condition,"[12] it is wrong to claim that birth is not the origin of death. Birth comes into existence first for the sake of death. Thus, Āryadeva says: "Birth exists for the sake of death." Because of being subject to such conditions as old age, illness, and misery, people are powerless and on the road to death. Because old age, etc., just like an executioner, quickly leads people into the Lord of Death's presence, people have a transient nature. Therefore, death will occur once again in the end, just as the heads of those condemned to die will roll. Since the Lord of Death is devoted to that very objective in the beginning, in the middle, and in the end, it seems as if death is mandatory and life is not, as life seems devoted to that same objective. For this reason, you are encouraged to reflect that even in the beginning you should not deceive yourself by desiring life.

§16. Ārya Śūra says in the *Jātakamālā*

> O king, beginning from that very first night,
> When a man takes up residence in the womb,
> Advancing with no delay,
> Every day he comes closer to Death. (JM XXXII.21)

§17. Consider the examples of the king's messenger sent out on a cold night, the woman leading the life of a wandering ascetic who walked by a camel, and the man requested to serve as an executioner.

§17 (1). In the first example, a messenger ordered to go out on a very cold night by a cruel, brutal, merciless king must indeed go and not remain behind. In the same way, a person's action is just directed toward death and not life, because life slips away moment by moment.

§17 (2). Also, in the second example, a woman leading the life of a wandering ascetic thought: "I'll go in that house." She started to walk by a female camel lying on the threshold. "She's a reason to leave," the camel thought, and it got up and ran away. Just as it fell under her power, so all people fall under the Lord of Death's power. The meaning is that Lord Death is in control.

§17 (3). Also, in the third example, an executioner was hired to kill someone. But he was unable to kill that other person and instead he killed the very person who hired him. Similarly, death is obligatory and life is not, since people cannot go on living. Life should be compared to the person who did the hiring and was killed.

The Uncertainty of Long Life

§18. Objection: Since life exists as long as the projecting force of karmic actions continues, life prevents death in this situation. Now, today people live for one hundred years and they think, "My first sixteen years have gone by but there are still eighty-four years yet to come. I will enjoy sensual pleasures for a while longer and later I'll make an effort to prevent death." So isn't the desire for life appropriate because long life spans do occur? To explain that this also is a wrong view, Āryadeva says:

You see the past as short
And the future as just the opposite!
You consider equals as if they were unequal.
That clearly is like a cry of fear! (CŚ I.3)

§19. Why do you regard the past as short and use your intelligence so carelessly? The time that has already gone by is just like the time yet to come! Whether the future will be long or short cannot be determined because the length of life is uncertain. In the same way, whether the past was long or short cannot be determined because its brevity or longevity depends on whether the future will be short or long. It is established that the time that has gone by and the time that is yet to come are equals because it is impossible to determine whether the time is short or long. Your belief that they are unequal, namely, that the past is short and the future is not, clearly indicates your fear of death. It is just like a cry of fear! Consequently, it is wrong to become overconfident by imagining that the future will be long. It is right to make an effort to become free of the fear of death.

§20 (1). Consider the story about the Brahmins who believed in the existence of a real person. An itinerant trader spent the night in a room of a village inn. He defecated in various spots and left very early the next morning. Among the travelers there were Brahmins who were left behind because they were asleep. The inn's watchman came in, seized them, and shouted angrily: "You idiots! Shame on you! Clean up the shit down there before I beat you!" Then all the Brahmins each cleaned up his excrement but not anyone else's. They are known as Brahmins who hold the heterodox belief in a real person because they seize as "mine" even what is impure. The expedient threat "you will be beaten" makes these Brahmins who hold the view of a real person clean up their excrement. Although the excrement is equally impure, they say, "this is mine, that is not," and see it as unequal. In the same way, even though past and future are equal in the sense that their brevity or longevity cannot be determined, human beings think that a short time has passed and a long time still remains, and they see them as unequal.

§20 (2). Also, consider the example of someone uttering a cry of fear. Someone on the road is frightened while he is near a group of thieves but claims that he is not afraid. He communicates by that denial that he is indeed afraid. Similarly, someone who thinks that a little time has passed and much time remains communicates a fear of death. For that very reason those cries of fear do not become sighs of relief!

Familiarity with Death Should Not Breed Contempt

§21. Objection: Although it is wrong for someone to imagine that the future is long, nevertheless, since human beings all have death in common, no fear of it occurs. Response: That claim should be refuted. Āryadeva says:

> You have no fear of death
> Because others have that in common too.
> Does something that harms someone else
> Make you suffer because of your envy? (CŚ I.4)

§22. Suppose harm were uncommon and did not injure others, and you were overcome by envy because you could not tolerate their well-being. Suppose also harm did not occur naturally. There would then be grounds for your confidence. But this is not the case. Harm inflicts pain by its very nature. The pain of being burned by fire does not torment the person who is burned because he envies others. But it is the kind of pain that completely engulfs its object and is overwhelming, regardless of envy. The pain of death is also like that. The fact that it is common is no reason for confidence. Sometimes it happens that envy causes pain. The emotion of envy, however, does not cause the agonizing pain that completely overwhelms its victim. For this reason, someone who is familiar with the grounds for fear is indeed afraid.

§23. Consider the examples of taxpayers and the bandit chieftain about to be executed.

§23 (1). When it comes time for citizens to pay their taxes, the person who pays first suffers. When everyone else has to pay, he no longer suffers. Death is not like that because it causes suffering, regardless of envy.

§23 (2). Also, the king proclaimed: "The bandits' chief must be executed." The bandit chief, who was about to be executed, suffered because of envy. That envy no longer exists when everyone is under a death sentence. But killing them will not benefit him! Similarly, foolish ordinary people do not fear death because they think it is common to everyone. Death does not benefit anyone!

There Is No Cure for Death

§24. Objection: Someone who uses medicines and life-prolonging elixirs manages at first to ward off the pain that accompanies the afflictions of old age and illness. He does not fear death because of the effort he exerts. Response: In order to frighten him, Āryadeva says:

> Illness can be cured; old age can be treated.
> Consequently, you may not fear them.
> There is no remedy for the final punishment.
> Clearly, you should be afraid of it! (CŚ I.5)

§25. Since illness can be cured and old age can be treated, you may not fear them. Since it is impossible for anything to ward off death, clearly, you should be afraid of it! That final punishment cannot be cured. Certainly, you must fear what cannot be cured: death that ends life. For this reason, it is wrong of you to deceive yourself by seeking a remedy for illness and old age.

§26. Take for example the story about the obstinate minister and the story about the washerman and the king's clothes.

§26 (1). A king had a minister who was obstinate and he sent his army to seize him. The minister remedied the situation by paying a bribe, and because of this the others let him go. In that situation there was a remedy. Then the king himself came and there was no remedy. Old age, illness, and death should be understood in just the same way.

§26 (2). A washerman, who was a domestic servant, damaged the clothes of some Brahmins and somehow he managed to repair them. When he damaged the king's clothes, he was unable to repair them. He had ruined the king's clothes. King Śālivāhana and some of his advisors were going to punish him. The washerman had damaged the king's garments, and since he could not deliver them, he pleaded for mercy:

> The water of the dark daughter of the southern ocean,
> Dear to Viṣṇu, known as the Godavarī River,
> Companion of the Ganges River,
> Which covers the shores for washing,
> Is not clear, even though the rainy season has ended,
> Because the pestle of your maddened elephant's tusk.
> Has stirred up grains of sand.

Such a plea cannot appease the Lord of Death. He certainly should inspire fear, in just the same way that an ignorant, bad-tempered enemy inspires fear!

The Certainty of Death

§27. Objection: Although ordinary people can't prevent death by human effort, death does not generate fear because now they don't understand its certainty. Response: That also is not the case. Thus, Āryadeva says:

> Like cattle about to be slaughtered,
> Death is common to all.
> When you see others die,
> Why do you not fear the Lord of Death? (CŚ I.6)

§28. If death were uncommon and invisible, it would be appropriate for you to utter those words. But someone who does not know about death is in the minority! Many have died and many are known to be dying. Take for example the death of cattle brought to be slaughtered. All have death in common. Each cow sees another one die. Because this is the same for human beings, why aren't you afraid? There are two reasons why death is not feared: either death has never been seen or it has been transcended. The second is impossible for you! The pariah Lord of Death stands right before you and blocks the path to life. So what's the point of being unconcerned? Of course, you become just like a cow by remaining unconcerned!

§29. Consider the example of cattle about to be slaughtered.

The cattle in the slaughterhouse are equals in death. When the butcher leads away one cow to be slaughtered, the others remain behind to be slaughtered. Death is common to everyone, just as it is for the cattle about to be slaughtered. When someone dies, the other fools remain carefree.

§30. Objection: Even though we certainly see death, we do not fear it because the time of death is uncertain. It is uncertain whether death will occur in one hundred years or in a thousand years. So what is the purpose of being preoccupied with it? Response: That also is not the case. Thus, Āryadeva says:

> If you consider yourself to be immortal,
> Because the time is uncertain,
> Then at some time
> The Lord of Death will destroy you! (CŚ I.7)

§31. In this case, if you consider yourself to be immortal because there is no certainty that you will die at this time, then you should be afraid because of the fact the time of your death is uncertain! To claim that you are not afraid for that very same reason is just extreme stupidity. In this world at some time—today or tomorrow—the Lord of Death will approach you, who are subject to death, and seize you. When you become weak, then you will understand. For this reason, after giving up hope that your life span will be long—one hundred years or a thousand years—and understanding the idea of death, it is appropriate to be careful.

§32. Consider the example of people approaching a flesh-eating demon one at a time. People come to be the food of a flesh-eating demon one by one. All people proceed toward death in this way.[13]

Risking Life for All the Wrong Reasons

§33. Objection: Although death is certain in this world, those who seek to win fame and honor and become heroes do not suffer, even though on the battlefield they face the danger of being struck down by sharp swords. They slaughter others with an assurance based upon their own scriptures. Consequently, a fear of death arises in cowards who are averse to danger but not in heroes. In response to that argument Āryadeva says:

> If you look for future advantages,
> Even though your life is not over,
> What intelligent person would say you have any love[14]
> For yourself when you put your life at risk? (CŚ I.8)

§34. You see only the gain of future advantages in this world because of your craving for them. You waste your life, which is the basis for enjoying the advantages that you work hard to acquire. That is wrong! You strive for future advantages by putting your own life at risk. What intelligent person would say that you are right to put your life at risk? No intelligent person would! Only a fool would say that! For this reason, you should think about losing your life and not think about such things as wealth and fame.

§35. Consider the story of the merchant's son and the story about the father who sold his son.

§35 (1). A merchant's son had many love affairs. Because he paid attention only to his own love for others and paid no attention to the lack of any reciprocal love, he was left destitute after the pleasure of his love affairs was over.

§35 (2). Also, there is the story about the Brahmin who had three sons.

The Brahmin said to his wife at the time of a famine, "We will have to sell one of our sons." The prince heard about this and came to take one of the sons. The father grabbed hold of the eldest son and the mother grabbed hold of the youngest son. The middle son told the prince, "Father will not sell the eldest. Mother will not sell the youngest. I understand that the middle one must be sold. Prince, lead me away."[15]

In just the same way as the Brahmin ascetic's middle son sold himself, people who work for wages also sell themselves and adapt themselves to society's customs.

Harmful Actions Put Life in Jeopardy

§36. Objection: If risking life for wealth is criticized, then it should be right to commit even harmful actions in order to protect life. In response, Āryadeva says:

> After you offer yourself as security,
> Why do you commit harmful actions?
> Of course, like the wise,
> You are completely free of attachment to yourself! (CŚ I.9)

§37. Some people addicted to alcohol offer themselves as security and drink alcoholic beverages in the tavern. They do not see their own future suffering, which will result from poverty or from being put under someone else's control. Why, because of your lust for this illusory object, do you likewise offer yourself as security to intense suffering in hell, etc., which you have done countless times, and commit harmful actions? One must suppose that you also are like enlightened people who lack attachment to themselves because they have no reason for it! This once again is wrong. Consequently, people who value their own welfare must not commit harmful actions.

§38. Take for example the story about the unscrupulous man sold by a prostitute and the story about the beer drinker.

§38 (1). An unscrupulous man had sex with a prostitute. He paid her nothing because he had already spent all the money he had accumulated earlier on drinking beer. Over time she bore him two sons. Not long after that, a foreign merchant came to the house. She said to the unscrupulous man, "Since we'll have other sons, we should sell our two sons to the foreign merchant." So that was done. When the merchant was about to return to his own country, the prostitute proposed to the unscrupulous man, "I'll go and remain behind as security in the foreign merchant's house, while you take the two children. Wash the youngest and then feed them." "I'll remain behind as security in the merchant's house while you take the children. You should wash the youngest and then feed them," he replied. So that was done. While she led the two children away and hid in a secret location, he remained behind. Because he had remained behind as security, the foreign merchant on the second day tied him up and returned home with him. Similarly, foolish people offer themselves as security and commit harmful actions. They alone must experience the maturation of those actions.

§38 (2). Also, a man who had no money came to a tavern. He said, "I'll pay the price." Then he drank much beer and did not pay. He was seized and beaten. In the same way someone who sells himself in this life and engages in harmful actions because he hopes to live for long time offers himself as security to the suffering of their maturation in the world to come.

Life Passes in a Moment

§39. Again, in response to him Āryadeva says:

> What is called someone's life
> Is nothing other than a moment of consciousness.
> People certainly do not know this.
> Consequently, self-knowledge is rare. (CŚ I.10)

§40. It is not very difficult to comprehend the destruction of a moment of consciousness because it passes so quickly from one thing to another. When individual letters [of the alphabet], beginning with a, are pronounced correctly, there is a difference in the time it takes to pronounce each letter. Consequently, a difference is understood between the time it takes to pronounce each letter and the time consciousness apprehends each letter. Also, because of the difference in the time this takes, it is established that consciousness is momentary. The smallest unit of elapsing time is called a moment. Sixty-five moments pass in just the time it takes a powerful man to snap his fingers. Consciousness is momentary in regard to that type of moment. All constructed things—for example, a thought—are momentary in the same way as consciousness is momentary because there is no impediment to their ceasing just as soon as they arise and because their impermanence requires that they cease just as soon as they arise. Thus, no sentient being has a life that lasts more than a moment. Since the nature of all constructed things is established in that way, it is wrong for people who expect to live a long time to consent to harmful actions so that they can indulge in pleasure for a very long time and accumulate even more pleasure.

§41. Objection: Why do people behave like that if it is wrong? Response: People, with such misleading ideas as "this is that" and "the self is that," attribute unity to a continuum of constructed things, a continuum that is not something different from the individual things that constitute it. For this reason, they act without understanding that it is momentary. Consequently, it is difficult to find among people anyone who understands the nature of the self. Someone who knows the nature of the self does not engage in harmful actions, because there is no longer a reason for error. Since people, for the most part, are prone to harmful actions, self-knowledge is rare in the world. Therefore, intelligent people, with great enthusiasm, should constantly exert themselves to analyze the nature of the self.

§42. Consider the examples of searching for clothes that have fallen into a stream and the swift pace of the god's sons, the Aśvins.[16]

§43 (1). After a long time had passed, a fool looked in that very same place where her clothes had fallen into the stream. In the same way, someone who has no knowledge of the self is regarded as a childish fool, even though advanced in age.

§43 (2). Also, no one at all, even the gods who travel in the intermediate space above the earth, can achieve the pace of the god's sons, the Aśvins. Similarly, there is no time shorter than life, which is destroyed in a moment.

Fools Expect to Live a Long Time without Growing Old

§44. Objection: Even though life is momentary, it is appropriate to be attached to it because we live for a long time without dying. In response, Āryadeva says:

> You like long life
> But you dislike old age!
> Alas! Your conduct seems right
> To a person like you. (CŚ I.11)

§45. You delight in living for a long time without becoming feeble, but you dislike old age, which you associate with wrinkles and white hair. That will not happen if you do not live very long! Alas! This perverse conduct of yours seems right only to a foolish ordinary person who is just as stupid as you are! But not to anyone else! Since you are growing older, you should not become attached to the continuous life stream.

§46. Take for example the young men who made fun of an old man in the garden.

"You're ugly," some young men said to an old man in the garden, and they laughed. They also want to live for a long time. Their conduct seems right only to stupid people like themselves! Consequently, someone aware of his own suffering must be troubled when, after someone else dies, he recognizes that others also share that same nature.

Inappropriate Mourning

§47. Objection: No one wants to get old and die. Still, there are reasons for mourning a son but not for ourselves. In response to someone who thinks like that, Āryadeva says:

> Why do you mourn because of your son, etc.,
> When you should mourn your own death?
> Why should the mourner, himself
> An object of scorn, not be criticized? (CŚ I.12)

§48. Dying means being mortal. It is appropriate that you, who are mortal, should grieve for yourself because you have not done what you should do. It is not appropriate that you should mourn your son, etc. It is appropriate that someone who has escaped the Lord of Death should mourn when others succumb to death. Shouldn't we criticize someone who has become the object of scornful attacks because he mourns others' deaths when he has that same mortal flaw? That is so! Why shouldn't intelligent people criticize you when you say, "It is appropriate that I mourn for my son, etc.," and you remain indifferent to the fact that it is appropriate that you should grieve for yourself? Consequently, you should feel very sad when others have succumbed to death but you must never completely cut yourself off from wholesome conduct by becoming obsessed with mourning.

§49. Consider the example of the Brahmin's servant who wore a badge.

A Brahmin's servant, who wore on her head as a badge the colored pattern made by a peacock feather, recognized other people who were employed as servants. But she did not recognize that she herself was a servant. Similarly, people forget that they themselves are mortal and mourn sons, etc., who have died.

§50. Objection: Upon reflecting "I am mortal," though it is proper to mourn for ourselves, grief still arises because of the pain incurred when a son goes to the other world without asking permission to leave. To show that this assertion also is wrong, Āryadeva says:

When someone, without being requested,
Voluntarily has become your son,
And then leaves without asking,
That is not inappropriate. (CŚ I.13)

§51. Your grief is inconsistent. Some human being, without being asked to do so, has come here and become your son. It is not wrong when he acts on his own, intent on going to the other world, which is his fate, and then leaves without asking your permission. It is not improper when someone who has come without being asked leaves without asking. It is improper to grieve for someone who has acted properly.

§52. Take for example the story about the woman who suddenly appeared.

A woman suddenly appeared in a garden and then remained there. The man who took her as his wife did not even know where she came from. Later, she disappeared in the very same way and he grieved because of her. Other men asked him, "Do you know where she came from?" "I don't know," he replied. "You don't know where she came from and you don't know where she went. Why, then, do you grieve for her?" In the same way, a fool grieves for a deceased son, without knowing where he has come from or where he has gone.

Recognizing the Signs of Mortality

§53. Since his fate was evident to his friends and close associates, without his uttering a single syllable, he did not go without asking. Āryadeva says to you:

It is because of your ignorance
That you did not notice your son's appearance. (CŚ I.14ab)

§54. Since you did not understand that his appearance indicated his departure, you should mourn your own ignorance and not your son.

§55. Moreover, if you ask about the appearance that made his fate evident to his friends, Āryadeva replies:

Growing older indicates precisely
That he is going to die. (CŚ I.14cd)

§56. Since his appearance had changed from one moment to the next, his friends recognized that he had been growing older. While living away from home, he had been deteriorating for a long time. Consequently, you should give up grieving and concentrate on becoming free of ignorance.

§57. Consider the example of the only son who left with a load of goods.

An only son left with a load of goods. His father began to mourn as his son started to leave. In the same way, people exert themselves to produce sons and then grieve when they encounter the result of birth.

Doting Fathers and Ungrateful Sons

§58. Objection: Even if aging indicates that he is going to die, the reason for the father's grief is his great affection for his son. In response, Āryadeva says:

> A son does not love his father
> In the same way his father loves him. (CŚ I.15ab)

§59. A son does not love his father in the same way as a father loves his son. Sons cause trouble hundreds of times and are remiss in acknowledging past favors. Because the greater share of their love is for their own sons, they forget the past and ignore their fathers at the same time, just as if their fathers were strangers! They become preoccupied with their own pleasures.

§60. People move downward because of the attachment to their sons. It is thus impossible for a father to rise higher because of his attachment to his son. A stream of mind guided by attachment flows downward, just like water, because the continuing force of karmic action accompanies that attachment. To explain further, Āryadeva says:

> The people of this world move downward.
> Even heaven is difficult to reach because of this! (CŚ I.15cd)

§61. Since it is difficult to find any reason for people under the influence of attachment to proceed upward, even heaven will be difficult to reach. Why even bother to mention liberation? Respect should be paid toward older people. Since sons who have treated their fathers badly descend to a bad rebirth, it is appropriate to grieve for them. But it is not appropriate to grieve just because they have died.

§62. Consider the examples of the lost asafetida and the sound of a bell.

§62 (1). A small of amount of asafetida runs out of a hole in a merchant's bag and disappears. In this way, all the asafetida will be lost.

§62 (2). Also, the sound of a bell gradually fades. Similarly, because bad behavior, such as wasting things, gradually destroys good behavior, even heaven will be difficult to reach. Why even bother to speak about liberation!

Trafficking in Love

§63. Moreover, a person afflicted by grief first should consider this: Is this love of yours for a son who is in agreement with you or in disagreement? Āryadeva says to him:

> When there is any disagreement
> No love can be found. (CŚ I.16ab)

§64. When someone does not agree with someone else, that person has no love for him. Thus, this so-called love does not extend to person who disagrees.

§65. Suppose that he loves a person who is in agreement with him. That may be true. Nevertheless, Āryadeva says:

> Love, then, arises
> Only like an exchange of merchandise! (CŚ I.16cd)

§66. The word "only" means it has just one cause. If love arises because someone thinks "he agrees with my position," then, since the benefit is in return for his compliance, the love that has arisen proves to be just a business transaction between two people who exchange merchandise. That is not love. So what is the point of grieving for a son?

§67. Take for example the story about how the king's grief at the death of his son vanished.

A king had a son whom he loved very much. When this son died, his ministers told him, "He has become rigid." When the king heard that, he became enraged and intended to beat his son because he had misunderstood them. Then his ministers told him, "He died." Relieved, the king instead beat a large drum for joy. Thus, people love someone who is compliant but not anyone else.

Love Is Fleeting

§68. Objection: Because a father's love for his son is constant, the assertion that love is conditional is wrong. In response, Āryadeva says:

> The pain that separation produces
> Vanishes quickly from human hearts.
> Observe the impermanence of love
> As shown by the elimination of pain. (CŚ I.17)

§69. Love has no constancy because observation shows that the pain separation produces vanishes quickly. Even the extreme grief a son's death produces vanishes quickly from human hearts because of the power that others have over its operation and cessation. If the bonds of love were not loose, the pain they produce would never be eliminated. But we see this elimination. Since love has no constancy, you should not torment yourself with the pain it has produced.

§70. Take for example the story about the behavior of the sons whose father named Happy threw himself into the river.

While the king was crossing the river, demons seized his boat. He had a minister whose name was Happy. This minister thought that he must protect his king. So after he had entrusted his sons into the care of the king, he jumped into the river. "Carry me away," he urged the demons. "Release your hold on the king." They released the king. When the minister's sons heard that their father had died, they became very upset. They became happy, however, when the king provided them with delightful things. The pain they felt because of being separated from their father vanished. Their father's death was recognized as the reason for their good fortune. Even grief is neither constant nor firm.

Grieving Hypocrites

§71. Objection: Even if we do not torment ourselves with grief over a loss because the bonds of love are loose, nevertheless, in conformity with the conventions of society, we must inflict pain on ourselves by such acts as beating our breasts, and tearing out our hair, and committing suicide. In response, Āryadeva says:

> When you have inflicted pain on yourself
> Well aware that it is in vain,
> That is hypocritical of you.
> Moreover, it is inappropriate for you. (CŚ I.18)

§72. In this situation you have inflicted pain on yourself in conformity with society's conventions. Even though you know that this has no value at all, you still continue to injure yourself. You make yourself suffer because of this hypocritical activity. Moreover, this is inappropriate for you. You become obsessed with conduct that has no merit so that you can gain advantages for yourself and engage in hypocritical acts just to impress others. It is wrong for you to do this. You should not distress yourself with the pain that other people's customs produce. Intelligent people do not go on this path which unscrupulous fools follow. Since you must maintain your self-control, you should not succumb to this occasion for grief.

§73. Take for example the story about the woman who killed herself.

A woman thought, "I'll teach this other woman how to kill herself." She was proud of being a teacher and killed herself while doing this. Even though this woman knew that she would die, she still did it! Similarly, those who are tormented by grief also beat themselves, even though they know that this is in vain.

The Cycle of Suffering

§74. Objection: Even if the infliction of pain is worthless, we still want to maintain a good reputation. For this reason, we don't relinquish the infliction of pain, which wouldn't occur if this wasn't the case. In response, Āryadeva says:

> As suffering increases,
> People in this world wander around.
> What is the purpose of increasing suffering
> For people who already suffer? (CŚ I.19)

§75. All these people wander around and are led here and there by their actions and their afflictions. These people do not escape suffering, which includes the pain of birth, old age, illness, and death, etc. People, who are tormented by suffering because of the pain of the cycle of death and rebirth and who are not free of attachment, become sons, daughters, and other relatives again and again in this and that rebirth. Then they move on all over again. The suffering that separation produces increases for the multitude of human beings who become fathers, mothers, and other relatives as they wander around in the cycle of death and rebirth. It is just like pouring salt on a wound! So what is the purpose of further increasing the allotment of suffering that separation causes for these people who have already suffered because it is their nature? If these people had no suffering and wanted suffering, it would be appropriate to increase their suffering. Since this is not the case, there is no need to increase their suffering!

§76. After meeting such people, who have created their own misfortune, what rational person would regret stopping it? Consequently, an intelligent person who wants to prevent others from suffering should understand the harm in the suffering of birth, etc., because of the association with the cycle of death and rebirth. Do not abandon the cycle of death and rebirth because it is the reason for your own and others' misfortune. After entering the abode of suffering, do not give up wholesome conduct.

§77. Consider the example of two brothers who learned of their parents' deaths.

Their mother died in the presence of one of the two brothers; and their father died in the presence of the other. They met to inform each other. One brother wept when he saw his brother. The other brother also began to cry. In the same way, suffering increases for people who already suffer.

The Inevitable Pain of Parting

§78. Objection: Even though we dislike parting because it causes pain, we like being together because it causes pleasure. In response, Āryadeva says:

> If you like being together,
> Why do you dislike parting?
> Doesn't experience show
> That meeting and parting go together? (CŚ I.20)

§79. When you or someone else likes being together with those whom you love, why do you dislike parting from them? Meeting and parting are seen go together. After a meeting has taken place, a parting will necessarily follow. Consequently, even though meeting causes pleasure, since the end is painful, you should attain liberation, which is free of both.

§80. Take for example the story about the Goddess of Good Fortune and the Goddess of Misfortune entering a house,[17] and the example of eating food that contains poison or a fishhook.

§80 (1). A man whose house the Goddess of Good Fortune had entered received her gifts. Then the Goddess of Misfortune followed her and entered his house. He asked the Goddess of Good Fortune, "Who is she?" "The Goddess of Misfortune," she replied. "Because of her I have not received any gifts," he complained. The Goddess of Good Fortune replied, "Wherever I am, she is present too." In the same way, wherever there is a meeting, there will be a parting also. Those who want only to associate with attractive people and do not want to part from them just engage in wishful thinking.

§80 (2). Someone who has eaten food that contains poison will inevitably die or will feel pain until death comes. In the same way, all the pleasures of meeting are associated with the pain of parting. Similarly, someone who wanted food that had a fishhook stuck in it, of course, had to pull out the piercing hook.

§81. Objection: Although parting is certain in the end, it is not considered in the beginning because meeting lasts for a long time. In response, Āryadeva says:

> The past has no beginning
> And the future has no end.
> Why are you concerned about meeting
> And not about parting, even though it is long? (CŚ I.21)

§82. No beginning is possible for the time that an ignorant person has passed in this cycle of death and rebirth; and parting prevails over all of this. There is no end to an ignorant person's future; and because no end has been reached, the future is the same as the past. Since all constructed things have the nature of being destroyed each moment, meeting with someone who has fallen into this beginningless, endless, vast, oceanic cycle of birth, old age, illness, and death lasts only a moment. Even though the meeting may seem long, why do you disregard the parting that governs both past and future? You regard the meeting as long, even though it is short. This is not right. Since the destruction that occurs moment by moment is very subtle, when you experience the meeting, you experience the separation. Consequently, you should always be distressed.

§83. Take for example the story about the man who was upset because another man had stolen his wife.

A man had gone to another country and lived abroad. Meanwhile another man took his wife for himself. The first man returned and heard about this when he was near the city gates. After he heard about it, he went to the house of that unscrupulous man. The pain of separation that arose at that time tormented him, even though the separation had not troubled him earlier. Now he started a fight. Similarly, because of a separation at the present time, people become disturbed by this or that, even though past and future concerns do not disturb them.

Time as the Enemy

§84. Objection: Even if the parting is long, it is not thought about, since the splendor of the seasons captivates the mind. In response, Āryadeva says:

> Beginning with a moment,
> Time invariably proceeds just like an enemy.
> Consequently, you should never become attached
> To those times that are your enemies. (CŚ I.22)

§85. The seasons of this world, spring, autumn, and winter, over time that gradually increases in duration—a moment, a second, a minute—end the moments of your life, just as an enemy does. For this reason, you should not become attached to those times that will deprive you of life. You should act carefully, just like someone who has discovered an enemy in the guise of a friend. You should become adept at recognizing time as an enemy.

§86. Take for example the story about the old maidservant who suffered.

As time, beginning with a moment, goes by, an old maidservant suffers because her masters treat her with contempt. She cannot retaliate. She is still attached to them, yet they feel no compassion for her. In the same way, people also become attached to time, beginning with a moment.

§87. During the hot season, someone tormented by the heat eagerly anticipates the cold season. During the cold season, someone tormented by the cold eagerly anticipates the hot season. There is no pleasure anywhere at all in this situation! Thus, you should reflect on the nature of constructed things as it really is and act in a way appropriate for a detached mind.

Entering the Religious Life

§88. Furthermore, if you should ask about what is right, we respond you should reject all of this and live a chaste religious life by going forth from home to homelessness.[18]

§89. Objection: Even if this is right, it is still not possible. Parting from relatives is extremely difficult. How can it be done? Because of the fear this parting produces, someone says, "I will not go and enter the forest." In response, Āryadeva says:

Fool! From fear of parting
You will not leave home.
What intelligent person would do what must be done
Because of the Lord of Death's rod? (CŚ I.23)

§90. You fool! You think that parting from your relatives is difficult and you don't leave home because of that fear. Parting is certain to occur at some time or another because of the Lord of Death's power. For this reason, it is indeed something that must be done. You don't leave home voluntarily to perform austerities, but inevitably you must leave home. What intelligent person would do something because of the Lord of Death's rod? You should put the means of liberation first and adopt an attitude that rejects egotism and selfishness.

§91. Consider the example of the villagers who suffer and then pay their taxes.

After the villagers incur intense pain, they all will certainly pay their taxes. No alternative exists. In the same way, the Lord of Death inevitably forces fools to part from their relatives, whom they must leave behind. They do not leave voluntarily.

§92. Objection: Even if we must inevitably leave relatives behind, first we become adults, get married, father sons, entrust the family responsibilities to them, and then we go. In response, Āryadeva says:

Although you think, "After I have done this,
I certainly will go to the forest."
What is the value of having done something
That should be rejected anyway? (CŚ I.24)

§93. You say, "I certainly will go to the forest," but since there are still a few things remaining to be done, you think that you will go after you have completed them. If both what you do and the purpose for which you do it will be cast aside after you have done them, then what is the point of doing them? You should not do them! For this reason, it is inappropriate to spend time on them. You should become adept at investigating what should be done and what should not be done.

§94. Take for example the story about the man who picked up a mango that had fallen into the dirt and threw it away, and the story about the foreigner who was polishing a stone.

§94 (1). A man picked up a mango that had fallen into the dirt. Someone else asked him, "What are you going to do with it?" "I'm going to wash it," he replied, "and throw it away." Just so, what is the point of pursuing things that should be cast aside?

§94 (2). Also, a foreigner had paused in his traveling and began to polish a stone.[19]

A merchant asked him, "What are you doing?" He kept on polishing the stone. When the merchant had gone, he continued on until he experienced pain, but he did not make that stone shine because there was no way to do so. People who wander in the cycle of death and rebirth should regard household duties in the same way.

Remembering Death

§95. Objection: Even if going to the forest is really best, someone who is in the grip of egotism and selfishness fears this. In response, Āryadeva says:

> How can someone who surely
> Cultivates the thought "I am going to die"
> Fear the Lord of Death,
> Since attachment has been abandoned? (CŚ I.25)

§96. In this world, an intelligent person who cultivates the thought "I am subject to the law of death" in accordance with scripture[20] and who repudiates the noise of worldly affairs does not fear even the Lord of Death, since attachment—even to a desire for life, known to be cherished—has been abandoned. How will there be fear either of going to the forest or of parting from a son? For this reason, you should strive to cultivate the remembrance of death.

§97. Consider the examples of wearing a finger ring to detect poison and the example of throwing away poisoned food.

§97 (1). Someone puts on a finger ring to detect poison.[21] Intelligent people similarly concentrate on the idea of impermanence in order to conquer the poison of the afflictions.

§97 (2). Also, just as good fortune comes from throwing away poisoned food, the supreme good surely comes from completely forsaking all attachment.

§98. This completes the commentary to the first chapter explaining the methods for rejecting the illusion of impermanence in the *Bodhisattvayogācāracatuḥśataka* composed by Āryadeva.

7

REJECTING THE ILLUSION OF PLEASURE

§99. The first chapter explained the method for rejecting the illusion of regarding the impermanent as permanent. This chapter will now explain the method for rejecting the illusion of regarding the painful as being pleasant.

Making Good Use of the Body

§100. Āryadeva says:

> Although the body may seem like an enemy,
> It must still be taken care of.
> A moral person who lives for a long time
> Generates much merit from it. (CŚ II.1)

§101. The body feels external pain caused by contact with sticks, knives, heat, cold, flies, bees, mosquitoes, scorpions, snakes, etc., and internal pain, namely, the four hundred and four illnesses caused by an imbalance of the elements. Exceptional people apprehend the nature of the body as it really is. They regard the body as an enemy because it is painful, because it is susceptible to injury, and because it is difficult to take care of.

§102. Objection: The body should not be cared for because it is considered to be an enemy. Response: Even though that is true, it should still be cared for because it serves a purpose.

§103. Objection: What is that purpose? Response: By making good use of the body, the entire collection of the bases for wholesome behavior is accumulated.[1] When the body is endowed with long life and virtuous behavior, many meritorious actions are done. But if it is not, this does not happen. For this reason, the body should be cared for.

§104. A mind repelled by the immediately preceding discussion of impermanence finds fault with the body in this respect: What is the use of having a body that invites trouble? Use the explanation given here to eliminate this objection:

> Although the body may seem like an enemy,
> It must still be taken care of.
> A moral person who lives for a long time
> Generates much merit from it.

§105. Take for example the story about the merchant's son who took care of a thief to whom he had close ties.

The merchant's son thought, "I will lose him as my companion when I go for a walk, etc." Because a close tie bound him to the thief, he took care of him, even when the thief was in prison. Similarly, the body should be taken care of in order to complete the collections of merit and knowledge, the causes, respectively, for attaining heaven and liberation.[2]

§106. Here we say:

> For his own advantage
> He protected the thief to whom he was closely bound.
> Similarly, an intelligent person should take care of the body
> So that moral conduct, etc., will increase.

Eliminating Attachment to the Body

§107. Objection: If the body is be cared for, we should be attached to it. In response, Āryadeva says:

> When people's pain arises because of the body
> And pleasure arises because of something else,
> Why do you cherish the body,
> Which is the vessel for every pain? (CŚ II.2)

§108. Whatever slight pain arises in the body, such as hunger or thirst, it arises only because of the body and not because of something else. Whatever slight pleasure arises in the body arises because of something else and not because of the body. For this reason, you should not cherish the body, which is the vessel for every pain. You should use moderation in caring for the body. This not a fault, for it will increase your life and your merit.

§109. Take for example the story about a man's attachment to a flesh-eating demoness.

A flesh-eating demoness in the form of a beautiful woman appeared right in front of a man who had entered the forest. She had no chariot of her own, so he helped her into his chariot. Not long after, a very ugly flesh-eating demoness stood right before him. He split her right down the middle with his sharp sword. Now there were two. Then he cut both of them in half and now there were four. In this way, these demonesses multiplied by twos. Then from above, a god who had been his friend advised him, "You should kill that woman riding in your chariot. When she is killed, all the flesh-eating demonesses will be killed." And he did just that. Reflection on pain and impermanence eliminates all attachment to the body. You should exert yourself so that attachment to the body will not occur. When there is no attachment, there will be no suffering.

The Prevalence of Pain

§110. Objection: Even if people's pain arises solely because of the body, there is still a remedy for it. Thus, various enjoyable things that produce great pleasure, such as food, drink, clothes, cushions, and vehicles, are not only the reason that much pain becomes less but also the reason that pleasure becomes abundant. It is wrong to fear pain, since there are few pains and many more pleasures. Response: You should fear pain. Thus, Āryadeva says:

> When pleasure does not become prevalent
> For people in the same way as pain does,
> Do you then consider
> Abundant pain to be minute? (CŚ II.3)

§111. When pain arises in the body, it becomes intense and pervasive. But this is not the case with pleasure. People know this well. When Devadatta reclined on cushions spread out on a soft carpet, surrounded by things that captivated his senses of vision, hearing, smell, taste, and touch, he was absorbed in his own pleasure. When bees, flies, and mosquitoes bit him, he forgot all about those pleasures and quickly became irritated and annoyed by the pain. Similarly, the greatest pleasure cannot withstand even one-sixteenth of the pain that arises on such occasions as a beloved son's death. This pain is bone-crushing and heart-breaking because of love. Consequently, pleasure cannot last when intense pain overwhelms it. If pleasure were very powerful, pain would not suppress it. The weak cannot prevail over the strong. In this regard it is wrong to claim that there is much pleasure in the body and little pain.

§112. Here we say:

> That power which easily suppresses others
> Is not weak and one cannot say
> That something which is suppressed
> By the power of something else is strong.

Consequently, you should not claim that the body, which suffers because of the pains external conditions cause, is pleasurable because these pains are so few.

§113. Take for example the story about Rāvaṇa's theft of Sītā.

It is true that Rāma suffered greatly when Sītā was abducted. He did not experience even the slightest pleasure. Similarly, you should regard pleasure in this cycle of death and rebirth as being submerged in the mud of a river of pain.

The Rarity of Pleasure

§114. Because pleasure is weak and pain suppresses it, Āryadeva says:

> People are inclined toward pleasure
> But those who are happy are hard to find. (CŚ II.4ab)

§115. A person who pursues pleasure and considers pain disagreeable flees from pain. But no one can find pleasure in a body whose very nature is painful. The more a person pursues pleasure, the more it remains far off in the distance. Since the desire for pleasure just increases the causes of pain, only pain is nearby. Consequently, happy people are very rare. Because this is so, Āryadeva says:

> Consequently, it seems that a person
> Amid this destruction pursues pain. (CŚ II.4cd)

§116. Even though people flee pain, pain follows these people, just as their shadow does. It is impossible to avoid their inherent nature.

§117. Take for example the story about the man chased by an elephant who hid in a well.

A man chased by a mad elephant in rut hid in a well because he had no rod. After he had gone halfway down the well, he thought, "I'm saved!" That mad elephant, however, still has him trapped. In the same way, people have the idea that they are happy because of their delusions. Pain, however, always traps them.

§118. Here we say:

> In this world a wretched person
> Rejects in an instant anything other than pleasure.
> Yet pain follows a dying person
> Just as a shadow does.

§119. This is the case because Āryadeva says:

> You can acquire pain freely
> But how can you acquire pleasure freely? (CŚ II.5ab)

§120. Pain is acquired easily because pain is constantly nearby and because no great effort is required to obtain it even when it is not nearby. Pleasure, however, is not acquired easily, since pleasure is extremely rare for the body whose very nature is painful, just as a cool breeze on a hot day is extremely rare! People do not fear the pain that is constantly nearby or even the pain from harmful actions. Even though people only want pleasure, they frequently engage in actions that have painful consequences.

§121. To counter this, Āryadeva says:

> Why do you value what is rare?
> And why do you not fear what is plentiful? (CŚ II.5cd)

§122. Objection: When does pain occur and what is it like? Response: Pleasure is not acquired easily whenever you want it. Since it is controlled by others, it is not acquired just by wanting it. People value pleasure, which is hard to get by desiring it and is under the control of others. A fool does not fear pain, which is easy to acquire and under its own control. Pleasure is sought because it is rare and desirable. Why, then, do you not fear abundant pain, which should be the object of your distress? Strenuous effort is appropriate under all circumstances. With this effort it is appropriate to reject nonmeritorious action. Thus, only pain—not pleasure—is natural in people and operates under its own control.

§123. Consider the example of breaking into the treasury.
Someone easily acquires pain by boring a hole into the king's treasury.[3] Pleasure is not like that.

§124. Here we say:

> People who do not understand
> Do not fear pain, even when it is familiar;
> And they willingly pursue pleasure,
> Because it is hard to obtain.

Pleasure as an Ally of Pain

§125. Furthermore, pleasure also ought be an object of concern because it is an ally of pain. Thus, it is right to reject it. Objection: How is it an ally of pain? In response, Āryadeva says:

> The body that experiences pleasure
> Becomes a vessel for pain. (CŚ II.6ab)

§126. The bodies of children who enjoy comfort are very delicate because they have been constantly indulged with the aim of experiencing pleasure. Just as the flame of a blazing fire sears a young tender leaf, contact with even a small amount of pain will injure them. But it will not injure their mothers and fathers, who patiently endure all those circumstances. Consequently, the greatest pleasures cause an increase of pain.

§127. Because this is so, Āryadeva says:

> These two—valuing the body and valuing an enemy—
> Are seen to be similar. (CŚ II.6cd)

§128. For someone who is in pain there is no difference between the body and an enemy. In short, these two are similar because they are alike in both being causes of pain.

§129. Take for example the story about the man who slept in a chariot.

During the hot season, in the middle of the day, a man slept comfortably in a chariot. The king saw him by chance and took pity on him. Later, when this man was reclining on soft cushions, he could not sleep because a single mustard seed had touched him. It is just like this when someone is brought up with the greatest comforts. The more the body is indulged with pleasure's prerequisites, the more it becomes a vessel for pain.

The Painful Nature of the Body

§130. Furthermore, since it is impossible for the body to be pleasurable, you should understand that it has the opposite nature. Thus, Āryadeva says:

> Even over a very long period of time,
> The body does not become the ally of pleasure.
> It is unreasonable to say that something else
> Suppresses its inherent nature. (CŚ II.7)

§131. Even over a long period of time, even though it is attended to with various things that bring about the experience of pleasure, the body does not become the ally of pleasure because pain is its inherent nature. Although mercury, lead, gold, and silver, which are naturally solid, will melt when they are in contact with fire, the property of melting does not belong to them because they have the inherent nature of being solid. In the same way, even over a long period of time, pleasure—which does not belong to the body—cannot be made to belong. Thus, the body is indeed endowed with pain.

§132. Consider the example of the young cuckoo.[4]

A young cuckoo reared by a crow is still a cuckoo and not a crow! Similarly, the body is not something pleasurable.

§133. Here we say:

> Blinded by ignorance, how can you
> Make the body, whose nature is painful,
> The ally of pleasure?
> Even after a long time, iron never becomes gold!

Two Kinds of Pain

§134. Objection: Even though pain exists, it is fortunate when we do not experience it. For example, we see that some people experience only pleasure from birth until death. These privileged people, placed in high positions, do not experience pain because it does not disturb them. Consequently, how is the body painful for these other people? In response, Āryadeva says:

> For the privileged pain is mental;
> For others it is physical.
> Day after day both types of pain afflict this world.
> Pain is twofold: physical and mental. (CŚ II.8)

§135. Pain is indeed twofold: physical and mental. In this world privileged people have all the prerequisites for pleasure. They come from the best families and have great wealth. But they have many desires and they suffer constant mental pain from not getting what they want. They suffer also from their abundant envy because the high positions they covet are difficult to get. Physical pain afflicts those from poor families who have inferior food, bedding, clothing, and shelter because of their low status. How does anyone find any opportunity for pleasure? Thus, both types of pain afflict this entire world day after day. Consequently, in this world there is no one who is happy by nature.

§136. Take for example the story about the elephant trainer's distress and satisfaction on seeing another man mounted on an elephant.

"Ride him," the king ordered a man mounted on a hard-to-control elephant. The man made the elephant go forward in the proper way. The king was pleased and rewarded him. The elephant's trainer saw the reward given to him and was upset. He suffered mental pain because he feared for his position. The second time the king ordered the unskilled man mounted on that elephant to ride him, he was unable to do so. The king then had that man beaten. That satisfied the elephant trainer. In this situation, the first man experienced mental pain and the second man experienced physical pain. Similarly, the privileged experience the mental pain of being treated with contempt and the poor experience the physical pain of being beaten.

§137. Here we say:

> After seeing people harassed
> By both types of pain,
> What compassionate person would say that
> They are happy?

The Power of Pain

§138. Objection: Even though both kinds of pain exist, they are not experienced because extreme pleasure suppresses them. Response: Since pleasure is controlled by the imagination, which pain controls, how can pleasure be powerful? Thus, Āryadeva says:

> Pleasure is under the control of imagination.
> Imagination is under the control of pain.
> Consequently, there is nothing at all
> That has greater power than pain. (CŚ II.9)

§139. When people imagine, "I am a donor, I am a lord, I enjoy desirable objects," mental pleasure arises while they use their imaginations in this way. Even though they have pleasure, they fear losing it later. They destroy their pleasure when they imagine that their enjoyable possessions might cease. Pleasure is under the control of imagination because the arising and ceasing of pleasure depends on it. Pain is not like this. There is, of course, no imagination that has the power to decrease pain and make it stop. For this reason, pain does not come under the control of the imagination in the same way that pleasure does. Instead the pain that arises destroys both the pleasure of enjoying desirable objects and the imagination that accompanies this arising of pleasure. While we may enjoy desirable objects, any pain can destroy this. After destroying all the pleasure, along with the imagining of it, only pain is experienced, not pleasure. Thus, pain is indeed more powerful—and pleasure is not—because the imagination of pleasure is under the control of pain.

§140. Take for example the story about the wife who suffered because another wife's son was well cared for.

The first of two wives had a son who had died. The other wife still had a son. Now the woman whose son had died saw the other woman tenderly caring for her son and she suffered very much. She was asked, "Are you crying over your beloved son who has died?" "I am not crying over him," she replied, "I am crying because her son still lives." On a subsequent occasion, when the second wife's son was ill, the first wife went to another village. After a few days had passed, she returned to her own village and saw a corpse being carried away from it. She imagined that it was the other wife's dead son. She used her imagination in this way and became very happy. Then a scorpion bit her on the leg. The pain of the scorpion's bite suppressed the pleasure that came from the power of her imagination. Consequently, there is not anything anywhere that has greater power than pain.

§141. Here we say:

> Pleasure is very difficult to acquire
> Because it has arisen from an illusion.
> But pain has arisen from what is real.
> For this reason, it is more powerful.

Pleasure Is Alien to the Body

§142. Objection: Even if pleasure is difficult to acquire, it belongs to the body because it does no harm. Pain is alien to the body because it inflicts harm. In response, Āryadeva says:

> As time passes,
> Pain increases.
> Consequently, pleasure is experienced
> As alien to the body. (CŚ II.10)

§143. As the body matures during childhood, adolescence, adulthood, and old age, we see an increase of pain but not of pleasure. Pleasure retreats into the background as the body matures and pain comes to the foreground. Consequently, we see that pain alone belongs to the body and pleasure is alien.

§144. Consider the example of traveling down a long road.

Day after day, the pain of exhaustion and the anxiety over the journey's diminishing provisions become more acute for the traveler on a long road. Similarly, the longer foolish ordinary people live, the more they acquire the pains of old age and move closer to death.

§145. Here we say:

> Since pain always comes forward,
> As if it were a friend,
> And pleasure leaves the body, as if it were an enemy,
> Pleasure is alien.

Pain Has Many Causes

§146. Objection: Even if pain is the body's nature, the causes of pleasure can remedy that. For this reason, our own bodies should not distress us. In response, Āryadeva says:

> The causes of people's pleasure
> Are not experienced to the same extent
> As are illnesses
> And other causes of pain. (CŚ II.11)

§147. In this world, the internal and external causes of the body's pleasure are not experienced to the same extent as are the causes of the body's pain. An imbalance of the elements causes pain to arise internally. Other illnesses are externally caused by the cold, etc., and contact with undesirable objects. Furthermore, since the body has few causes of pleasure and many causes of pain, it is wrong to claim that because there are causes of pleasure, pain should not distress us.

§148. Consider the example of the men who sought the king's daughter when she voluntarily made her choice of a husband, and the example of Māndhatā who stole Vaiśravaṇa's daughter.

§148 (1). When the king's daughter voluntarily makes her choice of a husband,[5] men who want to marry her will experience pain. She will be the cause for only one man's pleasure, but not for all the others. Many men seek her in marriage and cannot get her, and so they become unhappy. Thus, the reasons for people's pain are many and the reasons for their pleasure are few.

§148 (2). There is also the story about Māndhatā stealing Vaiśravaṇa's daughter. Because of its power in both stories, we see pain has many causes. The causes of pleasure are not like that.

Here we say:

> The wise know that in regard to the body
> Pleasure is like a drop of water.
> But pain is like the water of the ocean,
> And they wonder how there can be any pleasure in it!

The Irreversible Nature of Pain

§149. Objection: If there were no pleasure, we would not see its increase. Pleasure exists because we do see its increase. In response, Āryadeva says:

> When pleasure increases,
> Its reversal is observed.
> When pain increases,
> There is no corresponding reversal. (CŚ II.12)

§150. The more pleasure increases, the more we see the reversal of that increasing pleasure. If pleasure were to exist by its inherent nature, it would not change. Pleasure changes when it increases, but pain does not. When pleasure increases over a long time, it becomes weaker and is regarded with disfavor. When pain increases, it severely torments both body and mind because of the agony of even more intense pain. Thus, the body has pain as its inherent nature, since there is no change when pain increases. It does not have pleasure as its inherent nature.

§151. Take for example the story of Māndhatā's fall.

The unparalleled increasing pleasure of Māndhatā changed when he fell from heaven because he wanted Indra's throne. There is no change for suffering comparable to that.

§152. Here we say:

If happiness were to exist by its inherent nature,
Unhappiness would not occur from reversing it.
Because there is a reversal,
It does not exist by its inherent nature.

§153. Not only is pleasure weak by nature but also, Āryadeva says:

One sees the reversal of pleasure
Simultaneously with its conditions.
But there is no reversal of pain
Simultaneously with its conditions. (CŚ II.13)

§154. Conditions for pleasure, such as contact with heat and cold, when encountered, change into pain in the end. But conditions for pain, when encountered for a while, even without that contact being greatly prolonged, right from the beginning cause pain, just as if they were demons with eyes blazing red with rage. Consequently, pain has greater power because its conditions have greater power. The body indeed has pain as its nature—and not pleasure—because pain endowed with great power torments it.

§155. Take for example the story about King Aśoka's prison called "The Abode of Pleasure."

King Aśoka had a prison called "The Abode of Pleasure." At first anyone who entered it experienced pleasure by voluntarily adopting any one of the body's four postures.[6] Although these conditions for pleasure were present at first, pain occurred later. Similarly, even though its conditions are present now, pleasure will change later. But pain will not change.

The Pain of Dying

§156. Objection: If there were no pleasure, it would be impossible to say: "Devadatta is happy." Since this expression exists, pleasure exists. In response, Āryadeva says:

While you are dying,
Time has passed, is passing, and will pass.
It is entirely unreasonable to claim
That dying is pleasant! (CŚ II.14)

§157. Constructed things are dying moment by moment because it is their nature to be disintegrating every moment. Furthermore, while you are dying, time has passed, is passing, and will pass. This remains unchanged over the three times. Thus, it is entirely unreasonable to claim that dying is pleasant, since the process of dying extends over the three times. Therefore, it is not right to claim that pleasure exists on the basis of the expression "he is happy."

§158. Take for example the story of the servant who ate peppers and drank beer.

A young servant ruined his master's shoes. Then he ruined a stool. After that, he ruined a horse. He went from the house into the shed where peppers were stored. He went inside, ate the peppers, and then turned his attention to drinking beer. He stole from his master a thousand things. Then he stole from him two thousand things. His master scolded him, "You're doing what you shouldn't. While I've supported you, you've repeatedly done harm. You don't know what you've done or what you've wasted." "Even though I did what was wrong again and again," the servant responded, "you still trusted me! You don't know what you've done or what you've wasted." Similarly, fools say, "We are happy," even though they are dying from the time they are in the womb.

§159. Here we say:

> Someone who dies again and again is not happy.
> The source from which illness comes is no comfort.
> Where misfortune is prominent, good fortune is not.
> What has been accumulated wrongfully is not wealth.

Someone seized by the relentless Lord of Death never has any opportunity for even a small amount of pleasure.

The Body under Siege

§160. It is also wrong to superimpose the idea of pleasure on pain, since pain differs from pleasure and is abundant, even when it comes without showing itself openly. Thus, Āryadeva says:

> Hunger, etc., constantly attacks
> Beings who have bodies.
> It is entirely unreasonable to say that
> Being attacked is pleasant! (CŚ II.15)

§161. Because hunger, thirst, cold, heat, illness, etc., which are causes of pain and injure the body, are always close at hand, how can this harm, which is continual and uninterrupted, be pleasant?

§162. Take for example the story about the daughter-in-law who wanted to manage the household.

A daughter-in-law wanted to manage the household. Her mother-in-law put her to work on various tasks. Then what the daughter-in-law had anticipated with much pleasure became quite painful because of what she was ordered to do and not do. Similarly, people also suffer constantly because they seek food and drink as remedies for the pain of hunger and thirst. The idea of pleasure occurs because of an illusion.

§163. Here we say:

Pains continually subdue the body
Just as the king's men subdue thieves.
How will intelligent people consider
It reasonable to call this pleasure?

§164. Objection: Even if pleasure does not exist by itself, it exists in association with other factors. In response, Āryadeva says:

Since they each lack the ability,
All the elements work together in production.
It is entirely unreasonable to say that
Pleasure is found among these mutual antagonists. (CŚ II.16)

§165. In this world, pleasure and pain depend upon the body. The combination of the great elements, starting with the element earth, produces the body. Because each one of the great elements individually lacks the ability to produce the body, they must work together. Thus, if the earth element was not present when the first stage of the fetus develops, the other three elements would have no support. The fetus would then be aborted, since the earth element supports it. If the water element was not present, the second stage of the fetus would not occur. The second stage of the fetus develops when the water element binds it so that it will not break apart because of its individual atoms, as grains of sand would. If the fire element was not present, the fetus would decompose. Because the fire element makes it mature, it does not decompose. If the air element was not present, the fetus would not grow, develop, and become larger. Because of the air element, it grows larger. Since each one of the elements individually lacks the ability to produce the body without the others, all the elements must work together in production. These great elements, however, inflict harm on one another. The earth element impedes the motion of the air element. The air element scatters the earth element. The water element quenches the fire element and the fire element dries up the water element. Thus, these great elements are mutually antagonistic. Furthermore, the body indeed has a painful nature because these mutually hostile things cause the pain that arises within it and because pleasure cannot protect it.

§166. Consider the example of the six creatures tied together with a single rope[7] and the example of the suffering produced by four wives.

§166 (1). Mutually hostile creatures, a horse, a jackal, a snake, a bird, a deer, and a child-killing crocodile, whose domains are different, were brought together and tied up with one rope. None of them had any pleasure because they were all mutually hostile.

§166 (2). One of four mutually hostile wives was always acting in an arrogant way. The second one was always crying. The third was always angry; and the fourth was always acting crazy. They were unable to agree on how to provide the proper care for their husband's body when he requested their services. Because of their mutual antagonism, they did not attend to him properly. They also performed other actions improperly. How can there be pleasure among the four elements, since they are just like that?

§167. Here we say:

> Just as there is no pleasure when
> People who argue live in one house,
> So there is also no pleasure
> In these hostile elements when they come together.

The Pain of Frustration

§168. Objection: Even if the great elements are mutually hostile, since there is a remedy for that, pleasure exists. That is not right, because Āryadeva says:

> When there is not always a remedy
> For the cold, etc.,
> It is entirely unreasonable to say that
> Being frustrated is pleasant! (CŚ II.17)

§169. In this situation, when it is cold and someone wants to ease his fear of the cold, he resorts to blankets and puts on warm clothes, which are remedies for the cold. When it is hot, someone resorts to sandalwood paste and the *uśīra* and *priyaṅgaka* plants, which are cooling and remedies for the heat, and so on. When fear overwhelms someone bothered by the cold, he resorts to a remedy to get rid of that fear. This is not done for pleasure! If these remedies were naturally causes of pleasure, they would produce pleasure at all times. This is not the case. Consequently, the idea of pleasure as being a remedy for pain is wrong.

§170. Consider the example of a group of thieves driven away by a man with a stick and a rope in his hands.

When a powerful man wielding a stick and a rope drives away a group of thieves, who run here and there to protect themselves, they are not experiencing any pleasure! In the same way, when people afflicted with pain run here and there seeking warmth, etc., as a remedy for their pain, they are not experiencing pleasure, either.

§171. Here we say:

> Like a thief on the run who is always afraid,
> How can people who run here and here
> Because they fear the cold, etc.,
> Feel any pleasure?

All Work Is Painful

§172. Objection: People use such expressions as "Devadatta takes pleasure in sleeping," "He takes pleasure in sitting," and "He takes pleasure in going for a walk." Consequently, pleasure exists because ordinary language refers to it. In response, Āryadeva says:

> When there is no activity on earth
> That does not involve exertion,
> It is entirely unreasonable to say that
> Working is pleasant! (CŚ II.18)

§173. Here on earth we do not see any activity, sleeping, etc., that does not involve exertion. When someone becomes weak, he cannot lift even his own arms and legs without effort and someone else must carry him. When someone is able-bodied, he does not understand the pain involved in such activities as sleeping, stretching out, and contracting arms and legs. Consequently, he imagines that such activities are pleasant. After getting up every day, many activities are done to keep the body alive but not for pleasure. For this reason, working is not pleasant.

§174. Take for example the story about the prince plagued by his five teachers.

The prince was entrusted to five tutors so that he could study grammar, philosophy, economics, politics, and archery. He suffered continually. If one tutor released him, another grabbed hold of him. In the same way, foolish ordinary people also suffer continually because they must act in cooperation with the five aggregates, which are like a thief's executioner.

§175. Here we say:

> Working in order to keep the body alive,
> Always striving hard, making an effort,
> Working like this, a slave to the body—
> How can that be pleasant?

The Painful Consequence of Harmful Actions

§176. Objection: Pleasure exists because one is willing to undertake various pains for the pleasure of having power over the world. In response, Āryadeva says:

> You should protect yourself constantly
> From harmful actions in this world and in the next.
> It is entirely unreasonable to say that
> Having a bad rebirth is pleasant! (CŚ II.19)

§177. Intelligent people who want happiness reflect that human beings who desire power and undertake harmful actions for the pleasure of having power will experience as a result the pain of being beaten, bound, chained, and killed, which is the reason for their passing from this world. For this reason, intelligent people must protect themselves constantly from the pain that harmful action, undertaken for pleasure, will produce in this world and in the next. Consequently, it is entirely unreasonable to say that having a bad rebirth is pleasant.

§178. An approaching enemy is always feared when he is unknown and the time of his coming is unknown. Similarly, you should always protect yourself from harmful actions and from hell, etc., since you do not know when or where you will go.

§179. Here we say:

> Afraid of this world
> And afraid likewise of the next world,
> You should always protect yourself.
> How can that be pleasant?

No Relief of Pain

§180. Objection: After they have felt the pain of going on foot, people seek the pleasure of riding on horses, on elephants, or in chariots. If there were no pleasure, they would not ride. For this reason, pleasure exists. In response, Āryadeva says:

> The pleasure that people have
> In riding, etc., is not always present.
> How can that increase in the end
> When it is not begun in the first place? (CŚ II.20)

§181. There is no pleasure in riding, etc. If there were pleasure in this, there would be no pain in the end. Someone who experiences pain in the end has begun to suffer from the very beginning. If pain, subtle in nature, were not present from the very beginning, then later on it would not be recognized as pain after it has increased. Because pain arises both in the beginning and at the end—and pleasure does not—there is no pleasure in riding, etc.

§182. Consider the example of the fool satisfied by the remaining half ladle of food from the family cooking pot.

A fool thinks that the remaining half ladle of food from the family cooking pot will end his hunger. Similarly, foolish people think that riding, eating, drinking, sleeping, the postures the body assumes, etc., are just painful later.

§183. Here we say:

> If any trifling pleasure in riding, etc.,
> Were to exist in virtue of its inherent nature,
> Then it would not become pain in the end.
> An inherent nature does not disappear.

§184. Objection: Pleasure produced by the relief of pain exists. If it did not exist, pain would not be relieved. For this reason, pleasure exists. In response, Āryadeva says:

> In the same way that some are pleased
> When vomiting into a golden pot,
> Some people think that
> Relieving pain is pleasant! (CŚ II.21)

§185. When a rich man relieves his physical pain, he vomits into a golden pot. While he vomits into it, he sees his servant vomiting into a clay pot. He is proud and pleased with his own good fortune and wealth. He generates this selfish thought, "I have the pleasures of a rich man." The pain of vomiting, which both men share—whether they vomit into a golden pot or into a clay pot—is not pleasure! In the same way, uneducated ordinary people imagine that this or that relief of pain is pleasure because of an illusion.

§186. Consider the example of swallowing horse dung.

Someone thinks that swallowing horse dung will relieve pain and swallows it with pleasure.[8] Similarly, fools think that the relief of pain is pleasure.

§187. Objection: Consider the example of someone who shifts a burden from one shoulder to the other and thinks that this is pleasant. If there were no pleasure, the burden would not be shifted. For this reason, pleasure exists. In response, Āryadeva says:

> Were its arising to cease by undertaking it,
> What pleasure would there be even in undertaking pain?
> So consider what the Sage said:
> "Arising and ceasing are pain." (CŚ II.22)

§188. Someone who desires pleasure has intense pain because he has begun an activity that has exhausted him. Because he wants to stop that pain, he begins to engage in an activity that will allow him to experience pleasure. He thinks that he will have much less pain in the beginning, in comparison with the intense pain that he had in the end. The arising of a little pain causes the cessation of the earlier intense pain. When he begins to experience a little pain, the intense pain produced earlier ceases.

§189. The word "arising" should be taken to mean increasing. The meaning of the dual number[9] in regard to the statement "intense pain will cease because of the arising of a little pain" is explained as follows: pleasure is impossible in regard to *both* the occasions of arising and ceasing. Āryadeva says, "What pleasure would there be even in undertaking pain?" Undertaking pain would be no pleasure at all! As for the word "even": What pleasure would there be, *even* when pain stops? Indeed, no pleasure exists naturally *even* on both occasions, since it is only pain that arises and ceases. Thinking that it is pleasure occurs when an illusion is taken to be valid. This reasoning explains the example of the burden also. When analyzed in this way, there is no reason for even the slightest pleasure to exist. Consequently, the Buddha said, "Kātyāyana, even when arising, only pain arises. Even when ceasing, only pain ceases."[10]

§190. Here we say:

A fool imagines that
There is pleasure in undertaking pain.
If that were pleasure
It would not become pain!

§191. Consider the example of being tied up with cords of rattan.

Someone tied up with cords of rattan is later tormented by the sun and the rain. Similarly, with regard to employing a remedy for pain, an earlier pain does not stop when a later pain begins.

Pleasure Cannot Mask Pain

§192. Objection: Even if pain exists naturally, it is not evident because pleasure conceals it. In response, Āryadeva says:

An ordinary person does not see
Pleasure as masking pain.
There is no pleasure at all
That can conceal pain. (CŚ II.23)

§193. Objection: Why don't foolish ordinary people perceive pain? Response: If this so-called pleasure were established as existent by virtue of its inherent nature, it would be right to claim that the pain that it masks is unseen. There is no pleasure at all when this is analyzed. Consequently, how can something that does not exist conceal pain? Thus, it is wrong to claim that pleasure conceals pain.

§194. Take for example the story about the man who made the most of his tasting honey after he had fallen halfway down a well[11] and the story of the crow who entered an elephant's corpse and was carried away.[12]

§194 (1). A man chased by an elephant in the wilderness fell into an old well. Half way down he broke his fall by grabbing hold of a *dūrva* vine whose roots rats were devouring. On all sides, snakes stretched out; and down below a large python uncoiled itself. Because he had tasted a drop of honey that had fallen from above, he considered himself happy. Similarly, a fool chased by the elephant of death in the wilderness of the cycle of death and rebirth fell into the well of old age. Halfway down the road for human beings, he arrested his descent by grabbing hold of the *dūrva* vine's root, namely, the path of virtuous actions. On all sides, snakes, the afflictions of nonvirtuous thoughts, stretched out; and down below the great python of bad rebirths uncoiled itself. While the rats of his actions' maturation devoured the *dūrva* vine, the foundation of his life, he tasted the fallen drop of honey, his desire for sensual pleasures. While taking advantage of that experience, he considered himself happy. Not even the slightest pleasure was present!

§194 (2). Also, a crow entered the carcass of an elephant. Because it had rained, a flooding river disturbed that corpse; and the crow also died in that very place. That elephant was of little value and the danger was great. Similarly, foolish ordinary people engage in tasting sensual pleasures, which is like entering that carcass. They also do not see its danger and will die in the great ocean of the cycle of death and rebirth.

§195. Here we say:

> Since pleasure would conceal pain
> If it existed by virtue of its inherent nature,
> How can pain be concealed by
> Something that does not exist by virtue of its inherent nature?

Ignorance Causes Attachment

§196. Objection: If pain is established by its inherent nature, what's the point of explaining it? That's as good as saying that the sun is hot at noon! In response, Āryadeva says:

> An ordinary person should be told:
> "You are not free of attachment to what is painful."
> For this reason, the Tathāgatas said that
> Certainly, ignorance is the worst of all. (CŚ II.24)

§197. It's not the case that it shouldn't be explained here. Even though the body has the nature of pain, an ordinary person does not understand its nature as it really is because of ignorance and therefore should be told, "You are not free of attachment to your body, which is painful in nature." Because an ordinary person does not perceive that as it really is, the Buddha said, "The obstacle of ignorance—which is vast—is the greatest of the obstacles."

§198. Take for example the story about the maidservant who did not release her grip on the ass's tail.

A maidservant received her wages and after she had finished half of her work, she left it. Her mother told her, "Grasp well what you've taken hold of." At that time she had grabbed hold of a she-ass's tail. Even though her mother slapped her, she did not let go and insisted, "I must grasp everything well." Similarly, the Buddha also advised people in the grip of ignorance, "You should be distressed about suffering."

The Truth of Suffering

§199. Objection: Even though the body is impermanent, it still has pleasure. In response, Āryadeva says:

> Harm is certain for what is impermanent.
> What is harmed is not pleasurable.
> Therefore everything that is impermanent
> Is said to be suffering. (CŚ II.25)

§200. Harm is certain for an impermanent thing that is damaged by impermanence. What is harmed is also not pleasurable. Therefore, all things that are impermanent are said to be suffering because harm is the definition of suffering.

§201. Consider the example of pouring water on salt.

All the water poured on salt will become salty. Similarly, because everything that is impermanent is painful, constructed things have only a painful nature.

§202. Here we say:

> Since all constructed things
> In this world are harmed
> By being impermanent,
> All constructed things are indeed painful

Āryadeva's Intention to Free Disciples from Suffering

§203. The skillful methods of the wise, which clear the wilderness of the cycle of birth, old age, illness, and death, bring about freedom from desire. In this chapter, Āryadeva's intention was to make disciples, who are born into the world of the three realms and who are vast as the sky, disenchanted with the cycle of death and rebirth. His intention also was to lead them by means of nondual knowledge toward a pure realm, unsurpassed perfect enlightenment, which has great compassion as its cause.

The Definition of Suffering

§204. According to the word of the Buddha:

§204 (1). Birth is suffering. Old age is suffering.

Separation from what is pleasant is suffering.
Meeting with what is unpleasant is suffering.
Wanting and not getting what one wants is suffering.
In short, the five aggregates of attachment are suffering.

§204 (2). Similarly, the Buddha says: "Monks, this is also momentary."

§204 (3). And in the treatises on scholastic philosophy, the Buddha says: "The five aggregates of attachment are suffering."

§205. About the five aggregates, Vasubandhu says in the *Abhidharmakośa*:

§205 (1). They are suffering, its origination,
The world, the basis of views and existence. (AK I.8cd)

§205 (2). Also he says:

Pleasant, unpleasant, and neutral—
Contaminated things are without exception suffering,
Each according to its circumstances,
Because of their connection to the three types of suffering. (AK VI.3)

Bodhisattvas Strive to End the Suffering of Sentient Beings

§206. Thus, the dangers of the cycle of death and rebirth are explained. So that those who fear them and seek liberation will adopt the Mahāyāna teachings, the Buddha says, "Monks, there is no human being who is not known to have been in one or another kinship relation—father, mother, son, daughter, or other close relative—to those who wander about in the cycle of death and rebirth for a long time."

§207. Bodhisattvas who understand the Buddha's words become close relatives, mothers, fathers, etc., in the uninterrupted, beginningless cycle. This cycle is an ocean that tastes only of pain, and is the abode of crocodiles, alligators, sharks, and sea monsters, which represent birth, old age, illness, and death. It is a whirlpool of birth in the Lord of Death's realm, with its hell-beings, hungry ghosts, and animals; and it is agitated a hundred times, like the hollow of a beaten drum. Bodhisattvas endure plunging into this ocean so that they may help all sentient beings who have no guide cross over in the boat of the Mahāyāna.

§208. Thus, Āryadeva says:

A student emerges for someone.
A teacher emerges for someone else.
A person who knows skillful methods
Instructs ignorant people with various skillful methods. (CŚ V.12)

§209. This will be explained in detail in chapter five of this treatise. A Bodhisattva's actions produce endless pleasure a hundred times in the three realms, the desire, the form, and the formless realms, which correspond to the meditative states and meditative concentrations. A Bodhisattva adept in accumulating abundant pure, virtuous actions will undertake various activities. Devoted to all sentient beings and to making them happy with the radiant good fortune of heaven and liberation, a Bodhisattva will strive day and night to end the suffering of these sentient beings who, thoroughly disenchanted with the suffering of the cycle of death and rebirth, seek liberation.

§210. Nāgārjuna says in the *Ratnāvalī*:

§210 (1). After seeing that [world] in this way, the Bodhisattva also
Has a mind directed toward perfect enlightenment.
But it is only through compassion that
The continuity of rebirths lasts until enlightenment. (RĀ IV.66)

Also, he says:

§210 (2). Since he has no physical pain,
How can he have mental pain?
Through compassion, he experiences pain for people.
And for this reason, remains for a long time. (RĀ III.26)

§211. Also, similarly, in the *Samādhirājasūtra* the Buddha says:

Through insight I know that the aggregates are empty.
After knowing this, I do not associate myself with the afflictions.
I engage in ordinary activities only by convention.
I move about in this world, having finally attained Nirvana. (SR VI.12)

Refuting False Views of Pleasure

§212. Consequently, Āryadeva says to those who suffer the pain of death and rebirth in all the three realms:

§212 (1). Harm is certain for what is impermanent.
What is harmed is not pleasurable.
Therefore everything that is impermanent
Is said to be suffering. (CŚ II.25)

§212 (2). Also he says:

Pleasure is under the control of imagination.
Imagination is under the control of pain.
Consequently, there is nothing at all
That has greater power than pain. (CŚ II.9)

§213. Foolish ordinary people, who have blinded their mind's eye with the darkness of ignorance, have false pleasure that exists only because of their illusion that a thing that is unreal exists. They have joy that is false in nature because they take as authoritative the knowledge of those who inhabit the pleasurable rebirths, such as gods, humans, titans, horse-headed celestial musicians, great serpents, supernatural beings and bearers of knowledge.[13] This resembles the pleasure and joy that occur when one experiences desirable objects while dreaming.

The Refutation of Inherently Existent Pleasure

§214. Objection: How can substantially existent things such as pleasure occur in the three realms? Response:

> Against someone in whose view a substantially existent thing arises,
> The nihilist position, etc., should be advanced.
> That position that the world has an end
> And that the position that it has no end[14] are contradictory.

If a substantially existent thing ceases just as soon as it arises, then it will be annihilated. This is like saying that sprouts will arise from seeds destroyed by fire! Consequently, Buddhists and non-Buddhists regard differently a thing produced by causes and conditions. A thing that is empty of a real nature of its own is not substantially existent. These people pleased with the beauty of a garland created by a net of false conceptions must clearly be identified.

§215. In this treatise Āryadeva says:[15]

> Existence is like
> The circle of a firebrand, a magical creation,
> A dream, an illusion, the moon reflected in water, vapor,
> An echo, a mirage, and a cloud. (CŚ XIII.25)

§216. Objection: "First of all," Vasubandhu says, "this critic of pleasure should be questioned." Response: According to Āryadeva, how can a thing said to have an inherent nature exist? Consequently, those who advocate a substantially existent inherent nature and who lack conviction in the teaching of nonduality, which repudiates belief in existent things and nonexistent things, talk nonsense because they have erroneously understood the vast profound nature of the concept of nonduality.

§217. Therefore, Nāgārjuna says in the *Ratnāvalī*:

> After apprehending the form
> Of a previous object,
> Which the senses have already apprehended,
> The mind regards it as pleasant. (RĀ IV.53)

§218. After students understand that pleasure is in fact pain because it arises only from false conceptions and because it ceases just as soon as it arises, they become free of attachment to all three realms, the source of all suffering.

§219. I have said in the *Madhyamakāvatāra*:

§219 (1). Those outside the path of Nāgārjuna
Have no means of achieving tranquillity.
They are misled about conventional and ultimate truth,
And because they are misled they do not attain liberation.

§219 (2). Conventional truth is the means
And ultimate truth is the result of that means.
Whoever does not know the difference between these two[16]
Enters the wrong path because of that false conception. (MĀ VI.79–80)

§220. Objection: Suppose it is established that pain is an unpleasant feeling associated with an object that the five senses apprehend, is undesirable, and causes harm. Suppose also it is established that mental pleasure causes no harm and has the nature of physical pleasure associated with the great elements in the form of the senses. Response: This is just your opinion! Something that already exists because of its inherent nature does not arise, since it would follow that its arising again serves no purpose. The arising again of a pot and a cloth that are already present right in front of our eyes is just like what a magician does on the stage!

§221. Objection: Suppose that an existent thing were to arise. Since it would never change into something that has not arisen, pleasure arises. But a different mental state, such as pain, does not arise immediately after it. Response: This has not been observed nor is it accepted.

The Refutation of the Independent Existence of Pleasure

§222. Objection: Suppose that because it exists in virtue of its inherent characteristic.[17] A pleasant feeling does not arise in dependence on a painful feeling. If pleasure were different from pain, pain would not be dependently related to it. According to your system, pain would become pleasure! Response: There is nothing that is not dependently related, because Āryadeva says:[18]

There is no independent existence
For anything anywhere at any time.
Consequently, there is nothing permanent
At any time anywhere. (CŚ IX. 2)

§223. Also, the Buddha says in the *Anavataptanāgarājaparipṛcchāsūtra* (Discourse on the Questions of the Nāga King Anavatapta):

> The wise understand that things arise in dependence,
> And they do not rely on the extreme views.
> They understand that things have causes and conditions
> And that nothing lacks causes and conditions.

§224. Objection: Suppose that such things as the sprout and karmically constructed forces were dependent on a combination of causes and conditions, such as a seed, and ignorance, respectively. Response: Is the thing existent or nonexistent?[19] What is the use of a seed and ignorance for a sprout and karmically constructed forces that already exist because they have the inherent nature of being existent? If they had the inherent nature of being nonexistent, just like a barren woman's son, they would never come into existence. Things such as a sprout and karmically constructed forces are like dreams, mirages, and the moon's reflection in water. They defeat the conceptions of existence and nonexistence. They arise in dependence on a combination of their own causes and conditions.

§225. As long as the mind experiences a pleasant feeling, pleasure occurs because there is no opportunity for a painful feeling to arise. Since they are mutually hostile, like doubt and certainty, attachment and detachment, birth and death, and light and darkness, it is impossible for both feelings to exist at the same time in one moment of consciousness.

§226. Objection: Suppose arising and ceasing were possible in one moment and a pleasant feeling were to arise at the same time as a painful feeling ceases. Response: Arising and ceasing are two mutually hostile things. It is logically impossible that they would arise simultaneously. That would lead to the poisonous consequence of the error that Buddhas would have no cause, since everything connected to good and bad rebirths would be destroyed at the time it arises.

§227. Therefore, Nāgārjuna says in the *Lokātītastava*:

> There is no arising of a sprout
> From a destroyed or nondestroyed seed.
> You have said that all origination
> Is like the origination of an illusion. (v.18)

§228 (1). And he says in the *Yuktiṣaṣṭikā*:

> Those who hold that everything is impermanent
> Remain on the Buddha's path.
> It is surprising that one who has analyzed a thing
> Keeps on debating.
>
> §228 (2). When subjected to analysis,
> There is no apprehension of "it is this or that,"
> What intelligent person would then argue
> And debate "This or that is true"? (vv. 41–42)

The Illusory Purity of a Woman's Body

§229. If there were a substantially existent naturally pleasant feeling related to pain, then apprehending it as pleasant would not be an illusion, since it would exist by virtue of its inherent nature. Illusion means perceiving something as being exactly the opposite of what it really is. For example, in the prison of the cycle of death and rebirth, people whose mind's eye is covered by a net of ignorance become attracted to the body. They consider it pure because a thick veil of darkness covers their mind's eye. They think that a young woman's body, the source from which impurities emerge, is pleasurable and that she delights their eyes and their minds. They are pleased because they suppose their thoughts are true in nature. But to yogins her purity is an illusion.

§230. For this reason, Nāgārjuna says in the *Ratnāvalī*:

> §230 (1). Desire for a woman primarily arises
> From thinking that a woman's body is pure.
> In reality there is nothing pure
> In a woman's body.
>
> §230 (2). Her mouth is a vessel of impurities:
> Foul saliva and scum are on her teeth.
> Her nose is a vessel for snot and mucus,
> And her eyes are vessels for tears and filth.
>
> §230 (3). The interior of her body is a vessel for
> Excrement, urine, sputum, and bile.
> Someone who does not see a woman in this way
> Because of delusion, desires her body.
>
> §230 (4). If people are very much attached
> Even to the body, that stinking object,
> Which should be a reason for detachment,
> How can they be led to escape from desire?
>
> §230 (5). Women's figures—beautiful or ugly,
> Young or old—are all impure.
> From which attributes
> Does your desire arise?
>
> §230 (6). If it is wrong to desire an impure object,
> Even though it has an attractive color,
> A fine shape and in new condition,
> Then it is the same with a woman's body. (RĀ 48–51, 57–58)

§231. A woman's body has an impure nature because of the impurities it discharges. A foolish ordinary person, whose mind's eye is mistaken in regard to what is really not so, attributes purity to it. He finds pleasure in that object and thus the illusion that it is pure develops. We reject false ideas and illusions because Āryadeva says (CŚ III.7cd), "How can people who act without reason be stopped by reason?" When the sun is free from clouds, it does not set! Yogins reject the illusion of permanence and develop the habit of meditating on impermanence. The view of permanence is seen as nonsense. Similarly, the view that pain causes harm and is undesirable and that pleasure associated with the great elements in the form of the senses is substantially existent by nature is nonsense. Understand that constant intoxication with pleasure, the result of not seeing properly, is always an error and the source of a hundred misfortunes. To regard an impermanent thing as being permanent is an illusion because it exists in exactly the opposite way. It is the same with regarding an impure thing as pure.

The Illusory Self

§232. It is said:

> Those whose intelligence is blinded by ignorance
> Are confused by the heterodox philosophers.
> Where does what they hold to be an inner self
> Go when they lose consciousness?

§233. Āryadeva says:

> §233 (1). Since the inner self is not female,
> Not male, and not neuter,
> It is only from ignorance
> That your conviction is "I am male."
>
> §233 (2).What is called "propulsion"
> Does not arise from an intangible thing.
> Therefore, the self is not an agent
> Of the body's movement. (CŚ X.1, 5)

§234. Since it has no cause, the self imagined by heterodox philosophers does not exist. It is just like flowers in the sky or jewels on the heads of crows, water birds, parrots, or wolves. Someone who believes that an unreal inner self exists is mistaken because he attributes existence and permanence to a nonexistent thing. He is trapped in the prison of the cycle of death and rebirth. Reflection on the belief that there is no self is an antidote for the illusion of regarding its opposite as permanent. The view that there is no self is a position which is not distorted in nature. It is established as an antidote for the illusion of an unreal self and for the illusion of pleasure that is held in opposition to pain. For the sake of repudiating this group of four illusions, people who claim that the inherent nature of a thing is real should be told, "The four illusions, beginning with the belief in a self, are indeed false views. What you assert or observe is not true."

Definitive and Interpretable Discourses

§235. According to Āryadeva, whose intelligence is expert in regard to discourses on ordinary and supraordinary matters, this should not be understood as a criticism of pleasure. It should be understood clearly that this criticism of pleasure applies only to people who hold that things have an inherent nature, since they do not comprehend correctly the Buddha's discourses and they do not interpret correctly the nature of definitive and interpretable discourses.

An Interpretable Discourse on the Substantiality of Things

§236. The Buddha says:[20]

> Monks, if past forms did not exist, the noble learned disciples would not become dissatisfied with past forms. Monks, since past forms exist, the noble disciples are dissatisfied with past forms. Monks, if future forms did not exist, the noble learned disciples would not become dissatisfied with future forms. Monks, since future forms exist, the noble disciples are dissatisfied with future forms. Monks, if past feelings did not exist, the noble learned disciples would not become dissatisfied with past feelings. Monks, since past feelings exist, the noble disciples are dissatisfied with past feelings. Monks, if future feelings did not exist, the noble learned disciples would not become dissatisfied with future feelings. Monks, since future feelings do exist, the noble disciples are dissatisfied with future feelings. Similarly, monks, so long as past consciousness does not exist, the noble learned disciples would not become dissatisfied with past consciousness. Monks, since past consciousness does exist, the noble disciples are dissatisfied with past consciousness. Monks, if future consciousness did not exist, the noble learned disciples would not become dissatisfied with future consciousness. Monks, since future consciousness does exist, the noble disciples are dissatisfied with future consciousness.

§237. Because of their skill in prescribing medicine for their disciples, Buddhas, who have superior abilities in the liberating methods of great compassion, teach in this way about the existence of the past and future only because this conforms to the nature of foolish people's understanding. For this reason, the Buddha teaches in this scripture and in other discourses that the five aggregates are substantial things.

§238. If past and future things were to exist through their inherent nature, they would exist in the present and they would exist in the same way as pots, cloths, straw mats, and crowns exist at present right before our eyes. If a past nature were to exist, it must be either permanent or impermanent. First of all, it is not held to be permanent because of the consequence that this is the heterodox philosophers' belief. Second, it is not held to be permanent because something that has not originated dependently is nonexistent, just like horns on rabbits, etc. Finally, it is not held to be permanent because those who advocate distinctions succumb to both of these faults.[21] If it is then supposed that a past nature is impermanent, that also is not right. Why? Because the absurd consequence would follow that it ceases and exists in the past and in the future. An impermanent past thing cannot exist in the future. It is impossible for both past and present to exist in one thing at the same time, because ceasing and arising are mutually incompatible. It is not held that doubt and certainty exist in one consciousness or that birth and death occur at the same time! It is impossible that in one moment both the seed and its sprout exist, since the error of the sprout's having no cause would follow. In this world, wheat seeds are not collected from rice and sesame plants!

As I have said in the *Madhyamakāvatāra*:

> If you believe in origination without a cause,
> Anything could be produced from anything at any time! (MĀ VI.99ab)

A person who advocates this very vile doctrine that no cause exists should be kept at a distance and avoided!

Definitive Discourses on the Nonsubstantiality of Things

§239. Similarly, in another discourse the Buddha says:

> §239 (1). Monks, these five aggregates are mere names, mere theories, mere conventions. It is the same with past time, future time, space, and Nirvana. All internal and external things, the past, the future, the so-called "person" are mere worldly conventions.

Also, in another discourse the Buddha says:[22]

§239 (2). The Buddha, kin to the sun, explained:

> Form is like a mass of foam, feeling is like a bubble.
> Karmically constructed forces are like a banana tree's core.
> And consciousness is like a magical illusion.

> §239 (3). Thus, the energetic monk, fully aware and mindful,
> While he investigates things day and night,
> Should enter the tranquil state,
> The bliss, which is the calming of karmically constructed forces.

§240 And likewise in the *Samādhirājasūtra* the Buddha says:

§240 (1). A large lump of foam is carried away by the current
And, after investigating it, one sees no solid substance,
You should know all things in this way.

§240 (2). Just as the god Sthūlabinduka lets it rain
And the rain bubbles arise one by one,
Upon arising they burst, then, of course, there are no bubbles,
You should know all things in this way.

§240 (3). Just as, in the hot season at noon,
A person tormented by thirst might wander about
And see a mirage as a pool of water,
You should know all things in this way.

§240 (4). There is no water in that mirage,
But that deluded person wants to drink it.
Nonexistent water cannot be drunk.
You should know all things in this way.

§240 (5). Just as a person in search of the core
Might split in two a banana tree's green trunk,
And there is no core inside or outside,
You should know all things in this way.

§240 (6). A magician conjures up visible forms,
Wonderful elephant chariots and horse chariots.
Under these circumstances, nothing exists the way it appears there.
You should know all things in this way. (SR IX. 5–6, 16, 20–22)

§241. Therefore, someone who advocates that things have a real nature believes in illusions and sees permanence, pleasure, purity, and a self in what is impermanent, painful, impure, and lacking a self. This should not be accepted. Someone who has accepted the position that things exist, first should be questioned by using this critique of pleasure: "Is pain something that causes harm?" It is wrong to claim that "what does no harm is established as pleasure" because that contradicts what has been accepted.

§242. If you say that the Buddha and Āryadeva spoke in this way in conformity with the understanding of foolish people, then, even though this is so, why do you utter that statement that contradicts Āryadeva? It does not explain the master's teachings. You have not understood definitive and interpretable discourses. Buddhas, skilled in the liberating methods of great compassion, teach the views of impermanence, pain, impurity, and nonself as antidotes for the four illusions, the views of permanence, pleasure, purity, and self, in accordance with the understanding of those foolish ordinary people, whose mind's eye has been damaged by the eye disease of ignorance. These antidotes are the methods for liberating them from the oceanic cycle of death and rebirth.

§243. This concludes the commentary to the second chapter explaining the method for abandoning the illusion of pleasure in Āryadeva's *Bodhisattvayogācāracatuḥśataka*.

8

REJECTING THE ILLUSION OF PURITY

The Addiction to Sexual Pleasures

§244. Now the method for rejecting the illusion of purity will be discussed. Objection: Even if constructed things are painful in nature, pleasure will occur when we indulge a taste for enjoying desirable objects. For this reason, sexual pleasures should be pursued. In response, Āryadeva says:

> Even over a very long period of time,
> There is no limit to objects.
> Exertion in regard to your body
> Will have no effect, like an incompetent physician. (CŚ III.1)

§245. Objection: Someone whose mind longs to enjoy sexual pleasures will enjoy these sexual pleasures in the beginning, when he is young. Wealth will attract him in middle age; and toward the end he will think about pursuing religion.[1] Response: In that case, if sexual pleasures were few it should be possible for him to reach their limit in the beginning when he is a young man and be content. Even though he pursues them for a very long time, he will never reach their limit. If there is no limit, the exertions of someone who has enjoyed them and wants to stop will be ineffective. It is like an incompetent physician's efforts with regard to your body when he lacks the ability to cure the illness. This incompetent physician does not understand the symptoms of the illness, and his endless efforts will result only in fatigue. Your exertion will be ineffective in just the same way!

§246. Consider the example of a monkey covered by a leopard skin.

A monkey covered by a leopard skin always frightens other monkeys. Neither time nor place limits that fear. In the same way, even though people who enjoy sexual pleasures think a certain amount will satisfy them, there is no limit.

§247. Here we say:

> Just as water cannot dry up water,
> And heat cannot diminish heat,
> In the same way, indulgence in sexual pleasures
> Cannot curb the desire for sexual pleasures.

§248. Objection: Drinking water quenches thirst. In the same way, those who become sated with sexual pleasures will not crave them. In response, Āryadeva says:

> Just as an addict's craving
> For dirt cannot be stopped,
> The craving for sexual pleasures also increases
> In those people who are addicted. (CŚ III.2)

§249. In the same way as the craving for dirt will only increase for worms addicted to eating it, the craving for sexual pleasures also will increase in those people who enjoy sexual pleasures and are addicted to them. In the end the craving for sexual pleasures cannot be stopped. An addict of sexual pleasures encounters the right conditions and becomes adept at enjoying them because of the efforts previously mentioned. Desire treated by conditions of the same kind becomes even more powerful. So, how can there ever be any satisfaction for a person disturbed by a flood of sexual pleasures whose power increases moment by moment?

§250. Consider the example of overindulgence in sleep, etc., and the example of the deer tormented by thirst.

§250 (1). The more someone indulges in sleep, idleness, and sex, the more that desire increases. The afflictions are just like this.

§250 (2). Also, when the earth is very dry, deer, tormented by the heat of the midday sun in a cloudless sky, see a mirage resembling water that casts the image of a small stream. They think that it is water and run toward it. But they cannot quench their thirst. Similarly, people do not understand desire, which is like a mirage. They become attracted to its nature and pursue sexual pleasures.

§251. It is claimed that the pain of affliction ceases because enjoying sexual pleasures is satisfying. But how will that affliction stop?

Here we say:

> Just as fuel makes flames flare up,
> Just as people crossing makes the river rise,
> In the same way, by indulging their sexual pleasures,
> People increase their desires for sexual pleasures.

The Deceptive Beauty of Women

§252. Objection: Now, this advice may enable a man to reject an ordinary woman. But how can he turn his mind away from those shapely women, pleasant to embrace, whose limbs are alluring, who enchant both his eyes and his mind, and who melt the hearts of impassioned men with sidelong glances that reveal their hearts' desire, just as the touch of fire melts fresh butter? To quench this desire, Āryadeva says:

> Among all women not the slightest difference
> Is to be found in sexual intercourse.
> What use is the most beautiful woman to you,
> As others also can enjoy her beauty? (CŚ III.3)

§253. He used his imagination and he attributed superiority to her because of the way he imagined that delusive object. He made himself inferior, which only provokes contempt. When he uses logical reasoning to make that same object inferior, he becomes worthy of praise because of his detachment toward her.

§254. First of all, women are impure. They are formed by a collection of powerful organs' atomic particles. They naturally have a foul odor and their continually oozing bodies resemble the city's filthy sewers. Many men are obsessed with acquiring that impure thing, which is filled up just like an outhouse. Like the hole of an outhouse, it is dark, filthy, stinking, and attractive to a swarm of insects! Inside a woman is filthy, like a rotting heap of excrement, and outside only her skin encloses that filth. Even worse are sores inside her body that were acquired through past karmic action and cannot be healed.

§255. Apart from their own minds' misconceptions about that woman—who is an unparalleled and vast collection of reasons for detachment—there is no difference in the act of sexual intercourse for these selfish men who imagine her superior nature and become possessive. Her beauty is the object of the sense of vision. Consequently, all who have eyes and are within the visual range of her beauty share the enjoyment. So she is an object of enjoyment even for dogs and vultures! For this reason, it is wrong to generate attachment for such a common thing. Now, tell us what excellent qualities this superior woman has that have aroused your desire for her body. Otherwise, get rid of your desire to have the most beautiful woman.

§256. Take for example the story about the ugly woman and the story about the man who had sex with his own wife in the dark and mistook her for someone else's wife.

§256 (1)."You are ugly," her husband told an ugly woman. "A man obsessed with sex doesn't discriminate between beautiful and ugly women," she retorted. He did not understand her, so she put lentil soup in several bowls and called him when it was time to eat. "What is this?" he asked her. "It's lentil soup," she replied. "Now you see that I have put it in several bowls." "How are they different?" "It's just the same with having sex!"

§256 (2). Also, a man saw another man's wife, lusted after her, and thought: "Someday I will have sex with her." Later, his friend told him, "She is the very one you're seeking but don't say anything to her. She is a modest woman from a good family." Then, in the dark, that man had sex with a woman who was his own wife. He was quite happy and said, "There is no woman like her!"

§257. Here we say:

> Alas! What has concealed this human being in many ways?
> A dreamlike embrace reveals the [external] appearance.
> Desire has deluded those who pursue others.
> It is a wide net whose nature is darkness.

A Fool's Desire for Beautiful Women

§258. The most beautiful woman is not the cause even of a fool's desire. Āryadeva says:

> Whoever loves her
> Thinks that he is satisfied with her.
> Fool! Why are you attracted to her,
> Since you have this in common even with dogs, etc.? (CŚ III.4)

§259. Someone attracted even to an ugly woman thinks that she satisfies him. If only a beautiful woman aroused desire, he would want a beautiful woman all the time. But this is not the case. Of course, the cause of his desire is not a beautiful woman. Desire alone is the cause. Even without a cause, desire arises in dogs, asses, elephants, and pigs for the females of their own kind. So desire is common. Consequently, intelligent men do not make a beautiful woman the object of their desire for any reason whatsoever.

§260. Take for example the story about the demons who each preferred the beauty of their own wives.

Two demons each preferred the beauty of his own wife and quarreled over this. They approached a monk and asked him, "Whose wife is more beautiful?" The monk replied, "A wife is beautiful to the one who loves her."

§261. Here we say:

> If delusion is the cause of desire
> Then beauty is not the cause of desire.
> Moreover, that beautiful woman is not the cause of desire,
> Because any woman at all will arouse desire.

§262. Objection: It is difficult to find a woman whose every limb delights the mind. Whoever finds her would think it a miracle! Shouldn't he be attracted to her? In response, Āryadeva says:

The woman whose every limb
Is beautiful to you previously was common to all!
It is not at all surprising
That you should find her! (CŚ III.5)

§263. Women exist for the benefit of their husbands. Since it is doubtful that she is solely yours, it must be possible for every man to have her. So, why is it a surprise when the woman to whom you are attracted is found to be common property? Since she can be obtained like goods sold on the street, it is wrong for you to think that this is a miracle!

§264. Consider the case of the Vatsa king who obtained Vāsuladattā.

The king of Vatsa acquired Vāsuladattā,[2] who was a prostitute, and he thought that finding her was a miracle. But every man had shared her. Similarly, because she was the object that all men sought, a young woman became their common property. Later, she belonged just to one man.

§265. Here we say:

Like goods on the main road,
A woman can be found for a price.
Intelligent people do not think that
Finding her is any miracle.

A Good Woman Is Hard to Find

§266. Objection: We see that desire develops in men for women whose virtuous qualities they favor. It is appropriate to be attracted to a woman who has virtuous qualities. In response, Āryadeva says:

When a man experiences love
For a woman who has good qualities
And the reverse for the opposite,
As there is no constancy, which—former or latter—is true? (CŚ III.6)

§267. If desire arises for a woman who has virtuous qualities and hatred for the opposite, a superior woman is not the cause of this desire, since there is confusion about her faults and her good qualities. Good qualities and faults do not remain constant. Consequently, both will occur over time in the same woman. Since her good qualities and faults do not remain constant, desire for her does not depend solely on them. Before she had good qualities and later she has faults—which is true? If it is true that she has good qualities, isn't the first claim then false when this woman's faults appear? If it is true that she has faults, when this woman's good qualities appear, that second claim is false. Since there is no truth to either claim, neither desire nor hatred should develop. Thus, a desire for a woman who has good qualities is not appropriate.

§268. Consider the examples of talking a walk after eating and going to an outhouse.

§268 (1). We are pleased after eating well-prepared food. But there are drawbacks and we are not pleased about taking a walk after eating and going to the outhouse.

§268 (2). Also, a man came and wanted to use his friend's outhouse. When he uses it, he will be free of attachment because he sees its advantages and disadvantages. Similarly, one will become free of sexual desire by seeing the real nature of women.

§269. Here we say:

> If attachment to something exists
> Because it has good qualities,
> Then after rejecting a thing that has good qualities,
> A fool should not become attached to anything else.

§270. Objection: Because women who lack good qualities are thought disagreeable, no desire for them arises. Desire arises for women who have good qualities and are agreeable. In response, Āryadeva says:

> A fool's desire does not arise
> Solely for a woman who has good qualities.
> How can people who act without reason
> Be stopped by reason? (CŚ III.7)

§271. In this world the lust of men deluded by desire, overwhelmed by attachment, and lacking in shame and modesty does not arise solely for women who have good qualities. It arises for all of them! Just like a fire, these men do not discriminate between the presence and absence of virtuous qualities. They do not see reason because their delusion is so great. When something happens for a reason, it can be stopped by employing another reason. Reason cannot stop a fool who acts without reason. He acts without first taking reason into account. How can an impure form have good qualities? Consequently, it is wrong to claim that desire for women arises because they have good qualities.

§272. Take for example the story about the Brahmin woman who was crying because she was sorry for herself.

A Brahmin woman went to the forest to perform austerities so that she would become a mother. Some boys stopped her and she began to cry. They asked, "Are you crying because of the pain of losing someone?" "I'm not crying because of any loss," she replied, "I'm crying because I haven't experienced the pleasure of having sons." They asked her, "What's the point of this action?" She just cried and did not respond. She was unable to stop crying. In the same way, fools whose desire is not produced by good qualities find such desire difficult to eradicate.

§273. Here we say:

> Men who become infatuated with women
> Without examining their faults and their virtuous qualities
> Will be unable to turn away from women,
> Even if they try a hundred times!

§274. Objection: A woman will kill herself after her husband has died. A man won't do the same thing for a woman. Why shouldn't we be attached to women who have such love? In response, Āryadeva says:

> As long as she does not know someone else
> She is yours.[3]
> A woman must always be protected
> From opportunity, just as from serious illness. (CŚ III.8)

§275. As long as a woman does not experience the taste of another man because she has no opportunity to do so, she will love her husband and remain faithful to him. When she does experience the taste of another man, she will not love this one! You can rely on them to change when the opportunity for a quarrel arises! For this reason, women who can't be trusted should be protected from men, in the same way as they should be protected from serious illness. Women are hard to fathom; their way of doing things is difficult to comprehend. Consequently, intelligent men who are not attached to anything surely should not trust women!

§276. Take for example the story of the Brahmin woman who was uninterested earlier but later changed her mind.

A man desired a certain Brahmin woman. She told her husband, "A man came into my presence and I was afraid of him. When he comes again, I'll tell you." After she said that, she waited. When the man appeared again, she had changed her mind and was now attracted to him. She did not tell her husband that the man had come. Consequently, women should always be protected, for anyone can persuade them.

§277. Here we say:

> Women will follow their own desires,
> Even though they are protected.
> Consequently, a virtuous woman
> Who remains faithful to her husband is very rare.

Advice to Young Men on Sex

§278. Objection: A young man should indulge his sexual desires in the beginning when he is young. Those men who indulge their sexual desires in accord with social customs are not doing anything wrong. Response: What man with any intelligence would be attracted to a woman's filthy body? He is just like a dog! Moreover, in appearing before her, he has taken the word of people who do what is worthless as his authority. Intoxicated by drinking the wine of sexual desire and lacking in shame and modesty, he acts in a careless way. All his virtue has been destroyed. This man who acts in accord with that advice on women will come to regret his youthful conduct. Āryadeva says:

> An old man does not desire
> What he did when he was a young man. (CŚ III.9ab)

§279. When his faculties mature, when the elements forming his body weaken, and when he is free from sexual desire, he will examine his own past conduct. After he has reflected on the pain of this conduct, he will regret it. Thus, Āryadeva says:

> Do not those who are liberated
> Greatly regret that behavior? (CŚ III.9cd)

§280. When there is no pleasure taken in misunderstanding the truth and in bad behavior that inflicts pain each moment, liberation from the afflictions' bonds occurs. Abuse, difficulties, and their source [namely, desire] do not arise a hundred thousand times for intelligent and insightful people. Similarly, conduct that is adulterated with the stains of desire and mixed with pain does not arise.

§281. Take for example the story about the confused daughter-in-law who tied the calf's rope around her father-in-law's neck.

When the time of the festival had arrived, the family's daughter-in-law thought, "I must see the festival," and she tied the rope, meant for the calf, around the neck of her father-in-law. "What are you doing?" He protested and glared at her. She became very embarrassed. Similarly, at first an old man did not recognize that his sexual desire was excessive but later he found no pleasure in what he had done when he was young. Do not those who have thoroughly understood the truth about things greatly regret that conduct? You should reply! The implication is that such conduct should be severely criticized.

§282. Here we say:

> What was done because of confusion,
> Under the influence of desire and the influence of demons,
> Is now regretted and creates difficulties,
> Because the young man has grown older.

The Power of Delusion

§283. Objection: This pleasure is the best kind in the desire realm. Women are the cause of it. Women should be embraced for that reason. In response, Āryadeva says:

> Someone who lacks desire has no such pleasure
> And a sensible person does not have it.
> What kind of pleasure is there
> For someone who always turns his mind away? (CŚ III.10)

§284. Here in the desire realm the pleasures derived from women do not exist for a man who has no desire. When a man becomes aroused, the object of his desire takes on that desirable nature. His desire comes alive now that he has made something unreal into something real. Consequently, delusion prevails and because of delusion he does not understand the nature of the object. His own imagination has deprived him of his intelligence. He directs his mind toward an object created out of his own delusion. It is just like the phantom a magician creates! Because his mind is disturbed about something that is indeed different from the way he imagines it, he does not understand anything as it really is. Because he does not understand, he does not analyze pleasure properly. Apart from just his own deluded imagination, he has no pleasure at all. Thus, it is wrong to claim that women must be embraced.

§285 (1). Take for example the story about the fool who desired the queen but was busy with a rope.

The fool saw the queen; and after he saw her, he desired her. He bribed her maidservant with gifts. He asked, "Is it possible to meet with her?" "It's possible," she replied. Then she discussed this matter with the queen. "The king's palace is well guarded," the maidservant said, "nevertheless, when your majesty goes for a walk, this affair will be possible." The maidservant told the fool about this. At the end of one year, he had stockpiled perfume, incense, flowers, garlands, and cosmetics for the queen. "Tomorrow when the queen goes for a walk," the fool thought, "I'll meet with her." He made elaborate preparations in his own room. On that day, his teacher had lost a cow and sent him out to find it. After he had gone out, the queen came to his room. When he returned, she had gone. The fool whose mind was distracted experienced intense suffering for an entire year because of her. How will men whose minds are distracted by sexual desire obtain pleasure?

§285 (2). Also, a weaver was infatuated with the queen. He was crazy with desire. He asked everyone, "Have you seen the queen?" "Is she coming?" "Is she asking about me?"

§286. Here we say:

> Darkness has deprived of vision.
> A man deluded by desire for the pleasures of women.

He cannot see while he remains in that state,
Just as a reflection cannot be seen in muddy water.

Jealous Lovers

§287. Objection: The pleasures derived from women arise from sexual intercourse and without women they do not arise. For that reason, women must be embraced. Response: Why? Āryadeva says:

> You cannot have sexual intercourse
> All the time in accordance with your inclination. (CŚ III.11ab)

§288. Your inclination for enjoying women gradually increases from slight to moderate to intense. Day and night it increases without interruption! Your enjoyment does not increase in this same way. So, why don't impassioned men exhausted by sexual pleasure—which just lasts for a moment—relinquish women, as do men who are free of passion? To those men who cannot enjoy women in accordance with their inclinations, Āryadeva says:

> "She's mine; she doesn't belong to anyone else."
> What is the point of this possessiveness? (CŚ III.11cd)

§289. It is wrong to claim that a woman is loved for pleasure's sake, since it is impossible for you to enjoy her! When you engage in sexual intercourse, it should be possible for you to do it without jealousy. When you say, "She's mine; she doesn't belong to anyone else," this possessiveness and this rejection of anyone else but you enjoying her are wrong. The disturbance that possessiveness causes arises because of your self-serving attitude. To say, "What is done for my benefit should not be done for the benefit of anyone else," is not only possessiveness but is also a form of ignorance.

§290. Consider the examples of the Brahmin who hoarded food, the advice given to the king, and the blind man who could not see.

§290 (1). A Brahmin could not continue eating because the heat of his digestive fire had died down. He had plenty of good food to eat. But he did not want to give even a little of it to anyone else, and so he hoarded a large quantity of food.

§290 (2). Also, a king had many hundreds of wives living in his palace. This king did not engage in any activities with them and he did not relinquish them to anyone else. One day a monk asked the king, "Are you going to do anything with all these women?" "No," the king replied. Then the monk gave a talk on virtuous conduct to the king so that he would release these women. He released them because of this.

§290 (3). A blind man does not become enamored of women because of their beauty, since he cannot see. Nevertheless, he adopts a possessive attitude, "These women are mine; they do not belong to anyone else."

§291. Here we say:

If a man who has duties
Does not perform them,
What's the use of his possessiveness?
Is not this possessiveness foolish?

Desire Is Not the Same as Pleasure

§292. Objection: Ordinary men speak of desire as pleasure. It does not arise without sexual intercourse with women. So women must be objects of desire. In response, Āryadeva says:

If desire were pleasure,
Women would then be unnecessary.
Pleasure is not at all regarded as
Something that should be rejected. (CŚ III.12)

§293. If desire were pleasure, women would be unnecessary. We do not claim that pleasure should always be rejected because pleasure is faultless.[4] Like poison, desire repeatedly defeats men with the aid of women who are poisonous adversaries. For this reason, it is wrong to claim that desire is pleasure.

§294. Take for example the story about the man who threw away food.

Hunger and thirst tormented a family's impoverished son. One night he entered a house and there he saw ashes in one pot and water in another. He thought, "This is food." He then kneaded the ashes and ate them. After he was free of his hunger and thirst, he recognized that his "food" was ashes. Disgusted, he threw it away and came outside. The householder asked him, "What is this?" He explained. Then the householder placed many things before him and adopted him as a son-in-law. Similarly, if desire were pleasure, it would not be rejected.

§295. Here we say:

Because a man is addicted in this way
To women who resemble poison
And are the accomplices of a poison-like sexual desire,
How can he be happy?

Sex and Imaginary Pleasures

§296. Objection: Pleasure arises from sexual intercourse and women are its cause. Consequently, pleasure arises from women. In response, Āryadeva says:

Even in sexual intercourse with a woman,
Pleasure arises from something else.
What sensible person would maintain
That the cause of it is just a female companion? (CŚ III.13)

§297. In this world men have sexual intercourse with women, but sexual intercourse with women is not the cause of pleasure in this situation. Some men, even though they are not free of desire, respect their moral training. Unlike impassioned men, they would engage in sexual intercourse with women only under duress. A female companion would not be the cause of their pleasure.[5] If sexual intercourse with women were the cause of pleasure, there would be no difference at all between passionate men and dispassionate men, just as everyone suffers when burned by fire. Such a possibility does not exist. Consequently, such pleasure would arise only for those men whose perspective is fundamentally wrong and who think that what is impure is pure and what is painful is pleasant. They rely on this connection between their illusions and their senses. Pleasure arises because of its association with many conditions. The pleasure of sexual intercourse arises because of mistaken imagination. For this reason, what sensible person would claim that its cause is only a woman and not anything else? Only a fool would make that claim!

§298. Take for example the story about the fool who was pleased when his wife made him work.

His own wife gave orders to this fool: "Fetch the water for my bath!" And he obeyed. She ordered him to perform other services in the same way: "Get the wood! Heat the water! Massage me and rub me with oil!" There was no part of her body that he did not massage and he even enjoyed doing it! Similarly, impassioned men make themselves exhausted countless times and they think that pleasure is found only in women.

§299. Here we say:

Since pleasure arises
From many causes and conditions,
Those who know the truth
Know that there is not just one cause for it.

The Painful Itch of Desire

§300. Objection: If desire is criticized in this way because pleasure has many causes, why does an impassioned man repeatedly indulge his desires? A man surely will have pleasure by indulging his desires because pleasure arises from desire. In response, Āryadeva says, surely:

Like a leper scratching, he does not see
The danger of desire, because passion blinds him. (CŚ III.14ab)[6]

§301. A leper afflicted with a very severe skin disease scratches and does not see the error of scratching because immediate pain torments him. He scratches again and again, while failing to see the error of spreading his skin eruptions and stripping away his skin, and the oozing forth of blood and pus. He does not stop. In the same way as the leper does not see the error in this action, an impassioned man does not see the error in desire because the itch of desire overwhelms him. Again and again he enjoys sexual pleasures and does not stop. Since this is the case, Āryadeva says:

> Those who are without passion see impassioned people
> As being endowed with pain, just as the leper is. (CŚ III.14cd)

Since superior people, who are free of desire and released from the fault of desire's itch, see impassioned men as suffering in the same way as a leper does, the claim that an impassioned man is happy is never right.

§302. Consider the example of an addiction to gambling.

Gambling with dice and the leper's scratching are proven causes for exhausting one's wealth and damaging one's body, respectively. It is just the same with indulging a desire to have sex with women.

§303. Here we say:

> Dogs and pigs are seen as unclean.
> And in the same way sexual desire is seen as unclean.
> After seeing impassioned people mired in filth,
> What educated person would be happy about that?

The Tyranny of Women

§304. Objection: Although desires are impure, many kinds of activities that result from desire are pleasurable. In response, Āryadeva says:

> What happens in a famine
> To the protectorless tormented by hunger—
> That is the course for all impassioned men
> When united with women. (CŚ III.15)

§305. At the time of a famine, the pain of hunger and thirst overwhelm the poor whose relatives have died and have no one to protect them. They find it difficult to get food. Despite the gestures and entreaties the poor direct toward the rich, the rich have no compassion and treat them with contempt. Nevertheless, the poor still hope, "Later they will give us a little something." When they are treated with contempt and not given anything, that is seen to be a painful process. A similar process occurs for an impassioned man who wants to embrace a woman. He is intent on pursuing a pure young woman. A man who has that conviction has to endure patiently many kinds of contemptible acts. She smacks his head with a stick, spits on him, and beats him with a whip.[7] We see this happen to men who are blinded by their eagerness to enjoy sexual pleasures and who have no pride. Since this is the case, it is wrong to claim that the activity of an impassioned man when embracing a woman is pleasurable.

§306. Consider the example of the prisoner who tried to get water from cow dung.

A man put in prison tried to get water from cow dung. Similarly, impassioned men seek to indulge their desires with women by employing flattery.

§307. Here we say:

> After hearing about impassioned men's conduct
> And the way they act when embracing women,
> Men who are free of desire
> Will avoid women in this world.

The Filthy Nature of Women's Bodies

§308. Objection: Since a man embraces a woman because of his desire for pleasure and becomes jealous of other men on her account, the pleasure derived from women must exist. In response, Āryadeva says:

> Because of their pride
> Some become attached even to an outhouse!
> Some develop attachment for certain women,
> And some develop jealousy. (CŚ III.16)

§309. Because of his pride, a powerful and wealthy man was attached to his outhouse, a container for human excrement. For that reason, he did not allow others to use it. Since attachment and jealousy develop not only for women but also for outhouses, it is wrong to claim that pleasure exists because of the attachment and the jealousy that women arouse.

§310. Take for example the story about the miser who would not allow a servant girl water from his mountain peak.

A miserly king was proud of his sovereignty over a mountain peak. This proud man said, "What a difference there is between you and me!" He did not give her even a little water to drink because of his miserly attitude. Because of pride, attachment exists not only for things that are valuable but also for things that are not valuable.

§311. Here we say:

> Since a woman and an outhouse
> Are both containers of filth,
> Someone who knows the truth
> Would not eagerly desire her.

§312. Objection: There is still pleasure to be found in a woman's body, even though it is thought to be filthy. For this reason, it is appropriate to desire her. In response, Āryadeva says:

> It is reasonable that confusion
> And anger should arise for a filthy thing.
> But it is unreasonable that
> Desire should arise! (CŚ III.17)

§313. It is reasonable that someone might be confused and angry because he stepped in filth. It is possible confusion may have arisen because the covering of darkness obstructed his sight and he did not see it. It is also possible that anger may have arisen because its bad smell irritated him. It is not possible that desire might have arisen because that does not fit the situation at all! Since artificial means conceal its nature, it is reasonable for confusion to arise for a filthy female body. Since it smells bad, it is also reasonable for anger to arise. Since the body's nature is impure, it is entirely unreasonable for desire to arise. It is wrong to claim that it is appropriate to be attached to a woman's body because it is pleasurable.

§314. Consider the example of stepping in excrement at night.

At night someone stepped in excrement with both feet. When he saw it, he was angry. Later suppose he was attracted to it. Another man questioned him, "Why did you step in shit?" "Because the darkness hid it," he replied. The man asked him, "Then why are you angry?" "Because it is unpleasant!" Since there is no reason to, why even bother to ask, "Why are you attracted to it?" Consequently, it is reasonable for both confusion and anger to arise in regard to something that is impure but for desire to arise is completely unreasonable.

§315. Here we say:

> It is not reasonable at all
> To perceive it in that way.
> How can there be any desire for it?
> Alas! People are quite blind!

The Filthy Nature of the Human Body

§316. Objection: Although the body is impure, it should not be repudiated because people say it has no faults. Also people say, "Brahmins are pure because they come from the mouth of Brahmā" and "Women are completely pure." In response, Āryadeva says:

> With the exception of human beings,
> If a container of filth is repudiated,
> Why wouldn't one consider repudiating
> That [body] in which filth resides? (CŚ III.18)

§317. These Brahmins were born from an unclean body. If they consider contaminated vessels to be severely flawed, how could people who are not mentally impaired think that the perpetually impure matrix out of which they emerged is pure? Consequently, it is wrong to claim that a woman's body should not be repudiated.

§318. Take for example the story about the woman who vomited into a copper pot.

A rich man had in his possession a very beautiful woman who carried a copper pot. Men desired her, courted her, and sought her out. Then one day she went outside and vomited into that copper pot. After they saw that, they considered her damaged goods, plugged their noses, and went away. Similarly, fools do not see the impurities that reside in their own bodies as flaws. They think that just what comes out of the body is impure.

§319. Here we say:

> Fools, arrogant about their purity,
> And deluded by desire, say that the body
> Should not be repudiated because of its nature
> And because of the power acquired from chastity.

§320. Objection: People are attracted to a pure body. A woman's body is pure. For this reason, women should not be repudiated. In response, Āryadeva says:

> What intelligent person
> Calls that pure,
> On which the contamination
> Of all pure things is observed? (CŚ III.19)

§321. All pure things, flowers, perfumes, clothes, ornaments, etc., become impure merely by coming into contact with the body. It is not possible to call that body pure when pure things, aloewood, musk, and sandalwood scents, marigolds, other flowers, ornaments, etc., are considered contaminated by coming into contact with it. It is wrong to claim that a woman's body is pure, for intelligent people do repudiate a woman's body. A man's body should be considered equally impure in exactly the same way.

§322. Consider the example of the water of the river Ganges flowing into the ocean.

When the water of the river Ganges reaches the ocean, it becomes salty, just like the ocean's water. In the same way, all pure substances, food, clothing, etc., become just as impure as the body because of their contact with it.

§323. Here we say:

> Even though a fragrant
> And beautifully colored lotus is pure,
> After a person picks it, it becomes impure.
> Thus, the body is impure.

§324. Objection: In this world a person takes pride in a pure thing. If the body were not pure, no pride would occur. Pride does occur; consequently, the body is pure. In response, Āryadeva says:

> Someone who was inside a filthy enclosure
> And who could not live apart from it,
> Like a dung worm,
> Develops pride only out of ignorance. (CŚ III.20)

§325. Someone before he was born lived inside his mother's womb—which is like an outhouse—between her intestines and stomach. Like a dung worm, he was nourished by the fluid of her waste products. It is only from ignorance that he thinks "I am pure."

§326. Take for example the story about the young man put in a sewer.

A young man who had become involved with the wife of rich man arrived at that man's house. He was then seized and thrown into a sewer. There he was nourished by the sewage. One day because of a heavy rainfall one side of the sewer collapsed and he emerged from it. His relatives led him away and brought him into their house. They summoned a skilled physician. After several days much of his strength and color had been restored. On another occasion he had his body washed and oiled. When he went out into the middle of the main road, a poor man accidentally brushed against him with his clothes. The young man, inflated with pride, reviled him: "Shame on you! I am unclean because of this filthy clothing of yours!" Similarly, fools, their stomachs swollen with filthy substances, nourished by filthy substances in their mothers' wombs for nine or ten months before they emerge from an unclean opening, are just like dung worms. Out of ignorance, they develop pride in their wealth, in their purity, and in their power.

§327. Here we say:

> Even though they say that the body should not be reviled,
> There is no purity in the body
> Since its seed,
> Its food, and its foul smell are defiling.

No Remedies for the Body's Impurity

§328. Objection: If the body were not pure, we would not be able to remove the impurities. Because we can remove impurities, it is pure. In response, Āryadeva says:

> No method will purify
> The inside of your body.
> The effort you make cleaning the inside
> Is not like cleaning the outside. (CŚ III.21)

§329. You will be unable to clean the inside of your body, even though for a long time you resort to such actions as perfuming, washing, oiling, and using mantras to clean your body.[8] Consequently, how can the body, which is reviled because of the impurities that ooze out from inside it, be pure? Moreover, you are attached to your enjoyment of the body, the source of the impurities that emerge from it. Washing it, etc., does not make it pure. So, how can the body whose nature is impure be pure?

§330. Take for example the story about the villager's friend who built an outhouse and the story about the jackals and the *palāśa* flowers.[9]

§330 (1). The king employed the friend of a villager to build an outhouse. At one point, the villager's friend whitewashed it. The villager observed him purifying it with incense, etc. His friend laughed and said to him, "Right now it is clean!" Similarly, intelligent people laugh at fools who try to make their bodies pure inside by consuming sweet-smelling food and drink.

§330 (2). Also, two jackals were under a *palāśa* tree. One of them stood where a flower had fallen. He thought that the entire tree must be just like that flower and went on his way. The other jackal thought that the flower that fell from the *palāśa* tree was not the substance of the tree but rather what remained of the tree was its substance. In the same way, fools think that what comes out of the body is impure but what remains behind is pure!

§331. Here we say:

> Because this body emerged from the womb,
> Impurity is its nature.
> Since it is impure
> It is impossible to make it pure.

§332. Objection: Even though women's bodies contain urine, the ascetics who wanted to enjoy the pleasures of the sages' women did not avoid women.[10] For this reason, women should not be avoided. In response, Āryadeva says:

> If, like the leper,
> Containing urine were not common to all,
> All people would avoid someone who contains urine
> In the same way as they avoid a leper. (CŚ III.22)

§333. If this dripping, foul-smelling urine were uncommon, people who value their purity would also avoid a body defiled by this impurity, just as they avoid lepers because the bodies of lepers are putrid with foul, oozing pus and rotting skin lesions. But if something is common, how can it be avoided? Ordinary suffering is not attractive when repudiated for this reason. If leprosy were common in the same way that containing urine is, lepers could not be avoided, just as people who contain urine cannot be avoided. A leper is avoided because he is uncommon. But someone who contains urine cannot be avoided because it is common. If containing urine were not a flaw, why, then, are all people alike in regarding it in that way?

§334. Some people are like flies that get trapped by the honey in a small bottle. Others react like flies to a blazing iron ball because they see the danger. Those ascetics did not avoid women, since their philosophy is incompatible with ours in this respect. Consequently, it is wrong to claim that a woman's body should not be avoided.

§335. Take for example the story about the king who avoided water that would cause insanity and the story about the man who came to a country where everyone had goiters.

§335 (1). Fortune-tellers told a king that it was going to rain and that anyone who drank that rainwater would become insane. The king covered his well for his own safety. The rain fell and one of his relatives drank the rainwater and became insane. Even though the king was sane, people thought he was insane because his nature was the same as his relative's. The king heard about this matter and he thought, "If they already think that I am insane, they will ridicule me and destroy me." Then he drank the rainwater. Similarly, if there were just one person who contained urine, that person could be avoided, just as a leper is. But when everyone contains urine, where is the idea of purity to be found?

§335 (2). Also, all the people in a certain country were ugly and had goiters. A handsome man went there and they avoided him because they thought that he was extraordinarily ugly and lacked one of the body's usual parts.

§336. Here we say:

> If there were something that had no flaws
> The entire population would be attracted to it.
> But because a flaw is found
> Intelligent people will avoid it.

§337. Objection: A young man in the prime of his life who does not relish the pleasures to be had with young women adorned with all their best jewelry is thoroughly confused about the world! The application of fragrant perfume, for instance, will remove impurity. So it is not wrong for people to cherish purity. In response, Āryadeva says:

> Someone who lacks part of the body
> May be pleased with a substitute for his nose.
> In the same way, the desire for flowers, etc.,
> Is considered to be a remedy for its impurity. (CŚ III.23)

§338. Someone whose nose has been cut off may be pleased when he bears an artificial nose and thinks that all his body parts are complete.[11] Of course, he should be ashamed of his body's substitute part. That very thing gives him pleasure because he is a fool! In the same way, fools naturally long for sensual pleasures. Because of their ignorance, they think that perfumes, flowers, jewelry, etc., which are not natural to the body, are remedies for its impurity. Desire then arises. They think that their bodies and the bodies of others are pure because of these remedies. Of course, even wearing flowers, etc., is not enough to make the body continually fragrant with the finest scents, just as garlic doesn't continue to make it smell bad!

§339. Consider the example of a cat with butter smeared on its nose who enjoyed the taste of her food and the example of the man who was pleased when he saw his golden nose.

§339 (1). Someone smeared a cat's nose with butter and gave her a little morsel of food. The cat then thought that her food has been mixed with butter.

§339 (2). Someone who had lost his nose had a golden substitute made. He was pleased when he saw it. In the same way, fools develop attachment for the body after they have used flowers, etc., as remedies for its impurity.

§340. Here we say:

> Because of ignorance people are attracted
> By such things as perfumes, garlands, and clothes,
> Which conceal the open sores of this body,
> Which itself resembles an open wound.

Cultivating Detachment

§341. Objection: If flowers, etc., were not a cause of attraction, people would not become attracted to the body because of them.

§342. In response, Āryadeva says:

> It is unreasonable to call pure
> That toward which detachment develops.
> There is not anything anywhere
> That is invariably a cause of attraction. (CŚ III.24)

§343. There is no object that can be called pure because of its nature. First of all, people with unimpaired vision become detached when they look at the body. They see it as unattractive because it oozes impurities. It is not possible that the body is pure because it is the cause of their aversion. It is just like a piece of excrement! Even flowers, etc., are not invariably causes of attraction because aversion can arise even for them. Aversion for these flowers develops also in people detached from desire. Furthermore, what could always be a cause of attraction, since there is, of course, nothing that could be called pure because of its nature? For instance, even such things as flowers, assumed to be pure, become unattractive when they decay. If they were pure naturally, they would not change, since an inherent nature does not change. Consequently, they are not pure by nature. Also, if such things as flowers were always the causes of attraction, they would cause attraction to develop in all cases at all times. This is not so. Consequently, it is wrong to claim that flowers, etc., are causes of attraction.

§344. Take for example the story about the man who desired a young woman but no longer wanted her when he discovered that she was his own daughter.

A merchant went abroad when his daughter was born. Later, he returned home. His daughter had become a young woman. She was playing with other young women in the garden outside the house. When he saw her, a strong desire arose in him. Then he was told, "She is your daughter!" He lost that desire. So there is nothing that is invariably the cause of desire. That body toward which detachment should arise ought to be recognized as impure.

§345. Here we say:

> Since that very same thing
> Which gives rise to attraction
> Also gives rise to detachment,
> Attraction has no definitively established cause.

§346. Thus, the body is impure in the same way as it was previously explained that it is painful and impermanent and in the same way that it will be explained that it has no self. These four are not illusions. You should consider whether it is possible or not that these four that are not illusions exist in regard to one thing. Āryadeva says:

> In brief, the group of four—
> Impermanent, impure,
> Painful and the lack of an independent self—
> Are possible in one and the same thing. (CŚ III.25)

§347. Whatever is constructed and has arisen in dependence is impermanent because it is momentary. Whatever is impermanent is impure because it produces disgust. Whatever is impure is painful because it causes harm. Whatever is painful lacks a self because it is not under its own control. So, in short, these four that are not illusions are possible in one and the same thing. Although intelligent people recognize this, fools who are subject to illusion do not discern this. Instead they think that things have the opposite nature. Intelligent people understand the nature of things as it really is. Consequently, their minds are able to tolerate instruction about the absence of a self.

§348. Take for example the story about the man who was frightened because he saw the real nature of a flesh-eating demoness.

A flesh-eating demoness assumed the form of a man's wife. He treated her just as if she were his wife. When he saw her real nature, he was frightened because it caused him pain, because it disgusted him, because it was beyond his ability to control, and because it was changeable. He thought, "This is not my wife! This is a flesh-eating demoness!" Then he lost his desire for her. Intelligent people become detached in the same way, since they have seen the inherent nature of constructed things.

§349. Here we say:

> Whatever is constructed is not permanent.
> Whatever is impermanent is not pure.
> Whatever is not pure is not pleasant.
> Whatever is painful lacks an independent self.

§350. And:

> Because the four illusions
> Are possible in one constructed thing,
> All the afflictions
> Consequently are unreal.

§351. This concludes the commentary to the third chapter explaining the method for rejecting the illusion of purity, namely, the reflection on impurity, in Āryadeva's *Bodhisattvayogācāracatuḥśataka*.

9

REJECTING THE ILLUSION OF EGOTISM

Defining Egotism and Selfishness

§352. Objection: The method for rejecting the three previous illusions has been explained. Now explain the method for rejecting the fourth illusion. In response, Āryadeva says:

> What wise person would have pride
> In thinking "I" and "mine,"
> Since all objects in the cycle of existence
> Are common to all embodied beings? (CŚ IV.1)

§353. Since the king certainly has egotism and selfishness in abundance, primarily the king is advised here about their removal. In this context, egotism arises from the imagination of one's own superior characteristics: "I am the lord." Selfishness, however, arises in regard to notion of power over things appropriated as one's own: "These are my things." The word "pride" is used here in the sense of haughtiness, conceit, and arrogance. The word "existence" refers to the cycle of death and rebirth, namely, going round in the five places of rebirth[1] with the regular succession of death and rebirth, on the part of someone who is subject to action and the afflictions. Under those circumstances, what intelligent person who is alive now would take pride in egotism and selfishness? Of course, if there were somewhere someone whose sovereign power is extraordinary, then it would be appropriate for him to have pride based on it, that is, from his perception of that power: "I alone am the master of these things; these things are mine alone." This is impossible for a fool who goes around in the cycle of death and rebirth! For instance, all the objects of the senses, visible objects, etc., have originated from the karmic action that is common to all sentient beings. Consequently, the pride that results from embracing egotism and selfishness is inappropriate when directed toward those enjoyable objects that are common to all sentient beings, as a common arbor formed from a group of trees.

§354. Consider the example of a royal dancer. A royal dancer one minute assumes the role of a king; one minute he assumes the role of a minister; one minute, the role of a Brahmin priest; then, the role of a householder; and, finally, the role of a servant. In the same way, the king's role is temporary, since he dances on a stage made up of the five places of rebirth. Furthermore, in this connection it is said:

> §355. Since the possession of sovereignty
> Or wealth is acquired as a result of merit,
> It is not appropriate for intelligent people
> To take pride in a world that karmic action creates.

The Servant of the People

§356. Objection: Since all undertakings are under the authorization of the king, his pride, which has his authority as its cause, is appropriate. In response, Āryadeva says:

> Supported by one-sixth of your subjects' harvest
> What pride do you have?
> On every occasion your work
> Depends upon your being appointed. (CŚ IV.2)

§357. When people of the first eon began to take what had not been given to them, the majority of the populace paid a man strong enough to protect the fields with wages amounting to one-sixth of their harvested grain. Thus, he came to be called "a king" because he made the people happy with his work of protecting the fields. From that time on, the people supported every king with wages of one-sixth of the harvest. Consequently it is inappropriate for a king who has been given one-sixth of the harvest to think "the people's work is subject to my control" and be proud. Even though the king has exercised his authority over some servant's labor, some of the king's own actions depend on him. Thus, it is inappropriate for the king who thinks "my subjects depend on me" to be proud. Consequently, your majesty, if it is impossible to prove that this king is independent, inasmuch as he depends on this one person, why, then, bother to speak about his dependence on many people? For this reason, your pride is never appropriate under any circumstance.

§358. Consider the example of the man who was familiar with the wilderness.

A certain king set out from his own country on a conquest. With an outcaste whom he had commissioned as a guide, he traveled across the vast wilderness. That king, along with his army, depended on him. When that outcaste thinks "the king, along with his army, depends on me," he should not be proud on account of that. Similarly, the king should not be proud, because he thinks "the people depend on me."

§359. Here we say:

> If the king is entitled to be proud
> Because of his control over all activities,
> Is not his pride then inappropriate
> Because his wages amount to one-sixth of the harvest?

False Generosity

§360. Objection: The king is a generous lord and for this reason his pride is appropriate, since he has sovereign power over the conditions for the collection and donation of wealth. In response, Āryadeva says:

> Just as his subjects think of the king as a generous lord,
> After they receive what he has received,
> Similarly, after he has given what should be given,
> He thinks "I am a generous lord." (CŚ IV.3)

§361. The multitude of the king's subjects, after they have received their wages or their monthly salaries, which they should be given, consider themselves inferior and the king superior. They think "the king is a generous lord." In the same way, the king also, after he has given to the multitude of his subjects the wages and salary that he should give them, takes pride in thinking "I am a generous lord." In this situation the multitude of his subjects receives what they should receive, namely, the wealth produced from their labor that supports the king. They become downcast and humbled and do not act arrogantly toward the king. In the same way, the king also should not act arrogantly after he has given them what he should give.

§362. Consider the example of a servant who should receive wages.

A servant must be given wages. It is wrong for the person who pays her to act arrogantly, and for the servant to act arrogantly. In the same way, it is not appropriate for the king to act arrogantly when he collects or donates wealth.

§363. Here we say:

> If it is appropriate for king to be arrogant
> After he has given wages to his servants,
> In the same way, is it not also appropriate for merchants
> Who strive to obtain wealth to be arrogant?

The Precarious Position of the King.

§364. Objection: Since the king always enjoys the pleasures of whatever objects he desires, he is self-satisfied. For this reason, he is certainly proud. In response, Āryadeva says:

> On the contrary, others consider you,
> To be in a painful position.
> What produces pleasure for you
> Who live by working for others? (CŚ IV.4)

§365. People who control their senses say that having a strong desire for such objects as women, liquor, and jewelry is a painful position to be in because the senses are out of control. Consequently, since this sovereignty is the reason for much misfortune, it is a painful position. If you have a high position now, your ignorance will take effect later! Furthermore, you say that people attracted to sensual pleasures indulge in them in order to experience pleasure. What pleasure can there be in being afflicted with a livelihood, which has as its reward working for others and the continual suffering that protecting the majority of the people produces?

§366. Consider the example of the executioner who punishes thieves. An executioner who punishes thieves cannot be happy because of this vile work. The king is in the same position.

§367. We say:

> In this world he avoids
> What is right because of his desires.
> Don't others avoid
> What he is proud of?

§368. Objection: The king is the protector of his people. He certainly should be proud because he is their protector. If he were not, and if traditional customs were not observed, all of society would be ruined. In response, Āryadeva says:

> The king is the protector of the people
> But it seems that the king must be protected.
> Why should he be proud because of one
> And not the other? (CŚ IV.5)

§369. If he thinks "the protection of my people depends on me" and becomes proud, why, then, since his own protection depends on his people, does he not lose that pride when he understands that he himself must be protected? A king who is not supported by his people cannot govern his people.

§370. Consider the example of the married couple and the example of a lion and a forest.

§370 (1). "I suffer hundreds of times," a husband complained to his wife, "while you remain in the house with no troubles at all." His wife replied, "First, you do all the housework for twenty-four hours and then you'll understand!" He did just that and he came to regret what he had said.

§370 (2). Just as each one of a married couple supports the other, so the king protects his people and his people protect their king. Similarly, the lion protects the forest and the forest protects the lion.

§371: Here we say:

> The pride of an ignorant person
> Who rejects any remedy for pride
> And firmly holds onto pride
> Cannot be overcome by any means at all.

§372. Objection: When the king protects all his people in the same way as he does his son, he is victorious and he will receive one-sixth of the merit that belongs to those who perform meritorious acts. For this reason, pride is appropriate for the king who is abundantly endowed with good fortune because of his own and others' merit. In response, Āryadeva says:

> It is difficult to find among all the castes
> People satisfied with their own work.
> If you receive their demerit,
> It will hard for you to have a good rebirth. (CŚ IV.6)

§373. Today it is difficult to find any satisfaction among people whose work is caste-related because the five degenerations[2] mostly have occurred and these people primarily seem unreliable. If you are the recipient of one-sixth of their merit, in the same way, you also will receive one-sixth of their demerit. It happens that most of the time afflictions related to their castes overwhelm them and so they become shiftless. Those who associate with bad friends have no merit. It will be rare for you to have a good rebirth for this reason. First of all, a good rebirth is impossible for a king because of his own harmful actions. When the king shares in all his subjects' harmful actions as well, why even bother to speak about a good rebirth? Thus, people with impaired intelligence will be destroyed.

§374. Consider the example of the leper who wanted to drink milk and eat fish.

Because of his error, the leper not only failed to rely on medicine for treating his illness but he also drank milk and ate fish.[3] In the same way, because he remains in a state of carelessness, the king not only accumulates much demerit by himself but he also associates himself with the actions of those controlled by their caste.

§375. Here we say:

If in this world the king always
Lays claim to one-sixth of their actions,
Then he will find a good rebirth difficult,
Because most people have no merit.

The King Plays the Fool

§376. Objection: Since the king is the lord of the world and is independent, his pride is appropriate. In response, Āryadeva says:

Someone who acts after being advised by others
Is a fool on earth!
There is no one else equal to you
In being dependent on others. (CŚ IV.7)

§377. Someone who acts after others advise him may do a little or know a little, but he is not independent. People call him a fool. In this world there is no one else who is under the control of others in the same way as the king is. When many associates advise him, he becomes indecisive. Most of the time he remains dependent on others. He acts only after others advise him about what he should do and what he should not do. Because he remains dependent on others, people consider him very foolish and under the control of others. His pride is inappropriate for this reason.

§378. Consider the example of trained dogs and monkeys.

Dogs and monkeys listen to their master's instructions on what to seize and what to let go. Similarly, the king also is under the control of others because he has secret agents as his eyes.

§379. Here we say:

After being advised by his associates,
The king undertakes what he should or should not do.
So in this world the king is a fool,
Confused, and under the control of others.

A King Without Mercy

§380. Objection: Because the protection of all the people depends on the king, his pride is appropriate. In response, Āryadeva says:

He thinks "their protection depends on me"
And he takes wages from his people,
He commits harmful actions himself.
Who equals him in lacking mercy? (CŚ IV.8)

§381. If the king thinks "their protection depends on me" and takes wages from his people, then, following the tradition of virtuous kings, he must make an effort to protect the poor. He should accept that tradition and govern in that way. But he does not follow that standard. He commits such harmful actions as imprisoning, beating, threatening, banishing criminals, and executing people unable to pay his wages. He resorts to cruelty by depriving them of their lives and all their possessions. This shameless king takes wages from the people in compensation for their protection. He commits harmful actions so that their protection will ensue. Apart from him, who else in the world lacks mercy? Because he is adept at carrying out evil actions, he alone is considered to have no mercy.

§382. Take for example the story about the butcher's physician.

When a butcher was breaking bones into pieces, a bone fragment pierced his eye. He went to a physician. This physician applied an ointment to the butcher's eye and relieved his discomfort. But he did not completely eliminate the pain. Again and again the eye became irritated and the physician soothed the eye's irritation. But he did not completely eliminate the pain. The patient meanwhile had parted with most of his money. When that physician went away to another town, his son cured the butcher's painful eye. The king is just like that physician. He deprives the people of much of their wealth and does not completely carry out his obligations to his people.

§383. Here we say:

> A man who roars because of his eagerness for wages,
> Who is quite vicious and beats others,
> Apart from him, who else in the world
> Is so severely lacking in mercy?

§384. Objection: The king should not show mercy to people who are criminals. If he does not punish criminals, all his people will become degenerate. Consequently, he must punish criminals in order to protect his people. In response, Āryadeva says:

> If people who do harmful actions
> Are not the object of mercy,
> Then all foolish ordinary people
> Will not be the object of protection. (CŚ IV.9)

§385. If this person is not worthy of mercy because he has done wrong, who, would be worthy of mercy? Since he is not worthy of mercy, all foolish ordinary people will not be the object of the king's mercy. In this regard the word "fool" means to have the characteristics of a fool. The expression "ordinary person" refers to someone who is not on the noble path because of committing nonmeritorious actions. Those people characterized in both ways exceptional people call "foolish ordinary people." Merciful people will protect them because they have mercy on them. A merciful person thinks of stopping whatever is harmful to others. Protection is established because of mercy. Consequently, how will this merciless king bring about protection, which is the result of mercy? If he takes wages without protecting his people, then, surely, he is a thief who lives in cites and towns without being recognized as a thief!

§386. Consider the case of protecting life and property. If the king does not make people who engage in harmful actions the object of his compassion, then his own life and property will not be protected because he will have harmed everyone! When he is protected, all who engage in harmful actions will likewise be the object of his compassion.

§387. Here we say:

> Those who protect themselves with good conduct
> Do not need to be protected by the king.
> If he has made immoral people the object of his protection,
> He will protect them as well.

§388. Objection: If the king punishes evil people in order to protect his people, he incurs no harm because he benefits the good people. In response, Āryadeva says:

> Where do you not find
> Reasons for making yourself happy?
> Reasons, such as scriptural authority,
> Do not, however, destroy harmful actions. (CŚ IV.10)

§389. So-called reasons for making yourself happy are not found lacking anywhere at all. Even those people who take pleasure in such harmful actions as killing fish and butchering hogs claim that their caste justifies this slaughter of sentient beings. The king believes that punishment is his job and that there is nothing that is nonvirtuous about it. In this way, reasons that are satisfying are created. But the harm of these actions is not destroyed. It is just the same for the king. Since the king mostly engages in harmful actions, he will experience the maturation of that harm in bad rebirths. His heart, overwhelmed by the fire of misery, will break into many hundreds of pieces.

§390. Evil people may employ the rationale of a nonvirtuous point of view to deny the harm and to comfort themselves. There is no destruction of harm under those circumstances. Thus, just as superior people have the intention of benefiting others in order to do good, evil people have the intention of harming others in order to destroy them. How can there be an opportunity for a future high position for inferior people here on earth who have cruel and merciless minds and behave like demons toward others? Even scripture that says "Kings who carry out royal policy through punishment and pursue what is nonvirtuous are not victorious" indicates that they are harmful. We infer these kings are not victorious because they engage in harming others. Also, there is the analogy "they are like butchers," and the direct perception of yogins whose vision perceives the maturation of their actions. Consequently, these kings have committed harmful actions because scripture, inference, analogy, and direct perception prove that the harm exists.

§391. Take for example the story about the man who ate before his last meal was digested.

A man thought, "I will eat even though that last meal is not yet digested." He asked some Brahmins, "Should I please myself and eat?" They replied, "Eat." In the same way, they gave their consent to drinking water and sleeping, and all the other actions he asked about. He experienced pain after he had done all this. His physician asked him, "Why did you act like that?" "I didn't do anything without asking for advice," he replied. This person consulted others but severe pains seized him when he did was what wrong in order to please himself. In the same way, kings also do what pleases them. They make use of reasons for making themselves happy and commit harmful actions. Consequently, these human beings experience great suffering in hell, which these harmful actions have brought about. The kings have taken these treatises as authoritative; and because of their nonvirtuous conduct, unpleasant results will follow from their harmful actions.

§392. Here we say:

> If a king who inflicts harm under scripture's influence
> Does nothing wrong,
> Then why is it not virtuous behavior
> For those who escape from the cycle of death and rebirth?

Questioning the King's Behavior

§393. Objection: Properly protecting his people is virtuous behavior for the king, which he does so that he will reach heaven. He has no need of any other meritorious behavior. In response, Āryadeva says:

> If this so-called protection
> Is virtuous behavior for the king,
> Then why is it not virtuous behavior
> For those who manufacture affliction? (CŚ IV.11)

§394. Even though they benefit from their wages, an action motivated by gain is not virtuous behavior for carpenters and blacksmiths. In the same way, even though he provides proper protection, that is not virtuous behavior for the king who takes one-sixth of the harvest as his wages.

§395. Consider the examples of Kashmiri men who dig up the earth and the men who manufacture weapons.

§390 (1). Kashmiri men undertake such actions as digging a trench in order to protect their cities. Although they protect their community, their actions are not virtuous.[4] This is also the case for kings.

§395 (2). Also, even though they make weapons in order to protect society, the actions of those weapons' makers are not virtuous. This is also the case for kings.

§396. Here we say:

> If nothing else besides protection
> Were virtuous behavior for the king,
> Then it would be virtuous behavior also
> For laborers who have done their work properly!

§397. Objection: Since in this world all the people depend on the king, they should not criticize the king. In response, Āryadeva says:

> The people depend on the king
> But the king is criticized.
> Similarly, an intelligent person criticizes
> The craving for existence, the mother of all people. (CŚ IV.12)[5]

§398. Even if all the people, householders along with wandering ascetics, depend on the king, he is still considered a harmful man. The craving for existence, when it causes people to wander around in the cycle of death and rebirth, is a mother, since we see that people who have this craving are born and people who are free of this craving are not. Nevertheless, an intelligent person, whose vision is free of error, criticizes this craving, since it is the reason that all beings trapped in the prison of the cycle of death and rebirth wander around in this cycle. In the same way, an intelligent person will also criticize the king. Even though the king is the father of his people, he is still criticized because he is associated with violent actions, which will result in many bad rebirths.

§399. Consider the example of the merchants in an isolated location.

A group of merchants in an isolated location depends on a trader to provide the requisites for their protection, etc. Because he provides them at a very high price, he is criticized; and those merchants are not criticized. In the same way, although the people are dependent on the king for their welfare because he is their protector, the king is criticized because he is intent on reaping his own rewards.

§400. Here we say:

> Even if a virtuous king benefits his people,
> Intelligent people will still criticize him
> Because of the faults that remain,
> Just like a violent storm.

§401. Objection: Since a king who is highly intelligent and merciful properly protects his people, that is virtuous behavior for him. In response, Āryadeva says:

A sensible person does not acquire a kingdom.
And a fool has no mercy.
Even though he is their protector,
A merciless king has no virtuous behavior. (CŚ IV.13)

§402. The so-called royal way of life has become the basis for his pride and carelessness. How can one say that the king is not a fool if he rejects the path that benefits himself and others because of his attachment to mere power? He clearly directs his mind toward the excitement of worldly activity. Like a blind man, he does not perceive at all the impermanence associated with him and his pleasures. With a mind not directed in that way a human being should delight in moral behavior. Its excellent pleasing results, both seen and unseen, are never destroyed. But the king does not understand this. When he recognizes as good qualities a multitude of faults that are just the opposite, he is of course a great fool! For this reason, only a fool acquires a kingdom. The mercy of the king who is a fool does not last long because his arrogance makes its appearance. There is no virtuous behavior for the merciless king because he primarily engages in violence. It is wrong to claim that there is a highly intelligent and merciful king whose behavior is virtuous. A man who does not protect the people, even though he takes his wages everyday, is a thief and not a king!

§403. Take for example the story about the minister of the merciless King Ugradatta.

King Ugradatta's minister could not make the king's subjects pay their taxes. The king asked him, "Why couldn't you?" The king then became angry with his minister. The minister had a close friend and he told him about this. His friend advised him, "You must force them to pay." The minister then inflicted severe pain on them so that they would pay. The king appointed that close friend as a minister. He also committed many harmful actions because he wanted to please the king. Finally, when he was unable to kill all the tax-resisters with weapons, he destroyed them with fire. That fire killed many thousands of beings; and the king had given his consent to it. Thus, a fool has no mercy. When he has no mercy, how can he acquire virtuous behavior? This all applies to kings. For this reason, there is no virtuous behavior for them, even though they are protectors.

§404. Here we say:

Since compassionate people say that
Nonviolence is the root of virtuous behavior,
Consequently, there is no virtuous behavior
For a king who has no mercy.

Not All Sages Give Good Advice

§405. Objection: The king who engages in violence does not do anything wrong because sages establish it as his duty. In response, Āryadeva says:

An intelligent person should not undertake
Every action of the sages,
Since inferior, mediocre, and superior types
Are found even among them. (CŚ IV.14)

§406. In this world an intelligent person should not undertake every physical, verbal and mental action of the sages, since even among sages we find inferior, mediocre, and superior types. In this context, a sage is inferior when his treatises explain violence as virtuous behavior. A mediocre sage has doubts: "It may be so or it may not be so." A superior sage does not regard violence as virtuous behavior. For this reason, all sages' treatises should not be taken as authoritative. It is wrong to claim that the king who engages in violence because sages prescribe it as his duty does not do anything wrong.

§407. Take for example the stories about Viśvamitra, Vaiśiṣṭha, and Jāmadagnya. It is well known that one stole and ate something he should not have eaten, one went where he should not have gone, and one took life.

§407 (1). In this connection it is well known that Viśvamitra committed a theft and ate what he should not eat. To the dog-cookers[6] who wanted to take back the dog's meat he said:

While you are alive, your evil acts cannot be escaped.[7]
That penance exists because of the difference between us.
But when I am dead, I will not be able to escape this harm.
For that reason, of course I will eat this dog meat.[8]

§407 (2). It is well known that the Brahmin Vaiśiṣṭha had sexual intercourse with Akṣamālā, an outcaste woman, and she bore his sons.

§407 (3). Also, Jāmadagnya cut off the thousand arms of Arjuna Kārtavirya because he was angered by his stealing a calf.[9]

It is said:

Even though he is gentle and patient,
A sage's mind becomes extremely impatient and angry
Because of this or that evil person
Whose faults are offensive.

It happened that the king fell under the blade
Of the flawless Rāma's ax,
Since the cow lowed at milking time
Because her calf had been stolen.

Commanded to do so by his mother, Jāmadagnya made the earth free of the royal class twenty-one times. His mother spoke to him in this way:

An honest and patient ascetic,
Worthy of being honored one hundred times,

Does not look for a reason for people's death in battle.
Our enemies also do not look for one.

Although a powerful man does not achieve satisfaction
Through harmful actions,
Be a hero, take revenge!
Eradicate completely the root of our enemies!

Then the zinging sound of his bow was heard:

Passing over the tops of walls,
Destroying the warriors' houses,
The humming sound of Jāmadagnya's bow
Caused Kārtavirya's hair to stand on end.

§408. And here it is said:[10]

Those who know what is good for themselves
Should not make that treatise an authority.
People who have done that
Certainly will proceed to a bad rebirth!

Kings in an Age of Discord

§409. Objection: Since the ancient kings took the sense of the treatise as authoritative and properly protected a prosperous kingdom, the treatise is a valid authority. In response, Āryadeva says:

Previously the virtuous kings protected society
Just as they protected a son.
Now those who rely on the law of an age of discord
Have made it into a hunting ground. (CŚ IV.15)

§410. The virtuous universal monarchs, born before the age of discord, investigated what was proper and improper. They took as authoritative those treatises that agree with virtuous practices and rejected those that agree with harmful practices. They abided by the path of the ten virtuous actions.[11] These kings who loved their people protected society just as they would protect a beloved son. But now kings born in the age of discord rely on the evil nature of their own opinions and are obsessed by their desire for wealth. They take as authoritative treatises that agree with harmful practices and reject those that agree with virtuous practices. In this way, these kings who have no compassion devastate this world, just as if it were a hunting ground. Consequently, a treatise associated with harmful practices should not be taken as authoritative.

§411. Consider the example of the foreigner who squeezed an unripe sugar cane.

A foreign thief squeezed an unripe sugar cane because of ignorance. He just did something that was worthless and unprofitable. Similarly, if the king does not protect those who should be protected, there will be no profit for him in this world or in the next because of his lack of merit.

§412. Here we say:

> The wise compose a treatise
> Which does not differentiate
> Between one's own country and another's
> And which enables the people to be happy.

The Royal Thief

§413. Objection: In this world it is not a harmful practice for the king to attack his enemies' weak points because this is the treatise's opinion. In response, Āryadeva says:

> If it is not a harmful action
> For a king to attack weak defenses,
> Then that is even more the case
> For others, such as thieves! (CŚ IV.16)

§414. If it is not a harmful action for a king to attack his enemies' weak defenses or strangers' weak defenses, surely, then, because of this royal thief, it is not a harmful action for others either. Thieves who have discovered some weak defenses among the watchmen have stolen the property of others. They commit no harmful actions because first they have attacked weak defenses and second they are the best at attacking weak defenses! Since this last claim is not asserted, the prior claim that it is not a harmful action for a king to attack the weak defenses is not true either.

§415. Take for example the story about Prince Ajitasena.

It is said that a king told his minister, "When I die, you will crown my brother, Prince Ajitasena, king." When that king died, his minister attacked Ajitasena's weak defenses, killed the prince, and seized the kingdom for himself. His infamy as an evil man was well known in this world and in the next. In the same way, how will kings who attack weaknesses not be notorious and evil?

§416. Here we say:

> When a dark action is done
> A bright result will not arise.[12]
> Of course, the sprout of the fragrant Campaka tree
> Does not arise from the seed of a foul-smelling tree!

Dishonorable Sacrifices

§417. Objection: After a king in the jaws of battle has triumphed over his enemies, he takes great satisfaction in seeing the abundance of wealth acquired through his heroism. If he dies in battle, he surely will go to heaven because he has sacrificed himself. The *Bhagavad Gītā* says:[13]

> If you are killed, you will gain heaven;
> Or if you are triumphant, you will enjoy the earth.
> Therefore, son of Kuntī, rise up,
> Determined to fight the battle. (BG II.37)

§418. In response, Āryadeva says:

> The sacrifice of all of one's possessions
> For liquor and so forth is not respectable.
> I wonder why the sacrifice of oneself
> In battle is respectable. (CŚ IV.17)

§419. In this world people who give up all of their possessions for gambling, liquor, and prostitutes are not entitled to respect. Virtuous-minded people do not honor the sacrifice of these people, since they pursue an addiction. In the same way, the sacrifice of life in battle should not be respected, since this is the basis for harmful actions. Surely, how can it be right for someone who has no mercy, who has cruel intentions toward his enemy, who enthusiastically attacks in order to kill, and raises up his sword with a view toward bringing it down on his enemy's head, to go to heaven when his enemy kills him? Under those circumstances, it is wrong to claim that going to heaven is certain for someone who has died in the jaws of battle.

§420. Take for example the story about the cowherd's wife who offered her body to her father-in-law.

A certain cowherd's wife treated her father-in-law very disrespectfully while her husband was away from home. When his son returned, the old cowherd told him what had happened. He said, "If your wife ever again treats me disrespectfully, I will not stay in your house!" The cowherd was unafraid of his wife and devoted to his father. Consequently, he reprimanded his wife and told her, "If you ever again treat my father with contempt, you will not live in my house. You should do for him even what is very difficult to do, and you should give to him even what is very difficult to give." "Yes, yes," she promised him. The next time her husband was away from home, she very timidly and with great respect attended her father-in-law. During the day, she washed and anointed his body, presented him with flower garlands, and offered him food and drink. At night, after she had washed his feet with warm water and rubbed them with oil, she took off her clothes, and naked she proceeded to enter into an illicit union. She began to climb into his bed. The old cowherd exclaimed, "You evil woman! What have you begun to do?" She replied, "My husband told me that I should do for you what is very difficult to do and give you what is very difficult to give. There is nothing more difficult to do and nothing is more difficult to give." The old cowherd angrily retorted: "This is a good strategy to make me leave! You should be pleased! I will never again stay in this house!" After he said that, he left. His son returned and when he did not see his father, he questioned his wife, "What did you do?" She replied: "Husband, I deprived your father of nothing. With great respect and with pleasure, I bathed him, rubbed him with oil, and gave him food. I offered him everything!" Her husband sharply rebuked her and drove her from his house. After he had appeased his father, he brought the old man back into the house.

Just as the behavior of the cowherd's wife was wrong and her offer to give her body to her father-in-law was not honorable, the king's thoughts are also wrong and the sacrifice of his life in battle will not be honorable. Because people consider it wrong, the sacrifice of all one's possessions for such things as liquor is not worthy of respect.

§421. Here we say:

> If someone who has died in battle
> Surely ascends to the peak of Mt. Meru,
> Why, then, do all people who have died
> Not go to that very same place?

The King without Self Control

§422. Objection: In this world the king has pleasure because he serves as lord over all the people. In response, Āryadeva says:

> Your majesty, you are the people's lord,
> Yet you have no lord.
> Who would be happy to be a master
> Unable to control himself? (CŚ IV.18)

§423. In this world the king is the lord of all the people. Because of his authority, the people avoid improper actions and engage in proper actions to safeguard their lives and their property. Because the king experiences only pleasure, it is said that he has no teacher, no master, and that is what is meant by the expression "have no lord." That is the basis for his falling into a bad rebirth. How will anyone who has no master and no one to guide him have as his only pleasure doing what is proper? For this reason, when the situation calls for rejecting what is ruinous, if he has not controlled himself, he will not be happy. Consequently, the fact that he acts as lord over the people is not a suitable reason for his pleasure. In short, it is a reason for anxiety, not for joy, since the king lives in a state of carelessness!

§424. Consider the example of prostrations made to an ordinary old monk in the monastic community.

An old monk in the monastic community, an ordinary person,[14] who has no master, is pleased with the prostrations. Similarly, the king who has no master is pleased by people who bow and pay him homage.

§425. Here we say:

> In this world of human beings
> What intelligent person, born again into this state,
> Who seeks something different,
> Would be happy because he has no master?

Worthless Renown

§426. Objection: Since the king who resorts to mild punishment will not be renowned and the king who employs harsh punishment will be renowned after he has died, the king should resort to harsh punishment. In response, Āryadeva says:

> Even for the king who has died
> There is nothing of value to be had from renown.
> Being without virtue, would you
> And a dog-cooker not have great renown? (CŚ IV.19)

§427. If the king were to gain some advantage due to his renown after he has died, it might be proper for him to resort to harsh punishment. But there is no advantage due to renown, and that renown cannot eradicate evil. Suppose the king thinks "as long as my renown endures among the people, I'll have the advantage of renown because it won't disappear." We would respond: Surely, you also have accumulated a variety of nonvirtuous qualities, such as being a thief and merciless. Since you have many nonvirtuous qualities, when you die, you will be propelled into bad rebirths because of the evil accumulated by the great renown those nonvirtuous qualities have produced. If notoriety were to cleanse the stain of evil, it would cleanse the stain even of dog-cookers, since these dog-cookers are also renowned for cooking dogs. Since this is not so, renown does not serve any purpose at all. Consequently, the king who values his own welfare must not resort to harsh punishment.

§428. Take for example the story about the girl who killed herself.

A rich man's daughter had died. She was carried away with great expense. Another girl saw this and after she had seen it, she thought "I will also have such riches." She strangled herself and hung by a rope. She lost her life. In the same way, the king also does what is wrong for the sake of renown, namely, that his edicts will be remembered, even after the king himself has died.

§429. Here we say:

> If an immoral king who has died
> Were to have virtuous qualities because of his renown,
> Then why would not an immoral thief
> Also have them?

The Origins of the Ruling Class

§430. Objection: The king who has the [royal] lineage is worthy of the kingdom, but not someone else. For this reason, his pride is appropriate. In response, Āryadeva says:

> Since merit produces
> Sovereign power over all,
> It cannot be said that
> He is not the basis for sovereignty. (CŚ IV.20)

§431. That merit that he has will enable him to enjoy the earth and have supreme sovereignty. But that action is not restricted to just one individual. While it cannot be said that this human being is not the basis for sovereign power, it is inappropriate for him to be proud because of it.

§432. Consider the example of learning a trade.

People who have learned a trade are common in society. Anyone at all who wants to learn will learn it. Similarly, someone will acquire a kingdom after doing virtuous actions.

§433. Here we say:

> When I have done an action in the world
> And I experience its result,
> Then I should not envy that person
> Who has acquired power and happiness.

§434. Objection: Since it is taught that the duty of protecting the kingdom belongs just to the royal class and not to the other three, only someone of the royal class should protect the kingdom. For this reason, his pride is appropriate. In response, Āryadeva says:

> All methods of livelihood
> Are designated in society as caste.
> Consequently, no distinction due to caste
> Is found among all human beings. (CŚ IV.21)

§435. These classes, the royal class, etc., are means of making a living. Now in the first eon all beings that arose were self-generating because their birth did not depend on external factors, such as semen. Because they were generated only from mind, they had their own luminosity that arose from mind. They had magical powers, flew through the sky, and were nourished by bliss. They had all the marks of happiness and were lacking male and female sexual organs. It was impossible for caste to differentiate them because they all arose from a self-generated source. Later, these beings began to eat coarse food. When they became accustomed to very coarse food, channels for urine and excrement developed as a result so that the food could be expelled. When they saw the different physiques created by male and female sexual organs, beings who had the desire for sexual pleasures set about doing together what was wrong because they had been accustomed to it in their past lives. For this reason, birth from the womb developed. Then, when others were at fault in hoarding grain, some among their society began to take what was not given to them. Different classes came about because of the acceptance of different livelihoods. A large group of people commissioned a capable man to protect the fields. By accepting that work, he became known as a person of the royal class. Those people who sought to restrain their senses in order to perform austerities and turned their backs on the villages became known as Brahmins. Those who served the kings became known as the class of commoners. Those who engaged in harmful actions such as plowing were known as the lower classes. The different classes and the diverse castes arose from the differences in their work. Thus, Āryadeva says:

> All methods of livelihood
> Are designated in society as caste.

Because this is so, in society there are no [permanent] distinctions created by class. Because of the absence of such a distinction, class is not an appropriate reason for pride.

§436. Consider the example of classifying a pot according to its contents.

By classifying the pot's contents, one labels it accordingly as a pot of grain or as a pot of butter. Similarly, that work which was done in the first eon become known as caste.

§437. Here we say:

> Whether born lower-caste or upper-caste,
> Based upon that work
> By which one makes a living
> One will become that caste over time.

§438. Objection: Because the four lineages, the priestly class, the royal class, the commoner's class, and the lower class, have been established, human beings have class distinctions. In response, Āryadeva says:

> Since the past is far gone
> And the minds of women are fickle,
> Consequently, no one is
> From the class called the royal class. (CŚ IV.22)

§439. In this world birth comes from parents. It is difficult to acquire this so-called caste or class lineage because women are seen to be deceitful. Class should be rejected because a long time has elapsed and the minds of women are fickle. These women bear sons from their sexual intercourse with men of other class lineages. Since these adulterous women repudiate their class, pride in a class lineage is inappropriate. Thus, the so-called royal class does not exist on the basis of class alone. The kings of today mainly have their origins in the lower class. Their pride also is inappropriate.

§440. Take for example the story about Mārkaṇḍeya leaving behind a water pot, and the story about Vyāsa.

§440 (1). It is said that when the world was in the process of being destroyed and Mārkaṇḍeya was wandering around, the house and the pot had changed hands. He had left behind for safekeeping a golden pot at a Brahmin's house. After a long time had elapsed, he returned to that house. At the Brahmin's house, he asked, "Who is here?" "This is not a Brahmin's house," the inhabitants replied, "it is the house of a member of the royal class." "There was something that I left behind for safekeeping," Mārkaṇḍeya told them. "I entrusted a golden pot to a Brahmin." "There is no golden pot here," they said, "but there is one made of silver." Mārkaṇḍeya placed that silver pot in their hands and again after a long time had elapsed he returned to that house. Now it had become a commoner's house and the pot was made of copper. Once again he placed it in their hands and returned at a later time. Meanwhile the house had come to belong to members of the lowest class and the pot was now made of iron. This golden pot at different times took on diverse appearances and the house also was different because of the diverse appearances of its inhabitants. Similarly, the classes of society also undergo change. For this reason, there is no one from the class called "royal class."

§440 (2). Also, it is known that Vyāsa was born from a fisherman's daughter after the sage Parāsara covered Gandavati with a dense early morning fog on all sides. He was known as Dvaipāyana, "the Island-Born," because he was born on an island. He was known as Vyāsa, "the Compiler" because he compiled the Vedas.

§441. Here we say:

> Because time is endless
> And because the majority of women are fickle,
> An intelligent person in this world
> Does not take pride in class.

The Actions of Brahmins

§442. Objection: If someone does not become a member of the royal class because of his class at birth, then he will become a member of the royal class because of his actions in protecting the people. In response, Āryadeva says:

If even a person of the lower classes
Becomes a member of the royal class by his actions,
I wonder why a person of the lower classes
Does not become a Brahmin also by his actions? (CŚ IV.23)

§443. Now, if even someone who is not a member of the royal class by birth but who performs the actions of the royal class were to become royal, then, of course, even a member of the lower classes who performs the actions of a Brahmin will become a member of the Brahmin class and he will accept gifts and recite texts! Any person who does the work of someone else will assume that class status. In this connection it is wrong to claim that someone will become a member of the royal class by his actions.

§444. Consider the example of the boat going over to the other shore.

A river is situated between two banks. On one bank they say, "The boat has gone to the other shore" and on the other bank they say, "The boat has gone to the other shore." Neither bank is proven to be the other shore. Similarly, someone is not proven to be either a member of the royal class or a member of the Brahmin class. If a member of the lower classes becomes a member of the royal class by his actions, then in the same way a member of the lower classes will become a member of the Brahmin class by his actions!

§445. It is said:

A Brahmin who sells milk
Becomes a member of the lower class in three days.
He loses class the very same day
By eating meat, salt, or using lac.[15]

§442. Here we say:

If class were to exist because of actions,
Then class would have no [inherent] cause.
Because class from birth has been refuted earlier,
These classes do not arise from either birth or actions.

Sharing Power

§447. Objection: The king over time can share his royal power with many people because of his great sovereignty. Consequently, the king should seek great sovereign power. In response Āryadeva says:

Your majesty, you cannot share
Harmful actions in the same way as sovereign power.
Indeed what intelligent person would destroy
His future for the sake of someone else? (CŚ IV.24)

§448. It is true that a king has acquired great sovereign power over a long time. It is possible that he shared it with his people. But he cannot reign without oppressing the people. Many harmful actions inevitably will occur because he has oppressed the people. The harmful actions that he has accumulated as a result he cannot share in the same way as he shared his sovereign power. He alone must experience the suffering. Consequently, what intelligent person would think "I'll share my wealth in order to benefit someone else a little" and destroy himself in the future because he has accumulated so many harmful actions that will result in great misfortune? Consequently, this sovereign power is an occasion for shame, not for pride.

§449. Consider the examples of sacrificing a buffalo and the story of Śūnika's son.

§449 (1). Someone sacrificed a buffalo for himself and for the benefit of others. Many ate it, but the harm belonged to the man who killed it. In the same way, the king commits harmful actions for the sake of his kingdom and many enjoy the result.

§449 (2). Also Śūnika's son was unable to kill deer, etc., because he was afraid of the harm. His own people told him, "You must kill. The harm that will come out of this will be the same for all of us." He used this strategy and said, "I have an extremely painful feeling in my head. You all ought to share it." "We can't," they said. "Then why," he asked, "wouldn't the painful experience of hell be just the same?"

§450. Here we say:

> A person who seeks happiness in the next world
> Should do what is blameless in this world,
> And what will lead to
> Happiness in the next world.

§451. Objection: Surely the king has great power in this world. He should certainly be proud. In response, Āryadeva says:

> After they have seen others
> Who are endowed with equal or superior power,
> The pride that is produced by sovereignty
> Will not remain in intelligent people's hearts. (CŚ IV.25)

§452. Pride might occur from considering yourself superior to others. Intelligent people do not become proud because this status is uncertain and depends upon other things. Consequently, someone who wants to help people should reject pride. He should not treat others with contempt and act as if he were an eminent person or a lord. Someone who behaves in this way becomes a vessel for wealth because he engages in making people happy and contented.

§453. Take for example the story about Vāsula's wife.

His wife complained to the Brahmin Vāsula, "There is no woman who equals me in feminine beauty, and yet you do not honor me with suitable jewelry and clothing!" By a strategy of his, she entered the female apartments of a king named Rudra. There she saw the queen's maidservants and her pride in her beauty was shattered. Why even bother to mention how beautiful the queen was! In the same way, after the king has seen those who are equal or superior to himself, it is appropriate that he abandon his pride and egotism.

§454 Here we say:

First of all, it is not appropriate
For a king to be proud of his wretched kingdom.
How can there be an occasion for pride
When another king is his equal or his superior?

§455. This completes the fourth chapter that explains the method for rejecting the illusion of egotism in Āryadeva's *Bodhisattvayogācāracatuḥśataka*.

NOTES

Chapter 1

1. The eighth chapter of the *Catuṣpariṣasūtra* explains that the god Brahmā appeared before the meditating Buddha and requested him to teach. Because of his great compassion (*mahākaruṇā*) for all beings, the Buddha decided that he would open the door to immortality and teach. Lamotte 1949–80, 1.57–62, cites several parallel versions of this story (Vin I 5–7, *Mahāvastu* III 314–319, *Lalitavistara* 392–402).

2. Traditional accounts of this first council can be found in the Skandhaka section of each school's *Vinaya*. Jean Przyluski 1926–28 has studied several schools' accounts of this council. See Horner 1938–66, 5.393–406 for a translation of the Theravāda school's account. On the oral transmission of Buddhist teachings, see Collins 1992, Cousins 1983, and Norman 1997, 42–57.

3. Which Śatavāhana Dynasty king was the recipient of his letters has been much debated. See Gopalachari 1941, 28–29; Lamotte 1949, 1.xii–xiv; Warder 1970, 375; and Ruegg 1981, 5 n. 11.

4. *Ta-chih-tu Lun* (**Mahāprajñāpāramitopadeśa*) was translated by Kumārajīva and his team of translators into Chinese in the years 403–405 C.E. On the controversy over its attribution to Nāgārjuna, see Ruegg 1981, 32–33. The quotations from the *Aṭṭhakavagga / Arthavargīya* are discussed and translated by Lamotte 1949–80, 1.39–45.

5. The almost complete absence of historical writing in India makes the quest for the historical Āryadeva quite difficult. If the identification of the island Siṁhala with Sri Lanka is accurate, two fifth-century Sri Lankan historical chronicles, the *Mahāvaṁsa* and the *Dīpavaṁsa*, may prove helpful. The *Mahāvaṁsa* XXXV.29 records that after the King Voharikatissa heard the Buddhist monk Deva preach, he had several residences repaired; the *Dīpavaṁsa* XXII.41, 50 indicates that this same monk's preaching inspired King Voharikatissa's successors, Abhayatissa and Saṅghatissa, to provide medicine and shelter to the sick and to distribute rice gruel to the people. Lamotte, 1949–80, 3,1373 identifies the monk Deva with Āryadeva and places him in Sri Lanka in the latter half of the third century C.E., during the reign of these kings. See Lang 1986a, 7–8, and Tillemans 1990, 1.5.

6. Ruegg 1981, 71; Tillemans 1990, 1.13; and Scherrer-Schaub 1991, xxix, believe that Candrakīrti was active sometime between the mid-sixth to the mid-seventh centuries C.E. Lindtner 1979, 87–91, suggests the dates 530–600 C.E.

7. The description of this commentary as a *ṭīkā* instead of a *vṛtti* does not correspond to the descriptions of these two types of commentaries given by the tenth-century author, Rājaśekhara, who claims that the *vṛtti* comments on the entire work, whereas a *ṭīkā* "provides occasional elucidation of the meaning of the terms in the work upon which it comments, skipping from one place to another" (Griffiths 1999, 112–3). Candrakīrti's commentaries on Āryadeva's and Nāgārjuna's works elucidate the entire corpus of their verses and support Griffiths's skepticism about applying these definitions to Buddhist works from the first millennium. Griffiths 1999, 89–94 describes the various purposes of Indian commentaries.

8. On biographies of the Buddha, see Lamotte 1988b, 648–67; Bareau 1963–71, and Reynolds 1976.

9. Lamotte 1988b, 670–75, examines several versions of this story and its parallels to the Gospels' account of Simeon's encounter with the child Jesus.

10. I am indebted to an anonymous reviewer for drawing my attention to this colophon.

11. Sprung 1979 has translated sixteen of the *Prasannapadā's* chapters into English; see also Hayes 1994 and Wood 1994. On other translations into French and German, see May 1959. Scherrer-Schaub 1991 has translated the *Yuktiṣaṣṭikāvṛtti* into French.

12. Ruegg 1981, 3–4; Tuck 1990; and Hayes 1994 critically examine several prominent nineteenth- and twentieth-century Western interpretations of Nāgārjuna's philosophy.

13. See Tillemans 1990, 1.8–13, 30, for biographical data on Dharmapāla and his relation to epistemological wing of the Yogācāra school.

14. On the historical development of Madhyamaka thought from the time of Nāgārjuna and the roles played by various commentators, see Ruegg 1981, Della Santina 1986, and the chapter on Madhyamaka and the bibliographical essay in volume 2 of Akira Hirakawa's *History of Indian Buddhism*, forthcoming.

15. Boisvert 1995 and Hamilton 1996 discuss the five aggregates (*pañca-skandha*) and the role they play in forming human identity.

16. Matilal 1974, Bhattacarya 1974, and Ruegg 1981, 22 n. 49, also argue that *sādhya-sama* should not be interpreted as begging the question.

17. Tillemans 1990, 1.23–35, discusses the use of scriptural authority. See also Candrakīrti's commentary on CŚ XII.5 (Tillemans 1990, 1.120).

18. On MĀ I.1 and its references to nondual knowledge, see Wilson 1980, 5–6, and Huntington 1989, 119–22.

19. Tillemans 1990, 1.12, notes that despite this description of Dharmapāla as a poet (*snyam dngags mkhan*), no trace of his poetry remains. The Buddha seems to anticipate the conflict between mainstream practitioners and those affiliated with the new Mahāyāna movement over which sūtras were the word of the Buddha and which were poetical creations (S II 267). In this passage he uses the analogy of a drum that had begun to split; each time it was mended, new material was used, until the original drumhead had disappeared and only the repairs remained. Some monks in the future, he predicts, will listen to discourses created by poets (*kavikata*) and will not hear or understand discourses "whose meaning is profound, reaching beyond the world, and concerned with emptiness."

20. Tillemans 1990, 1.87–114, 135–73, translates Dharmapāla's commentary on chapters 12 and 13 of the *Catuḥśataka*.

21. On the difference between ultimate truth (*paramārtha-satya*) and conventional truth (*saṃvṛti-satya*), see Sprung 1973; Huntington 1983, and 1989, 48–50; Garfield 1995, 296–99; and Williams 2000, 147–49.

22. Huntington 1989, 232–33 n. 47 has translated pages 107–9 of Candrakīrti's commentary on conventional truth in MĀ VI.28.

23. Ruegg (1981, 53 n. 148) writes that Tāranātha identifies Dharmadāsa as Asaṅga's and Vasubandhu's student, who transmitted their teachings on Vijñānavāda to Dharmapāla. Tillemans (1990, 1.11 n. 26) says that Sum pa Ye shes dpal 'byor's religious history also confirms this lineage and adds: "It is tempting to speculate that some aspects of Dharmapāla's philosophical stances which seem to resemble Asaṅga's might have been communicated to him by this Dharmadāsa."

24. Cummings 1982 has reproduced photographs of these bas reliefs along with the Jātaka stories they depict. See also Brown 1997.

25. On Buddhist uses of the image of house/home, see Collins 1982, 165–71.

26. The body is the first of four objects toward which mindfulness is directed; feelings, thoughts, and *dharma* (Pāli: *dhamma*) are the other three. Gethin 1992, 29–68, examines Pāli and Sanskrit sources on the four applications of mindfulness.

27. Trainor 1993, 70–71. Contemporary Sri Lankan monks still observe this meditation practice, although they now frequent the morgue and the hospital autopsy room rather cremation grounds (Gombrich 1984, 84).

28. E. H. Johnson has translated the *Saundarananda* [1928] 1975. On the Pāli Jātaka version and the *Dhammapada* commentary's version of story, see Wilson 1996, 112–22.

Chapter 2

1. On the performance of these rituals, see Knipe 1977 and Parry 1994.

2. Olivelle 1996, xxiv–lvi, provides an excellent introduction to the social world in which these texts were composed, their position within the Vedic corpus, and their interpretations of Vedic rituals.

3. The expression "realm that is free of death" (*amataṃ padaṃ*) is used to describe Nirvana. Dhp VIII.15 makes it clear that experiencing the deathless realm of Nirvana, even for a day, far surpasses the Vedic conception of "nondying" and living for one hundred years.

4. On the practice of polygamy, see Kane 1968–77, 2/1.550–54. The legal literature indicates that legitimate reasons for taking another wife include the birth of only daughters, a wife with a bad temper and quick tongue, and an unfaithful wife. Some sources restrict a Brahmin to four wives, whereas a king may have as many as he wants.

5. Geshe Ngawang Dhargyey told this story in the spring of 1978 in his lecture on the *Catuḥśataka* at the Library of Tibetan Works and Archives, Dharamsala, India.

6. Strong 1992, 93–117, examines Māra's defeat at the hands of Upagupta. The monk Upagupta uses his superior power to tie Māra up and force him to perform acts of devotion to the Buddha's image. Some of these stories portray Māra as bound by a garland of human and canine corpses.

Chapter 3

1. See Lamotte 1976, 294–98, on the Buddha's illnesses, and Walters 1990 on the disputed issue of the Buddha's pain and its relation to his past actions.

2. Tillemans 1990,1.131, translates Candrakīrti's commentary on CŚ XII.19: "As for the Jains—who lack any practice of hygiene and are hence clothed [only] by the ever-increasing filth of their foul-smelling bodies, their bodies lacking [even] a bathing-cloth—they support various sufferings such as cold, wind, the sun and plucking out of their hairs."

3. See Leslie 1989 on these legal texts (*dharma śāstra*) and their definition of the duties a perfect wife should perform.

4. The lengthy description of Rāvaṇa's abduction of Sītā and Rāma's grief occurs in book three of the *Rāmāyaṇa.* See Pollock 1991, 182–229.

5. The *Mandhātu Jātaka* (Ja II 311–13 no. 258) tells the story of Mandhātā's fall. He was not satisfied with ruling his kingdom on earth for 84,000 years or with ruling the heaven of the four guardian kings. For further references in Buddhist texts to this story, see Lamotte 1949–80, 2.931 n. 1.

6. Parry 1994, 204: "Literally *sapindikaran* might be rendered 'making one flesh.' Consistent with the meaning of *pind* as 'body,' the *sapinda* relatives of the legal treatises are those with whom one shares body particles." Parry discusses this belief's effect on how Hindus deal with the pollution of death (1994, 217–22, 266). On the legal theory behind this belief see Kane 1968–77, 2/1.452.

7. See Collins 1982, 249–51, on Buddhist texts' use of raging rivers and streams as images of desire out of control.

8. Masefield 1989 has translated the *Vimānavatthu*; on the *Vimānavatthu*'s stories of divine pleasures, see Collins 1998, 311–16.

9. The *Ta-chih-tu Lun* includes a version of the Buddha's *Āśiviṣopamasūtra* (Lamotte, 1949–80, 1.702–7). Lamotte summarizes this allegorical story: "A man being guilty of some offense, the *king* (*rājan*) gives him a *coffer* (*karaṇḍaka*) containing *four poisonous snakes* (*āśiviṣa*), and orders him to rear those snakes. Terrified, the man takes flight, but the king sends *five killers* (*vadhaka*) in his pursuit. A *sixth killer*, guessing his intentions, advises him to comply with the king's orders. Suspecting a trap, the man continues on his way and comes to an *empty village* (*śūnyagrāma*). A *good person* (*satpuruṣa*) warns him of the imminent arrival of *six big thieves* (*mahācaura*) and persuades him to leave the village as soon as possible. The man continues on his way and comes across a *stretch of water* (*udakārṇava*): the *near bank* (*oratīra*) was highly dangerous, while the *far bank* (*pāratīra*) was entirely safe. The man builds a *raft* (*kaula*), gets on it and *manoeuvering his hands and feet* (*hastaiś ca pādaiś ca vyāyāmjaḥ*), manages to *cross* (*tīrṇa*) the stretch of water. The *king* is Māra; the *coffer* is the human body (*kāya*); the *four poisonous snakes* are the four great elements (*mahābhūta*) entering into the compositions of the body; the *five killers* are the five psychophysical aggregates (*skandha*) constituting the false personality; the *sixth killer* is joy and pleasure (*nandirāga*). The *empty village* represents the six internal bases of consciousness (*ādhyātmikāyatana*), eye, etc. The *good person* who advises flight is the good Master (*śāstṛ*): he puts the man on guard against the *six thieves*, that is, the six external bases of consciousness (*bāhyāyatana*), colour, etc. The *stretch of water* is the sea of yearning (*tṛṣṇā*), fed by the rivers of craving (*kāma*), becoming (*bhava*), false views (*dṛṣṭi*) and ignorance (*avidyā*). The *near bank*, full of dangers, is the world (*loka*), the aggregation of perishable things (*satkāya*); the *far bank* is *Nirvāṇa.* The *raft* which the man uses is the noble eight-

fold path (*āryāṣṭāṅgamārga*). The manoeuvering of hands and feet is the vigour (*vīrya*). And finally the man who has *crossed* is the Arhat" (1976, 138 n. 28).

10. See Tatz 1985, 18–19, 71–76, for the causal connection between the four elements and various physical illnesses.

11. See La Vallée Poussin 1988–90, 3.899–910, for an English translation by Pruden of the relevant section from La Vallée Poussin's French translation of a Chinese translation of Vasubandhu's *Abhidharmakośabhāṣyam*.

12. States of mind become contaminated (*sāśrava*) when they are infected by sense desire, the desire for continued existence and ignorance. Collins 1998, 671, explains that "the idea seems to be one of bad states of mind flowing in and out of a person in his/her interaction with the world."

13. On the pleasure experienced in meditation, see Collins 1998, 208–10.

14. Lamotte 1988a provides a brief history of how the Buddhist scholastic tradition has differentiated between these definitive (*nitārtha*) and interpretable discourse (*neyārtha*).

15. See Lopez 1988 for a detailed discussion of Candrakīrti's interpretation of Mahāyāna sūtras.

Chapter 4

1. See Collins 1993 for an annotated translation.

2. The derivation of the word "person" (*puruṣa*), as Anne Klein 1995, 45, points out, is from the Sanskrit root √*prī*, meaning "to fill," and is linked with nouns that signify enclosure (city, town, citadel) as well as with earth and excrement.

3. In Geshe Dhargyey's oral version of this story (spring 1978), the role of the itinerant trader is played by Uncle Tompa, a legendary Tibetan trickster. When one of the travelers asked for his name, he replies "Anus," anticipating the scene when the watchman will return and ask who is responsible for the mess. The fool says "Anus did it." The angry watchman proceeds to beat him, despite his repeated cries that "Anus did it."

4. *Gautama Dharmasūtra* 7.22 prohibits Brahmins from doing the work of outcastes; *Gautama Dharmasūtra* 8.12 prohibits the king from inflicting corporal punishment on Brahmins (Olivelle 1999, 89–90).

5. The intentional emission of semen prompts a meeting of the community which then places the monk on probation. See Faure 1998, 83–86.

6. The performance of these rituals fulfills a man's debt to his ancestors and ensures that the deceased person's soul passes on to a good destiny and joins with ancestors in the divine realm. For detailed descriptions of these rituals, see Kane 1968–77, 4.470–515; Knipe 1977; Gold 1988, 88–94; and Parry 1994, 191–222.

7. Leslie 1989, 287. Cf. MDŚ III.45–48.

8. Johnston 1928 [1975] 45, "I take the verse to be an answer to the argument that there are many well-known instances of women acting with genuine devotion, but Professor Charpentier suggests to me a different rendering based on G's emendations *muktajīvitān* and *caiva*, that women will mount the funeral pyre (as in the tale of the unchaste woman who mounted her husband's pyre to prove her faithfulness to him and was carried off from it by her lover disguised as a madman), that they will attach themselves even to those condemned to death (as in *Jātaka* no. 318 and the poem of Caura), that they will submit to restraints but in no case is their friendship genuine."

9. Candrakīrti and the *Vinaya* concentrate on curbing heterosexual desire. Jones 1979, 79, finds that the only suggestion in the *suttas* of warnings against

homosexual behavior in this context: "If a monk says of another 'he is dear to me' he may be adversely affected should the beloved monk fall into error, go elsewhere, become mentally unstable or die." See also Zwilling 1992 and Faure 1998, 81, 214.

10. Jones 1979, 87–89. See also O'Flaherty 1973, 42–52 for additional versions of this story in both Buddhist and Hindu sources.

11. Five verses (vv. 13–17) describing their encounter were excised by the Victorian translator H. T. Francis.

12. See Lang 1986b; Wilson 1996, 36–39, 73, 94–95; and Blackstone 1998, 63–71, on the issue of women's bodies as sources of temptation.

13. Hamilton 1996, 187, quotes a "wonderfully lurid" description of the human body from Buddhaghosa's *Visuddhimagga* which speaks of these nine streams "perpetually oozing from the nine orifices, like a chronic open carbuncle, from both of whose eyes eye-filth trickles, from whose ears ear-filth, from whose nostrils snot, from whose mouth food and bile and phlegm and blood, from whose lower outlets excrement and urine."

14. The *Ta-chih-tu Lun* quotes a verse with a similar theme, translated in Faure 1998, 55: "This body [of yours] is a swamp of dirt, / a filthy heap of impurities. / In these wandering latrines, / How could one revel?"

15. For an analysis of this story, see Strong 1992, 76–85, and Wilson 1996, 95–105.

16. See Wilson 1996, 82–93, and Blackstone 1998, 67–69. Wilson 1996, 86–87, points out that the bodies of paupers and criminals were abandoned on the cemetery grounds and proved useful for monastics who sought disfigured and decaying bodies for the practice of meditating on impure subjects (*asubhabhāvanā*). Since prostitutes sold their bodies near the burning grounds, "it is not surprising that the thoughts of Buddhist monks practicing *asubhabhāvanā* there would occasionally have wandered from the signs of foulness displayed in dead bodies and turned to thoughts of illicit pleasure."

17. See Hamilton 1995, 51–60, and 1996, 171–89. Much of Hamilton's analysis focuses on the Indian monk Buddhaghosa, whom she accuses of importing Brahmanical beliefs about physical impurity into Buddhism. Cf. Wilson 1996, 50–56, who finds Hamilton's position unconvincing.

Chapter 5

1. See Pollock 1991, 43–47, on the existential and functional divinity of the king.

2. O'Flaherty 1976, 33–34, and Strong 1983, 47–48, interpret this story as a myth explaining the fall from the golden age. Tambiah 1976, 13, describes it as "an elective and contractual theory of kingship." Cf. Collins 1996 on the application of the "social contract" model. Collins 1993, 317–31, argues for seeing a "Buddhist-ascetic hierarchial model of society" and shows (326–31) how key elements in the story that precipitate the "fall" are described in the same language that is used in the *Vinaya* for violations of the monastic code of conduct.

3. On the expression "great appointee" see Collins 1993, 345–46, 379–86.

4. *Rāmāyaṇa* III.6.11 also says that a king who receives one-sixth of the harvest as wages and does not protect his kingdom fails in his duty. This practice is mentioned in MDŚ VII.130–32, 37, and in several of the *Dharma sūtras* translated in Olivelle 1999 (*Gautama* 10.24; *Baudhāyana* 18.1; *Vaiśiṣṭha* 2.42). See Kane 1968–77, 3.185–99 for a detailed explanation of the king's right to tax his people. Several of the sources Kane draws on argue that taxes are the king's wages.

5. Candrakīrti derives the word *rāja* (king) from the Sanskrit root √*raj* (to delight). The Pāli version (D III 93) explains that the king "delights others with the *dhamma*." See also Norman 1997, 159, and Lingat 1973, 215.

6. On the prohibition against low-class śūdras studying the Vedas and performing Vedic rites, see Kane 1968–77, 2/1.154–58.

7. See Collins 1998, 480–96, 602–15, for an analysis and translation of this text.

8. On the concept of a universal monarch, literally "wheel-turning" king (Pāli: *cakkavatthi*, Sanskrit *cakravartin*), see Strong 1983, 44–49, and Collins 1993, 379–84; 1998, 28–29, 66, 470–76.

9. Nattier 1988, 23–47, discusses Maitreya and his association with the myth of a golden age.

10. See Collins 1998, 460–66, on the *Kurudhamma Jātaka* and other stories of the Buddha's previous births that describe the rule of good kings.

11. The story is told in *Mahābhārata* XII.139 by the sage Bhīṣma, who counsels Yudhiṣṭhira on righteous behavior in time of distress. MDŚ X.108. See also the interpretation of this story in White 1991, 75–77, and Glucklich 1994, 200–202.

12. MDŚ IX.23 refers to this story. The context suggests that she "married up" and took on his social status. Doniger comments: "Akṣmālā ('Wearing a Rosary') , better known as Arundhatī, married the priestly sage Vaiśiṣṭha and became the paragon of wifely fidelity, though she suspected him, insulted him, abandoned him, and was cursed therefore to become a small, ugly, hardly visible star of evil omen (*Mahābhārata* I.124, 27–29)" (1991, 199 n. 23).

13. See van Buitenan 1975, 3.446–47. Goldman 1977, 23–25, 138–44, rejects the argument that Jāmadagnya's slaughter of the royal classes may reflect a real war or campaign of genocide and explains the story as a "mythic tradition" of tension between the priestly Bhṛgu clan and the royal classes.

14. See Glucklich 1988, 32, 112–13; Lingat 1973, 211–12; Pollock 1991, 96. Olivelle 1999, 251 translates *Vaiśiṣṭha Dharmasūtra* I.43–44, which prescribes that the king should receive a sixth part of a Brahmin's meritorious acts, instead of taxes.

15. See Day 1982, 57–63; Glucklich 1994, 213–35; and Kane 1968–77, 3.21–23 on the king's use of the rod. Kane 3.389–406 describes the wide variety of punishments at the king's disposal, from fines to dismemberment and death. The nature and severity of the punishment varies, depending on the class of the offender. Only Brahmins are exempt from capital punishment.

16. See Strong 1983, 211–13, for a translation of the *Aśokāvadāna* legends surrounding the creation of this prison.

17. Thapar 1963, 256–57; Lingat 1989; and Tambiah 1976, 54–72, examine both the historical records and the legendary accounts of Aśoka's reign in their explanations of how Aśoka functions as model for kingship in Theravādin Buddhist countries.

18. Olivelle 1993, 116–17, discusses several instances from the epics and Buddhist texts of kings who abdicate in old age and retire to the wilderness.

19. Collins 1998, 423–33, cites this story as a prime example of the Buddhist critique of kingship ("Why All Kings Are Bad").

Chapter 6

1. Buddhist iconography depicts the Bodhisattva Mañjuśri in the form of a sixteen-year-old youth. According to Tibetan tradition, the salutation to

Mañjuśrī indicates that this text belongs to the group of texts on scholastic philosophy (Abhidharma), the third of the traditional "three baskets" (*tripiṭaka*) of the Buddha's word.

2. The afflictions are emotional and intellectual defilements that poison the mind. The three basic afflictions (*kleśa*) are desire, anger, and confusion.

3. When Candrakīrti quotes from the *Catuḥśataka* in his commentary on Nāgārjuna's *Mūlamadhyamakakārikāḥ*, he omits the numeral four from the title. This has caused confusion because the Chinese edition of the Buddhist canon contains another text of Āryadeva's, the **Śatakaśāstra* (Taishō 1569), which Kumārajīva translated in 404 C.E. Much of this text is similar in content to the last two hundred verses of the *Catuḥśataka*, but the two texts are not identical. See Lang 1986a, 30–14, and Tucci 1929, 3–58.

4. Candrakīrti quotes only a part of the dedication (*anirodham anutpādam . . . yaḥ pratīyasamutpādaṃ*) and expects his audience to fill in the rest from memory. I have translated the entire dedication (*anirodham anutpādam anucchedam aśāśvataṃ / anekārtham anānārtham anagamam anirgamaṃ / yaḥ pratīyasamutpādaṃ prapañcopaśamaṃ śivaṃ / deśayāmāsa saṃbuddhas tam vande vadatām varam //*).

5. Candrakīrti's comment on the world of death (*mṛtyuloka*) is similar to the derivation of the word *loka* from the root √*luj* (to be destroyed): "It is being destroyed and for this reason it is called world. S IV 53: *lujjati kho loko ti vuccati.*

6. The first interpretation of the three worlds refers to the three realms: (1) the realm of desire (*kāmadhātu*) contains beings in hell, hungry ghosts (*preta*), animals, humans, titans (*aśura*), and the gods of the six lower heavens; (2) the form realm (*rūpadhātu*) contains gods born there because of their mastery over meditative states (*dhyāna*) and those gods whose forms have only the sense organs of vision and hearing; (3) the formless realm (*ārūpyadhātu*) contains gods who are born in mental form as a result of their mastery over the formless meditation attainments (*samāpatti*). For charts illustrating these worlds, see Kloetzli 1983, 33–39. The second interpretation reflects a different spatial configuration. The gods live in the worlds above the earth; humans live on the surface of the earth; and serpentine supernatural beings (*nāga*) live in waters underneath the earth.

7. The "demon of death" (*mṛtyu-māra*) is one of four "demons" the Buddha conquered. Māra, taking the form of chief of the gods (*devaputra-māra*), is the demon who sent his army (and his three voluptuous daughters) in a vain attempt to prevent the Buddha from becoming enlightened. Death and the other two, "the demon of the afflictions" (*kleśa-māra*) and the "demon of the aggregates" (*skandha-māra*), are the impersonal aspects of Māra. See Wayman 1959, 112–16, and Boyd 1975, 109–15.

8. The signs of death may refer to the divine messengers sent to warn people of the consequences of careless behavior. In the *Devadūtasutta* (M III 178–87), the Lord of Death asks a man seized by the guardians of hell if he had seen the five messengers—a baby, an old person, a sick person, a punished thief, and a corpse—and why he failed to understand that he too was subject to birth, old age, sickness, death, and the punishment of hell.

9. The expression "done what should be done" (*kataṃ karaṇīyaṃ*) forms part of the description of an enlightened Buddhist: "birth is exhausted, the chaste religious life fulfilled, what should be done has been done, nothing more remains of this life" (*khīṇā jāti vusitaṃ brahmacariyaṃ kataṃ karaṇīyaṃ nāparaṃ itthattāya*).

10. I read *drag* "harsh" instead of the Derge edition's reading *drug* "six" (32b6) and the Peking edition's reading *dug* "poison" (35b6).

11. Nāgārjuna (SL 13ab) identifies the Buddha as the author of this advice: "The Sage said: 'Carefulness is the realm of the deathless. Carelessness is the realm of death.'" The half verse Candrakīrti quotes corresponds to Dhp II.1ab (= *Udānavarga* IV.1ab).

12. Here Candrakīrti refers to the eleventh link (birth) and the twelfth link (old age and death) of the chain of dependent origination: "old age and death have birth as their condition (*jātipratyayaṃ jarāmaraṇaṃ*)." Nāgārjuna treats the subject of dependent origination (*pratityasamutpāda*) in the twenty-sixth chapter of the *Mūlamadhyamakakārikāḥ*.

13. This may refer to the *Sutano Jātaka* (Ja III 325–30 no. 398), in which a king saves his own life by offering to send one man a day to a flesh-eating demon.

14. Translated according to the Peking edition of CŚṬ (39b7) of the text: *byams pa zhes mkhas pa su zhig*. rGyal tshab prefers the reading of the Derge edition of *Catuḥśataka*: *rnam dpyod ldan zhes su zhig smras* (Who would call this intelligent?). See Sonam 1994, 70 and 340 n. 25.216.

15. Candrakīrti quotes this verse from Vālmīki's *Rāmāyaṇa* (I.60.20; cf. Goldman 1984, 239–42. King Ambarīṣa must atone for his carelessness in allowing Indra to steal the offering for sacrifice by finding a human substitute. He offered the Brahmin Ṛcīka a thousand cows for one of his sons. Ṛcīka refused to sell the oldest son; his wife refused to sell the youngest. The middle son, Śunaḥśepa, agreed to be sold.

16. The Aśvins, twin horse-headed sons of Dyaus, the sky god, are known for their speed.

17. The *Sirikālakaṇṇi Jātaka* (Ja III 257–63 no. 382) identifies Kālakaṇṇī (Black-Nose) as the daughter of Virūpakkha, guardian deity of the west, and describes her as dark in color and the friend of greedy, envious, and angry people. Siri (Good Fortune) is the daughter of Dhataraṭṭha, guardian deity of the north, and is described as gold in color and the friend of righteous, honest, and kind people.

18. The expression "going forth from home to homelessness" (*agārasmā anagariyaṃ pabbajanti*) indicates the rejection of the lay person's home life for the homeless life of the monk or nun. Dutt 1962, 5–65, traces the development of the Buddhist order from a "community of the homeless" to an organized and settled life in monasteries.

19. The text of this story is difficult to translate. In Sonam 1994, 78, the traveler grinds the stone in a vain effort to make it square. Cf. Suzuki 1961, 1.236–37. In this story a Zen master begins to polish a piece of brick against a stone. When his student asks him what he is doing, the Zen master replies that he is trying to make it into a mirror. The student says that no amount of polishing will ever make that brick into a mirror. The Zen master then replies: "No amount of sitting cross-legged will make you a Buddha!"

20. In the *Devadutasutta* M III 183, the Lord of Death asks a man bound for hell: "Did you not think 'I am subject to death?'"

21. MDŚ VII.218cd advises a king that he should always wear jewels that have the power to destroy poison.

Chapter 7

1. The bases for wholesome behavior (*kuśala-mūla*) are the absence of desire, the absence of hatred, and the absence of confusion.

2. Candrakīrti associates the two collections of merit and knowledge (*puṇya-jñāna-sambhāra*) with two distinct results. The meritorious actions of an unen-

lightened person reap a heavenly reward. The acquisition of knowledge is associated with the enlightened person's liberation from the cycle of death and rebirth. In Nāgārjuna's *Ratnāvalī* III.13, these collections together are the cause of Buddhahood. See also Lindtner 1982, 225–48, on the **Bodhisambhāra* (Taishō 1660), a text on these two collections that is attributed to Nāgārjuna. Candrakīrti quotes the *Bodhisambhāra* in his commentary CŚ XII.13. See Tillemans 1990, 1.127, 241–42 n. 195.

3. See the *Sīlavīmaṃsa Jātaka* (Ja I 370–71 no. 86) and Glucklich 1994, 199–200. A Brahmin stole from the king's treasury and initially was allowed to do so out of respect for his social status. The third time he grabbed a fistful of coins he was brought before the king, who had him punished.

4. This may refer to the *Kokālika Jātaka* (Ja III 102–3 no. 331). When a young cuckoo reared by a crow uttered a cry, the crow knew it was not her offspring and killed it by pecking it with her beak.

5. Kane 1968–77, 2/1.523 notes that the simplest form of this type of "self-choice" (*svayaṃvara*) marriage arrangement occurs when a girl has no parent or guardian who can find a husband for her and chooses her own husband. According to Jamison 1996, 224, 238, 303, this form of marriage was largely restricted to a king's daughters.

6. The four postures, literally "ways of going" (*īryapatha*), are walking, standing, sitting, and lying down.

7. The Buddha (S IV 97) compares the competing distractions of the six sense bases (*saḷāyatana*) to six different creatures—a snake, a crocodile, a bird, a dog, a jackal, and a monkey—that a man had caught and tied together. Each struggled to escape to its own domain: the snake struggled to escape to the anthill, the crocodile to water, the bird to air, the dog to the village, the jackal to the burning ground, and the monkey to the forest.

8. Das 1902, 532, cites an unidentified Tibetan medical text: "horse dung (strained) removes worms and bilious vomiting."

9. The dual number indicates that the verb has two subjects ("arising and ceasing"). Unlike English, in which the verb is either singular or plural, Sanskrit has a third category, the dual. The Tibetan translation uses the particle *-dag* to translate the Sanskrit dual number.

10. Cf. the nun Vajirā's response to Māra (S I 135): "It is just pain (*dukkha*) that arises, that persists and passes away. Nothing but pain arises and nothing but pain ceases." See also Sonam 1994, 93 and 341 n. 14 for a citation from the *Vinayaksudrakavastusūtra*: "When Kātyāyana's son is born, only suffering is born. / Also when he ceases, only suffering ceases."

11. Basham 1958 refers to non-Buddhist sources of this famous parable and provides an abridged translation from taken from a Jain Prakrit source, Haribhadra's *Samarādityakathā*. The parable occurs also in the *Mahābhārata* (Mbh XI.5.2–22).

12. A similar tale about a greedy crow occurs in the *Sonaka Jātaka* (Ja V 255 no. 529). This crow remained feasting on the carcass of an elephant floating in the flooded waters of the Ganges River while the waters swept it out into the sea. The crow, sated by the elephant's flesh, was unable to save itself from drowning.

13. The titans or anti-gods (*aśura*) are proud, jealous beings who fight with the gods. In Tibetan paintings of the Wheel of Life, the divine realm is split into the realm of the gods and the realm of the titans. The horse-headed celestial musicians (*kiṁnara*), great serpents (*mahoraga*), supernatural beings (*siddha*), and bearers of knowledge (*vidyādhara*) are minor deities.

14. The positions that the world has an end and the world has no end are two of fourteen topics that the Buddha did not address. See Collins 1982, 131–35.

15. Tillemans 1990, 1.197–99, has translated Candrakīrti's commentary on this verse.

16. In MKV 492–93, Candrakīrti examines the two truths in detail. See May 1959, 225–29, and Sprung 1979, 230–32. Candrakīrti also discusses the two truths in MĀ 101–19, 175–78. See Huntington 1989, 160–61, 166–67, 231–34 (nn. 38, 47, 49), and 246–47 n. 109. "In reality," Candrakīrti concludes (MĀ 119), "there are not two truths but only one since the Buddha has said: 'Monks, this is the unique ultimate truth, namely, Nirvana which is nondeceptive'."

17. Here the term inherent characteristic (*svalakṣaṇa*) seems to be used as an equivalent for inherent nature (*svabhāva*) in arguing for the independent existence of a thing.

18. May (1980) translates Candrakīrti's commentary on this chapter and verse of the *Catuḥśataka*.

19. Candrakīrti begins his response here by forcing his opponent into a dilemma: either the effect is existent in virtue of its inherent nature (*svabhāva-sadbhūta*) or it is nonexistent in virtue of its inherent nature (*svabhāvāsadbhūta*). If existent, there would be the absurd consequence that an effect that already exists is produced. If nonexistent, there would be the absurd consequence that an effect that can never be produced (the barren woman's son) is produced. Candrakīrti considers this topic at much greater length in MĀ 83–100). See the translation and notes in Huntington 1989, 158–60, 227–31 nn. 13–34. See also Candrakīrti's commentary on Nāgārjuna's MMK XX.19–23 (MKV 404–7); de Jong 1949, 53–55; and Garfield 1995, 116–17, 265–66.

20. Candrakīrti in MKV 444 quotes an abridged version of this discourse.

21. The Vibhajyavādins (advocates of distinctions) are a splinter group of the Sarvāstivādins, who affirm the existence of past, present, and future things. See Bareau 1955, 167–80, and Dutt 1977, 223–26.

22. Candrakīrti quotes these verses (= S III 142–43) also in MKV 41–42. Nāgārjuna in *Śūnyatāsaptati* v.56 and Āryadeva in CŚ XIII.22–23 also use the same images.

Chapter 8

1. The pursuit of sensual pleasures (*kāma*), wealth (*artha*), and religion (*dharma*) are three of the four traditional goals; the fourth is liberation (*mokṣa*). See Kane 1968–77, 2/1.8–11. The poet Kālidāsa in *Raghuvaṃsa* 1.8 describes the royal life of the Raghus "who studied the Vedas in their childhood, indulged in pleasures during their youth, lived as sages in their old age, and gave up their life while practicing yoga" (Olivelle 1993, 176).

2. Lamotte 1988b, 10–11, identifies Vatsa as one of the four great kingdoms at the time of Buddha. Udayana acquired Vāsuladattā from her father King Caṇḍa Pradyota in a matrimonial alliance. On the cycle of stories connected with this king and his wives, see Burlingame 1969, l.63.

3. Or following the variant reading in the Derge edition (66b2): "loves a husband" (*khyo la sdug*).

4. Although desire is an affliction that poisons the mind, not all pleasure is harmful. Carnal pleasure (*sāmisa*) is associated with the objects of the five senses; noncarnal (*nirāmisa*) pleasure is associated with the cultivation of meditation. On the pleasures of meditation, see Collins 1998, 207–13, 304–09.

5. In cases cited in the *Vinaya* (Vin I 33–40), monks who are forced to have sex against their will and show remorse are judged not guilty of sexual misconduct. In some of these stories women grab men's penises against their will, or sit down on them while they are asleep; in others a group of young men force monks to have sex with nuns, lay women, and prostitutes. See Horner 1938, 1.51–62. Faure 1998, 76, quotes a *Vinaya* commentary that details four phases of a sexual act: "the initial entrance, the time of staying in, the time of taking out, and the subsequent period. If the monk feels pleasure during any of these four phases, he is guilty; otherwise he is innocent."

6. The Buddha uses the leper as an example to illustrate the dangers of sensual pleasures in the *Māgandiyasutta* (M I 506). The example occurs also in Nāgārjuna's *Suhṛllekha* v.26 and in *Ratnāvalī* II.68: "There is pleasure when a sore is scratched / But to have no sores is even more pleasant than that. / Similarly, there is pleasure in worldly desires / But to have no desires is even more pleasant than that."

7. Leslie 1989, 243, notes that such texts as Vātsyāyana's *Kāmasūtra* describe sexual intercourse as battle in which a woman takes an active role: "when a woman is (or pretends to be) jealous, a great quarrel arises; she cries, becomes angry, strikes her lover, pulls his hair, kicks him repeatedly on his arms, head, chest, and back, and rebukes him with harsh and reproachful words." See also Wilson 1996, 214 n. 90.

8. Kane 1968–77, 2/1.649–68, 685–86, discusses in detail various methods, including the recitation of Vedic mantras, that the legal texts prescribe for cleansing the body and preserving purity.

9. Buddhaghosa cites a similar story in chapter VI of the *Visuddhimagga* (Ñyāṇamoli 1975, 202).

There was a jackal chanced to see / A flowering *kiṁsuka* in a wood
In haste he went to where it stood: / "I have found a meat-bearing tree!'
He chewed the blooms that fell, but could / Of course, find nothing fit to eat;
He took it thus: "Unlike the meat / There on the tree, *this* is no good."
A wise man will not think to treat, / As foul only the part that fell,
But treats as foul the part as well / That in the body has its seat.

10. Candrakīrti may have in mind stories in which the ascetics Agni and Śiva seduced the wives of sages. See O'Flaherty 1973, 172–75; 1975, 104–12.

11. O'Flaherty 1980b, 84, observes that a women's nose is cut off as a punishment for making sexual advances; in quarrels arousing sexual jealousy, the opponent's nose is cut as "symbolic castration." See also Leslie 1989, 56–57, for textual references to noses being cut off as punishment.

Chapter 9

1. These are the abodes of gods, humans, animals, hungry ghosts (*preta*), and hell-beings.

2. These five degenerations (*kaṣāya*) are the degeneration of life-span (*āyuḥ*), the degeneration of views (*dṛṣṭi*), the degeneration of afflictions (*kleśa*) the degeneration of sentient beings (*sattva*), and the degeneration of the eon (*kalpa*).

3. Candrakīrti does not explain why these are ineffective treatments. It may be that the white color of milk and the flesh of most fish is involved. Glucklich says that "If leprosy is a discoloration of the skin, reflective in the later medicine of a *guṇa* imbalance that originates in the bones and reflects an inner cor-

ruption (*doṣa-kṛta*), then the multicolored coloring plant (the black *rajani*) is an appropriate homeopathic treatment" (1994, 97–98).

4. They kill worms and other insect life when they dig into the earth. This intentional act of killing will have harmful consequences in the next life.

5. Compare the commentary on *Dhammapada* XXI.5: "Here it is craving that is called 'mother because it produces beings in the three planes of existence, [as one can see] from the statement 'craving gives birth to the person'" (Dhp 1987, 321).

6. White 1991, 72, suggests that the term *śvapāka*, often taken as a synonym for *śvapacas*, "dog-cookers," may be glossed as *śva-pā-ka*, from the root √*pā* "to nourish, suckle" so that the *śvapākas* would be a race or people "nourished by dogs," "suckled by dogs," or even "children of dogs."

7. Translated according to the Sanskrit; the Tibetan text (P 89b3) *gson pas sdig pa'i las ni rgal nus te* differs: "A harmful action can be overcome by living."

8. The verse seems to say that as long as an outcaste (*caṇḍala*) is alive he cannot escape the penance of his birth, the result of harmful actions done in the past. If the Brahmin Viśvamitra remains alive, he can perform suitable penances to escape the consequences of his actions.

9. According to the version in the *Āraṇyakaparvan* (Mbh III.116.43–62), King Kārtavirya spurns the hospitality of the sage Jamadagni's wife and then abducts his calf. In the version of the *Śantiparvan* (Mbh XII.49.30–33), Kārtavirya's sons abduct the calf. No motive for the abduction of the calf is given in either version.

10. This verse is not in the Tibetan translation.

11. The ten are almsgiving, morality, liberality, honesty, mildness, religious practice, nonanger, nonviolence, patience and nonoffensiveness.

12. In the *Kukkuravatikasutta* (M I. 389), the Buddha explains that actions of body, speech, or mind that are harmful are dark actions and have a dark result, rebirth in the hells. Bright actions are actions of body, speech, and mind that do no harm and have a bright result, rebirth in the heavens.

13. The Tibetan translation of Candrakīrti's commentary quotes this verse but it is not in the surviving Sanskrit manuscript.

14. Here the term "ordinary person" (*pṛthagjana*) applies to a monk who is not included among the "exceptional persons" (*āryas*) because he has not severed any of the ten bonds linking him to the cycle of birth and death: belief in a real person (*satkāyadṛṣṭi*), doubt (*vicikitsā*), adherence to mere rules and rituals (*śilavrataparamarśa*), sensual desires (*kāmarāga*), anger (*vyāpāda*), desire for the realm of form (*rūparāga*), desire for the formless realm (*arūparāga*), pride (*māna*), excitedness (*auddhatya*), and ignorance (*avidyā*). On these "ordinary" monks, see Masefield 1986, 21–24.

15. According to *Yajñavalkyasmṛti* III.40 (cited in Kane 1968–77, 2/1.128) a Brahmin loses the right to perform the duties of upper classes when he sells lac, salt, or meat; the sale of milk, curds, or liquor reduces him to the status of a śūdra.

BIBLIOGRAPHY

Primary Sources

Abhidharmakośa and Bhāṣya. Edited by Swami Dwarikas Shastri. Varanasi: Buddha Bharati, 1970–73.

Aṅguttara Nikāya. Edited by R. Morris and E. Hardy. 5 vols. 1885–1900. Reprint, London: Pali Text Society, 1955–61.

Aṣṭasāhasrikāprajñāparamitā. Edited by P. L. Vaidya. Buddhist Sanskrit Text Series 4. Darbhanga: Mithila Institute, 1960.

Atharvaveda. Edited and translated by Satya Prakash Sarasvati. New Delhi: Veda Pratishthana, 1992.

Bhagavad-Gītā. Edited and translated by R. C. Zaehner. London: Oxford University Press, 1969.

Bṛhadāraṇyaka Upaniṣad. Edited and translated by S. Radhakrishnan. *The Principal Upaniṣads*. London: George Allen & Unwin, 1978.

Buddhacarita. Edited and translated by E. H. Johnston. Lahore: University of Punjab, 1936. Reprint, New Delhi: Oriental Books Reprint Corporation, 1972.

bZhi brgya pa'i rnam bshad legs bshad snying po. Sarnath: Pleasure of Elegant Sayings Printing Press, 1974.

Catuḥśataka. Edited and translated by Karen Lang in *Āryadeva's Catuḥśataka: On the Bodhisattva's Cultivation of Merit and Knowledge*. Copenhagen: Akademisk Forlag, 1986.

Catuḥśatakaṭīkā. Edited by Haraprasād Shāstrī in "Catuḥśatika of Ārya Deva," *Memoirs of the Asiatic Society of Bengal* 3 no. 8 (1914): 449–514.

Cone Edition of the bstan 'gyur. Microfiche. Stony Brook, N.Y.: Institute for the Advanced Study of Religion, 1974.

Dbu ma bzhi brgya pa'i 'grel pa. Sarnath: Pleasure of Elegant Sayings Printing Press, 1974.

Dbu ma bzhi brgya pa'i tshig don rnam par bshad pa klu dbang dgongs rgyan. New Delhi: Ngawang Thogay, 1978.

Dhammapada. Edited and translated by John Ross Carter and Mahinda Palihawadana. New York: Oxford University Press, 1987.

Dīgha Nikāya. Edited by T. W. Rhys-Davids and J. Estlin Carpenter. 1890. Reprint, London: Pali Text Society, 1960–67.

Dīpavaṁsa. Edited and translated by Herman Oldenburg. Berlin, 1879. Reprint, New Delhi: Asian Educational Services, 1992.
Jātakamālā. Edited by P. L. Vaidya. Buddhist Sanskrit Text Series 21. Darbhanga: Mithila Institute, 1959.
Jātakāṭṭhakathā. Edited by V. Fausbøll. 6 vols. London: Pali Text Society, 1877–96. Reprint, London: Pali Text Society, 1962–64.
Kāśyapaparivarta. Edited by A. von Stael-Holstein. Shanghai, 1926. Reprint, Tokyo: Meicho-fukyu-kai, 1977.
Lalitavistara. Edited by P. L. Vaidya. Buddhist Sanskrit Text Series 1. Darbhanga: Mithila Institute, 1958.
Madhyamakāvatāra. Edited by Louis de La Vallée Poussin. Bibliotheca Buddhica 9. St. Petersburg, 1912. Reprint, Osnabrück: Biblio Verlag, 1970.
Mahābharata. Edited by Vishnu S. Sutthankar et al. 5 vols. Poona: Bhandarkar Oriental Research Institute, 1971–76.
Mahāvaṁsa. Edited and translated by W. Geiger. London: Pali Text Society, 1908–12.
Majjhima-nikāya. Edited by V. Trenckner and R. Chalmers. 3 vols. 1888–1902. Reprint, London: Pali Text Society, 1960–64.
Mānava Dharma Śāstra. Edited by J. Jolly. London: Trübner, 1897.
Milindapañho. Edited by V. Trenckner, London: Williams and Norgate, 1880. Reprint, London: Pali Text Society, 1962.
Mūlamadhyamakakārikāḥ. Edited by J. W. de Jong. Madras: Adyar Library, 1977.
Prasannapadā Madhyamakavṛtti. Edited by Louis de La Vallée Poussin. Bibliotheca Buddhica 4. St. Petersburg, 1903–13. Reprint, Osnabrück: Biblio Verlag, 1970.
Rāmāyaṇa. Edited by L. M. Mehta et al. Baroda: Oriental Institute, 1960.
Ratnāvalī. Edited by Michael Hahn. Vol. 1. Bonn: Judica et Tibetica, 1982.
Rig Veda. Edited by Barend A. van Nooten and Gary B. Holland. Cambridge, Mass: Dept. of Sanskrit and Indian Studies, Harvard University, 1994.
Samādhirājasūtra. Edited by P. L. Vaidya. Darbangha: The Mithila Institute of Post Graduate Studies and Research in Sanskrit Learning, 1961.
Saṃyutta Nikāya. Edited by L. Feer. 5 vols. 1884–98. Reprint, London: Pali Text Society, 1973–90.
Śatapatha Brāhmaṇa. Edited by W. Caland and revised by Raghu Vira. Delhi: Motilal Banarsidass, 1983.
Saundarananda. Edited and translated by E. H. Johnston. Lahore, 1928. Reprint, Delhi: Motilal Banarsidass, 1975.
Sde dge Tibetan tripiṭaka bstan 'gyur. Edited by K. Hayashima et al. 17 vols. Tokyo: Sekai Seiten Kanko Kyokai, 1977–79.
Suhṛllekha. bShes pa'i spring yig. Edited by A. Sonam. Sarnath: Pleasure of Elegant Sayings Printing Press, 1971.
Suttanipāta. Edited by D. Anderson and H. Smith. London: Pali Text Society, 1948.
Thera- and Therī-Gāthā. Edited by H. Oldenberg and R. Pischel. 2d ed. London: Pali Text Society, 1966.
Tibetan Tripiṭaka, Peking Edition. Edited by D. T. Suzuki. 168 vols. Vol. 98 (Ya). Tokyo-Kyoto: Tibetan Tripiṭaka Research Institute, 1956–61.
Udānavarga. Edited by F. Bernhard. 2 vols. Göttingen: Vandenhoeck and Ruprecht 1965–68.

Vinaya-piṭakam. Edited by H. Oldenberg. 5 vols. London: Pali Text Society, 1879–83.
Visuddhimagga. Edited by C.A.F. Rhys-Davids. 2 vols. London: Pali Text Society, 1920–21.

Secondary Sources

Altekar, A. S. 1956. *The Position of Women in Hindu Civilization*. Delhi: Motilal Banarsidass.
Armstrong, Karen. 2001. *The Buddha*. New York: Penguin Putnam.
Babb, Lawrence A. 1975. *The Divine Hierarchy: Popular Hinduism in Central India*. New York: Columbia University Press.
Bareau, André. 1955. *Les Sectes bouddhiques du petit véhicule*. Saigon: École Française d'Extrême-Orient.
———. 1963–71. *Recherches sur la biographie du Bouddha dans les Sutrapiṭaka et les Vinayapiṭaka anciens*. 3 vols. Paris: École Française d'Extrême-Orient.
———. 1982. "Un personnage bien mysterieux: l'epouse du Bouddha." In *Indological and Buddhist Studies*, edited by L. A. Hercus, 31–59. Canberra: Faculty of Asian Studies, Australian National University.
Basham, A. L. 1958. "The Man in the Well." In *Sources of Indian Traditions*, vol. 1, edited by Wm. Theodore de Bary, 53–55. New York: Columbia University Press.
Beal, Samuel, trans. [1884] 1984. *Si-Yu-Ki: Buddhist Records of the Western World*. Reprint, Delhi: Motilal Banarsidass.
Bhattacarya, Kamaleswar. 1974. "A Note on the Interpretation of the Term *sādhyasama* in Madhyamaka Texts." *Journal of Indian Philosophy* 2 (September): 225–30.
Blackstone, Kathryn R. 1998. *Women in the Footsteps of the Buddha: Struggle for Liberation in the Therīgāthā*. Richmond: Curzon.
Boisvert, Mathieu. 1995. *The Five Aggregates: Understanding Theravāda Psychology and Soteriology*. Waterloo: Wilfried Laurier University Press.
Boyd, James W. 1975. *Satan and Māra: Christian and Buddhist Symbols of Evil*. Leiden: E. J. Brill.
Brown, Peter. 1988. *The Body and Society: Men, Women, and Sexual Renunciation in Early Christianity*. New York: Columbia University Press.
Brown, R. L. 1997. "Narrative as Icon: The Jātaka Stories in Ancient India and Southeast Asic Architecture." In *Sacred Biography in the Buddhist Traditions of South and Southeast Asia*, edited by J. Schober, 64–109. Honolulu: University of Hawai'i Press.
Burlingame, Eugene, trans. 1969. *Buddhist Legends: Translated from the Original Pali Text of the Dhammapada Commentary*. 3 vols. London: Pali Text Society.
Chimpa, Lama, and Alaka Chattopadhyaya, trans. 1970. *Tāranātha's History of Buddhism in India*. Simla: Institute for Advanced Study.
Clark, Elizabeth, and Herbert Richardson, eds. 1977. *Women and Religion*. New York: Harper.
Collins, Steven. 1982. *Selfless Persons: Imagery and Thought in Theravāda Buddhism*. New York: Cambridge University Press.
———. 1992. "Notes on Some Oral Aspects of the Pali Literature." *Indo-Iranian Journal* 35, no. 2 121–35.

———. 1993. "The Discourse on What Is Primary (Aggañña-Sutta)." *Journal of Indian Philosophy* 21 (December): 301–93.

———. 1996. "The Lion's Roar on the Wheel-turning King: A Response to Andrew Huxley's 'The Buddha and the Social Contract.'" *Journal of Indian Philosophy* 24 (December): 421–46.

———.1997. "The Body in Theravāda Buddhist Monasticism." In *The Body in Religion: Comparative and Devotional Approaches*, edited by Sarah Coakley, 185–204. New York: Cambridge University Press.

———. 1998. *Nirvana and Other Buddhist Felicities: Utopias of the Pali Imaginaire*. New York: Cambridge University Press.

Corless, Roger, trans. 1995. "The Chinese Biography of Nāgārjuna." In *Buddhism in Practice*, edited by Donald S. Lopez Jr., 525–31. Princeton: Princeton University Press.

Crosby, Kate, and Andrew Skilton, trans. 1996. *The Bodhicaryāvatāra*. New York: Oxford University Press.

Cousins, L. S. 1983. "Pali Oral Literature." In *Buddhist Studies: Ancient and Modern*, edited by Phillip Denwood and Alexander Piatigorsky, 1–11. London: Curzon.

Cowell, E. B., et al., trans. [1895–1907] 1973. *The Jātaka, or Stories of the Buddha's Former Births*. 6 vols. Reprint, London: Pali Text Society.

Cummings, Mary. 1982. *The Lives of the Buddha in the Art and Literature of Asia*. Ann Arbor: Center for South and Southeast Asian Studies, University of Michigan.

Das, Sarat Chandra 1902. *A Tibetan-English Dictionary*. Calcutta: Bengal Secretariat Book Depot.

Day, Terence. 1982. *The Conception of Punishment in Early Indian Literature*. Waterloo: Wilfrid Laurier University Press.

De Jong, Jan Willem, trans. 1949. *Cinq chapitres de la Prasannapadā*. Paris: Paul Geuthner.

———. 1976. *A Brief History of Buddhist Studies in Europe and Asia*. Varanasi: Buddha Bharati.

Della Santina, Peter. 1986. *Madhyamaka Schools in India*. Delhi: Motilal Banarsidass.

Dietz, Siglinde. 1984. *Die buddhistische Briefliteratur Indiens*. Wiesbaden: Harrassowitz.

Doniger, Wendy. 1994. "Playing the Field: Adultery as Claim-Jumping." In *The Sense of Adharma*, edited by Ariel Glucklich, 169–88. New York: Oxford University Press.

———. 1995. "Begetting on Margin: Adultery and Surrogate Pseudomarriage in Hinduism." In *From the Margins of Hindu Marriage*, edited by Lindsey Harlan and Paul B. Courtright, 160–83. New York: Oxford University Press.

Doniger, Wendy, and Brian K. Smith, trans. 1991. *The Laws of Manu*. Harmondsworth: Penguin.

Dutt, Nalinaksa. 1977. *Buddhist Sects in India*. Varanasi: Indological Book House.

Dutt, Sukumar. 1962. *Buddhist Monks and Monasteries of India*. London: Allen and Unwin.

Faure, Bernard. 1998. *The Red Thread: Buddhist Approaches to Sexuality*. Princeton: Princeton University Press.

Frauwallner, Erich. 1995. *Studies in Abhidharma Literature and the Origins of Buddhist Philosophical Systems*, translated by Sophie Francis Kidd. Albany: State University of New York Press.

Garfield, Jay L., trans. 1995. *The Fundamental Wisdom of the Middle Way: Nāgārjuna's Mūlamadhyamakakārikā*. New York: Oxford University Press.
Gethin, R.M.L. 1992. *The Buddhist Path to Awakening: A Study of the Bodhipakkiyā Dhammā*. Leiden: E. J. Brill.
Glucklich, Ariel. 1988. *Religious Jurisprudence in the Dharmaśāstra*. New York: Macmillan.
———, ed. 1994. *The Sense of Adharma*. New York: Oxford University Press.
Gold, Anne Grodzins. 1988. *Fruitful Journeys: The Ways of Rajasthani Pilgrims*. Berkeley and Los Angeles: University of California Press.
Goldman, Robert P. 1977. *Gods, Priests, and Warriors: The Bhṛgus of the Mahābharata*. New York: Columbia University Press.
———, trans. 1984. *The Rāmāyaṇa of Vālmiki*. Vol. 1. Princeton: Princeton University Press.
Gombrich, Richard F. 1984. "Temporary Ordination in Sri Lanka." *Journal of the International Association of Buddhist Studies* 7 no. 1: 41–65.
———. 1996. *How Buddhism Began: The Conditioned Genesis of the Early Teachings*. London: Athlone.
Gonda, Jan. 1950. *Notes on Brahma*. Utrecht: J. L. Beyers.
———. 1969. *Ancient Indian Kingship from the Religious Point of View*. Leiden: E. J. Brill.
———. 1985. *Change and Continuity in Indian Religion*. New Delhi: Munshiram Manoharlal.
Gopalachari, K. 1941. *Early History of the Andhra Country*. Madras: University of Madras.
Griffiths, Paul J. 1999. *Religious Reading: The Place of Reading in the Practice of Religion*. New York: Oxford University Press.
Gyatso, Janet. 1998. *Apparitions of the Self: The Secret Autobiographies of a Tibetan Visionary*. Princeton: Princeton University Press.
Hallisey, Charles, and Anne Hansen. 1996. "Narrative, Sub-Ethics, and the Moral Life: Some Evidence from Theravāda Buddhism." *Journal of Religious Ethics* 24 (December): 305–27.
Hamilton, Sue. 1995. "From the Buddha to Buddhaghosa: Changing Attitudes toward the Human Body in Theravāda Buddhism." In *Religious Reflections on the Human Body*, edited by Jane Marie Law, 46–63. Bloomington: Indiana University Press.
———. 1996. *Identity and Experience: The Constitution of the Human Being According to Early Buddhism*. London: Luzac.
Harrison, Paul. 1995 "Searching for the Origins of Mahāyāna: What Are We Looking for?" *Eastern Buddhist* 28 no. 1: 48–69.
Hayes, Richard. 1994. "Nāgārjuna's Appeal." *Journal of Indian Philosophy* 22 (December): 363–72.
Heesterman, Jan. 1985. *The Inner Conflict of Tradition: Essays in Indian Ritual, Kingship, and Society*. Chicago: University of Chicago Press.
Hopkins, Jeffrey, trans. 1998. *Buddhist Advice for Living and Liberation: Nāgārjuna's Precious Garland*. Ithaca, N.Y.: Snow Lion.
Horner, I. B. 1938–66. *The Book of the Discpline*. 6 vols. London: Pali Text Society.
Huntington, C. W. Jr. 1983. "The System of Two Truths in the Prasannapadā and the Mādhyamika Soteriology." *Journal of Indian Philosophy* 11 (March): 77–107.
———, trans. 1989. *The Emptiness of Emptiness: An Introduction to Early Mādhyamika*. Honolulu: University of Hawai'i Press.

Ingalls, Daniel H. H., trans. 1965. *An Anthology of Sanskrit Court Poetry*. Cambridge: Harvard University Press.

Jaini, Padmanbh S. 1977. "Saṃskāra-duḥkhatā and the Jaina Concept of Suffering." In *Revelation in Indian Philosophy*, edited by Harold Coward and Krishna Sivaraman, 153–57. Berkeley: Dharma Publishing.

Jamison, Stephanie. 1996. *Sacrificed Wife / Sacrificer's Wife: Women, Ritual and Hospitality in Ancient India*. NewYork: Oxford University Press.

Jones, John Garrett. 1979. *Tales and Teachings of the Buddha: The Jātaka Stories in Relation to the Pāli Canon*. London: Allen and Unwin.

Jones, J. J., trans. 1949–56. *Mahāvastu*. 3 vols. London: Pali Text Society.

Kaelber, Walter. O. 1989. *Tapta Marga*. Albany: State University of New York Press.

Kalupahana, David. 1986. *Nāgārjuna: The Philosophy of the Middle Way*. Albany: State University of New York Press.

Kane, P. V. 1968–77. *History of Dharmaśāstra*. 5 vols. 2d ed. Poona: Bhandarkar Oriental Research Institute.

Karetsky, Patricia Eichenbaum. 1982. "Māra, Buddhist Deity of Death and Desire." *East and West* 32 (December): 75–92.

Keenan, John P. 1997. *Dharmapāla's Yogācāra Critique of Bhāvaviveka's Mādhyamika Explanation of Emptiness*. Lewiston, N.Y.: Edwin Mellen.

Khoroche, Peter, trans. 1980. *Once the Buddha Was a Monkey: Ārya Śūra's Jātakamālā*. Chicago: University of Chicago Press.

Klein, Anne Carolyn. 1995. *Meeting the Great Bliss Queen: Buddhists, Feminists, and the Art of the Self*. Boston: Beacon.

Kloetzli, Randy. 1983. *Buddhist Cosmology: From Single World System to Pure Land*. Delhi Motilal Banarsidass.

Knipe, David. 1977. "Sapiṇḍikaraṇa: The Hindu Rite of Entry into Heaven." In *Religious Encounters with Death*, edited by Frank Reynolds and Earle H. Waugh, 111–24. University Park: Pennsylvania State University Press.

Lamotte, Étienne. 1949–80. *Le Traité de la grand vertu de sagesse de Nāgārjuna*. 6 vols. Louvain-la-Neuve: Institut Orientaliste.

———. 1976. *The Teaching of Vimalakīrti*. Translated by Sara Webb-Boin. London: Pali Text Society.

———. 1988a. "The Assessment of Textual Interpretation in Buddhism." In *Buddhist Hermenutics*, edited by Donald S. Lopez Jr., 11–27. Honolulu: University of Hawai'i Press.

———. 1988b. *History of Indian Buddhism: From the Origins to the Śaka Era*. Translated by Sara Webb-Boin. Louvain-la-Neuve: Institut Orientaliste.

Lang, Karen, trans. 1986a. *Āryadeva's Catuḥśataka: On the Bodhisattva's Cultivation of Merit and Knowledge*. Copenhagen: Akademisk Forlag, 1986.

———. 1986b. "Lord Death's Snare: Gender-Related Imagery in the 'Theragāthā' and the "Therīgāthā.'" *Journal of Feminist Studies in Religion* 2 no. 1: 63–79.

———. 1990. "sPa tshab Nyi ma grags and the Introduction of the Prāsaṅgika Madhyamaka into Tibet." In *Reflections on Tibetan Culture: Essays in Memory of Turrell V. Wylie*, edited by Lawrence Epstein and Richard Sherburne, 127–41. Lewiston, N.Y.: Edwin Mellen.

———. 1992. "Āryadeva and Candrakīrti on the Dharma of Kings." In *Asiastische Studien* 46 no. 1: 31–43.

———. 1993. "On the Middle Indic Forms Found in Candrakīrti's Quotations from the Ninth Chapter of the *Samādhirājasūtra*." In *Aspects of Buddhist*

Sanskrit, edited by K. N. Shastri, 426–59. Sarnath: Central Institute for Higher Tibetan Studies.

———, trans. 1995. Āryadeva and Candrakīrti on Self and Selflessness." In *Buddhism in Practice*, edited by Donald S. Lopez Jr., 380–98. Princeton: Princeton University Press.

La Vallée Poussin, Louis de 1988–90. *Abhidharmakośabhāṣyam*. Translated by Leo. M. Pruden. 3 vols. Berkeley: Asian Humanities Press.

Leach, Edmund. 1983. "Against Genres: Are Parables Lights Set in Candlesticks or Put under a Bushel?" In *Structuralist Interpretations of Biblical Myth*, edited by Edmund Leach and D. Alan Aycock, Cambridge: Cambridge University Press.

Leder, Drew. 1990. *The Absent Body*. Chicago: University of Chicago Press.

Lefeber, Rosalind, trans. 1994. *The Rāmāyaṇa of Vālmīki*. Vol. 4. Princeton: Princeton University Press.

Leslie, Julia. 1989. *The Perfect Wife: The Orthodox Hindu Woman According to the Strīdharmapaddhati of Tryambakayajvan*. New York: Oxford University Press.

Lincoln, Bruce. 1991. *Death, War, and Sacrifice*. Chicago: University of Chicago Press.

Lindtner, Christian. 1979. "Candrakīrti's *Pañcaskandhaprakaraṇa*, I. Tibetan Text." *Acta Orientalia* 40: 87–145.

———, trans. 1982. *Nagarjuniana: Studies in the Writings and Philosophy of Nāgārjuna*. Copenhagen: Akademisk Forlag.

Lingat, Robert. 1973. *The Classical Law of India*. Berkeley and Los Angeles: University of California Press.

———. 1989. *Royautés bouddhiques: Aśoka et la fonction royale à Ceylan*. Paris: Éditions de l'École des Hautes Études en Sciences Sociales.

Lopez, Donald S. Jr. 1988. "On the Interpretation of the Mahāyāna Sūtras." In *Buddhist Hermenutics*, edited by Donald S. Lopez Jr., 47–60. Honolulu: University of Hawai'i Press.

Masefield, Peter. 1986. *Divine Revelation in Pali Buddhism*. London: Allen and Unwin.

———, trans. 1989. *Vimāna Stories*. London: Allen and Unwin.

Matilal, B. K. 1974. "A Note on the Nyāya Fallacy *sādhyasama* and *petitio principii*." *Journal of Indian Philosophy* 2 (September): 211–24.

May, Jacques, trans. 1959. *Candrakīrti Prasannapadā Madhyamakavṛtti*. Paris: Maisonneuve.

———, trans. 1980. "Āryadeva et Candrakīrti sur permanence (I)." In *Indianisme et Bouddhisme, mélanges offerts à Mgr. Étienne Lamotte*, 215–32. Louvain: Institut Orientaliste.

———, trans. 1981a. "Āryadeva et Candrakīrti sur permanence (II)." *Bulletin de l'École Française d'Êxtreme-Orient* 69: 75–96.

———, trans. 1981b. "Āryadeva et Candrakīrti sur permanence (III)." *Études Asiatiques* 35 no 2:47–76.

———, trans. 1982. "Āryadeva et Candrakīrti sur permanence (IV)." *Études de Lettres* (University of Lausanne) 3: 45–76.

———, trans. 1984. "Āryadeva et Candrakīrti sur permanence (V)." *Acta Indologica*: 115–44.

McFague, Sally. 1975. *Speaking in Parables: A Study in Metaphor and Theology*. Philadelphia: Fortress.

Miles, Margaret R. [1989] 1991. *Carnal Knowing: Female Nakedness and Religious Meaning in the Christian West*. Reprint, New York: Vintage.

Ñāṇamoli, Bhikku, trans. 1975. *The Path of Purification*. Kandy: Buddhist Publication Society.

Ñāṇamoli, Bhikku, and Bhikku Bodhi, trans. 1995. *The Middle Length Discourses of the Buddha*. Boston: Wisdom.

Naudou, J. 1968. *Les Bouddhistes kaśmiriens au moyen age*. Paris: Presses Universitaires.

Nattier, Jan. 1988. "The Meaning of the Maitreya Myth." In *Maitreya, the Future Buddha*, edited by Alan Sponberg and Helen Hardacre. Princeton: Princeton University Press.

———. 1991. *Once Upon a Future Time*. Berkeley: Asian Humanities Press.

Norman, K. R. 1997. *A Philological Approach to Buddhism*. London: School of Oriental and African Studies, University of London.

Obermiller, E., trans. 1931–32. *Bu-ston's History of Buddhism*. 2 vols. Heidelberg: Harrosowitz.

O'Flaherty, Wendy Doniger. 1973. *Asceticism and Eroticism in the Mythology of Siva*. Oxford: Oxford University Press, 1973.

———. 1975. trans. *Hindu Myths: A Sourcebook Translated from the Sanskrit*. Harmondsworth: Penguin.

———. 1976. *The Origins of Evil in Hindu Mythology*. Berkeley and Los Angeles: University of California Press.

———. 1980a. "Karma and Rebirth in the Vedas and Purāṇas." In *Karma and Rebirth in Classical Indian Traditions*, edited by Wendy Doniger O'Flaherty, 3–37. Berkeley and Los Angeles: University of California Press.

———. 1980b. *Women, Androgynes, and Other Mythical Beasts*. Chicago: University of Chicago Press.

———. 1984a. *Dreams, Illusions and Other Realities*. Chicago: University of Chicago Press.

———, trans. 1984b. *The Rig Veda*. Harmondsworth, Middlesex: Penguin.

———. 1985. *Tales of Sex and Violence*. Chicago: University of Chicago Press.

———. 1988. *Textual Sources for the Study of Hinduism*. Chicago: University of Chicago Press.

Ogawa, Ikkyo. 1977. "Jikanron ni taisuru Daijōbukkyō Shiten—Gesshō zō 'Shihyakuron Sahaku' Daijūisshō." *Annual Report of the Researches of the Otant University* 29: 1–56.

Olivelle, Patrick, trans. 1992. *The Saṃnyāsa Upaniṣads: Hindu Scriptures on Asceticism and Renunciation*. New York: Oxford University Press.

———. 1993. *The Āśrama System: The History and Hermeneutics of a Religious Institution*. New York: Oxford University Press.

———, trans. 1996. *Upaniṣads*. New York: Oxford University Press.

———, trans. 1999. *Dharmasūtras: The Law Codes of Ancient India*. New York: Oxford University Press.

Pagel, Ulrich, trans. 1995. *The Bodhisattvapiṭaka*. Tring, U.K.: Institute of Buddhist Studies.

Parry, Jonathan. 1994. *Death in Banaras*. Cambridge: Cambridge University Press.

Paul, Diana, trans. 1979. *Women in Buddhism: Images of the Feminine in Mahāyāna Tradition*. Berkeley: Asian Humanities Press.

Pollock, Sheldon, trans. 1986. *The Rāmāyaṇa of Vālmīki*. Vol. 2. Princeton: Princeton University Press.

———, trans. 1991. *The Rāmāyaṇa of Vālmīki*. Vol. 3. Princeton: Princeton University Press.

Przyluski, Jean. 1926–28. *Le Concile de Rājagṛha*. Paris: Paul Geuthner.

Ramanan, K. Venkata. 1966. *Nāgārjuna's Philosophy as Presented in the Mahāprajñāparamitāśāstra*. Rutland, Vt.: Charles Tuttle.

Ray, Reginald. 1994. *Buddhist Saints in India: A Study in Buddhist Values and Orientations*. New York: Oxford University Press.

Reynolds, Frank. 1976. "The Many Lives of Buddha: A Study of Sacred Biography and Theravāda Tradition." In *The Biographical Process*, edited by Frank Reynolds and Donald Capps, 37–61. The Hague: Mouton.

Rhys-Davids, C.A.F., and S. Z. Aung, trans. 1915. *Points of Controversy*. London: Pali Text Society.

Robinson, Richard. 1967. *Early Mādhyamika in India and China*. Madison: University of Wisconsin Press.

Ruegg, David Seyfort. 1981. *The Literature of the Madhyamaka School of Philosophy in India*. Wiesbaden: Harrassowitz.

Scarry, Elaine. 1985. *The Body in Pain: The Making and Unmaking of the World*. New York: Oxford University Press.

Scherrer-Schaub, Cristina Anna, trans. 1991. *Yuktiṣaṣṭīkāavṛtti. Commentaire à la soixantaine sur la raisonnement ou du vrai enseignment de la causalité par le maître indien Candrakīrti*. Brussels: Institut Belge des Hautes Études Chinoises.

Schoening, Jeffrey D., trans. 1995. *The Śālistambha Sūtra and Its Indian Commentaries*. 2 vols. Vienna: Arbeitskreis für Tibetsiche und Buddhistiche Studien Universitat Wien.

Schopen, Gregory. 1997 *Bones, Stones, and Buddhist Monks: Collected Papers on the Archeology, Epigraphy, and Texts of Monastic Buddhism in India*. Honolulu: University of Hawai'i Press.

Seneviratne, H. L. 1999. *The Work of Kings: The New Buddhism in Sri Lanka*. Chicago: University of Chicago Press.

Sharma, Arvind, et al. 1988. *Sati. Historical and Phenomenological Essays*. Delhi: Motilal Banarsidass.

Shulman, David. 1985. *The King and the Clown in South Indian Myth and Poetry*. Princeton: Princeton University Press.

———. 1993. *The Hungry God: Hindu Tales of Filicide and Devotion*. Chicago: University of Chicago Press.

Smith, Brian K. 1989. *Reflections on Resemblance, Ritual, and Religion*. New York: Oxford University Press.

———. 1994. *Classifying the Universe: The Ancient Indian Varṇa System and the Origins of Caste*. New York: Oxford University Press.

Sonam, Ruth, trans. 1994. *Yogic Deeds of Bodhisativas: Gyel-tsap on Āryadeva's Four Hundred*. Ithaca, N.Y.: Snow Lion.

Sprung, Mervin, ed. 1973. *Two Truths in Buddhism and Vedanta*. Dordrecht: Reidcl.

———, trans. 1979. *Lucid Exposition of the Middle Way: The Essential Chapters from the Prasannapadā of Candrakīrti*. Boulder: Prajñā.

Strong, John, trans. 1983. *The Legend of King Aśoka*. Princeton: Princeton University Press.

———. 1992. *The Legend and Cult of Upagupta: Sanskrit Buddhism in North India and Southeat Asia*. Princeton: Princeton University Press.

Suzuki, D. T. 1961. *Essays in Zen Buddhism*. 3 vols. New York: Grove.

Suzuki, Koshin. 1989. "A Study of Candrakīrti's *Bodhisattvayogācāracatuḥśatakaṭīkā*, I. *Taishō daigakuin kenkyūronshū*: 266–55.

Tambiah, S. J. 1976. *World Conquerer, World Renouncer*. Cambridge: Cambridge University Press.

Tatz, Mark. 1985. *Buddhism and Healing: Demiéville's Article Byō from Hōbōgirin*. Lanham, Md. University Press of America.

Thapar, Romila. 1963. *Aśoka and the Decline of the Mauryas*. Oxford: Oxford University Press.

Thurman, Robert A. F., trans. 1984. *Tsong Khapa's Speech of Gold in the Essence of True Eloquence*. Princeton: Princeton University Press.

Tillemans, Tom J. F., trans. 1990. *Materials for the Study of Āryadeva, Dharmapāla and Candrakīrti*. 2 vols. Vienna: Arbeitskreis für Tibetische und Buddhistische Studien Universitat Wien.

Trainor, Kevin. 1993. "In the Eye of the Beholder." *Journal of the American Academy of Religion* 61 no. 1: 57–79.

Tsong kha pa. 2000. *The Great Treatise on the Stages of the Path to Enlightenment*. Vol. 1; edited by Joshua W. C. Cutler and translated by the Lamrim Chenmo Translation Committee. Ithaca, N.Y.: Snow Lion.

Tucci, Giuseppe. 1929. *Pre-Diṅnāga Buddhist Texts on Logic*. Gaekwad's Oriental Series 49. Baroda: Oriental Institue.

Tuck, Andrew. 1990. *Comparative Philosophy and the Philosophy of Scholarship: On the Western Interpretation of Nāgārjuna*. New York: Oxford University Press.

van Buitenen, J.A.B., trans. 1973–77. *The Mahābhārata*. 5 vols. Chicago: University of Chicago Press.

Walleser, Max. 1990. *The Life of Nagarjuna from Tibetan and Chinese Sources*. New Delhi: Asian Educational Services.

Walshe, Maurice, trans. 1987. *Thus Have I Heard: The Long Discourses of the Buddha*. London: Wisdom.

Walters, Jonathan S. 1990. "The Buddha's Bad Karma: A Problem in the History of Theravāda Buddhism." *Numen* 37 no. 1: 70–95.

———. 1999. "Suttas as History: Four Approaches to the Sermon on the Noble Quest (Ariyapariyesanasutta)." *History of Religions* 38 no. 2: 247–84.

Wangyal, Geshe. 1978. *The Door of Liberation*. New York: Lotsawa.

Warder, A. K. 1970. *Indian Buddhism*. Delhi: Motilal Banarsidass.

Wayman, Alex. 1959. "Studies in Yama and Māra." *Indo-Iranian Journal* 3 vol. 1 4–73, vol. 2 112–31.

———, trans. 1977. *Yoga of the Guhyasamājatantra*. Delhi: Motilal Banarsidass.

White, David Gordon. 1991. *Myths of the Dog-Man*. Chicago: University of Chicago Press.

Wijayaratna, Mohan. 1990. *Buddhist Monastic Life: According to the Texts of the Theravāda Tradition*. Translated by Claude Grainger and Stephen Collins. Cambridge: Cambridge University Press.

Willemen, Charles, Bart Dessien, and Collett Cox. 1998. *Sarvāstivāda Buddhist Scholasticism*. Leiden: E. J. Brill.

Williams, Paul. 1989. *Mahāyāna Buddhism: The Doctrinal Foundations*. New York: Routledge and Kegan Paul.

———. 1997. "Some Mahāyāna Buddhist Perspectives on the Body." In *The Body in Religion: Comparative and Devotional Approaches*, edited by Sarah Coakley, 205–230. Cambridge: Cambridge University Press.

———. 2000. *Buddhist Thought: A Complete Introduction to the Indian Tradition*. London: Routlege.

Wilson, Elizabeth. 1995. "The Female Body as a Source of Horror and Insight in Post-Ashokan Buddhism." In *Religious Reflections on the Human Body*, edited by Jan Marie Law, 76–99. Bloomington: Indiana University Press.

———. 1996. *Charming Cadavers: Horrific Figurations of the Feminine in Indian Buddhist Hagiographic Literature*. Chicago: University of Chicago Press.

Wilson, Joe. 1980. *Chandrakirti's Sevenfold Reasoning: Meditation on the Selflessness of Persons*. Dharmasala: Library of Tibetan Works and Archives.

Wood, Thomas E. 1994. *Nāgārjunian Disputations: A Philosophical Journey through an Indian Looking-Glass*. Honolulu: University of Hawai'i Press.

Woodward, F. L., and E. M. Hare, trans. 1917–30. *The Book of the Kindred Sayings*. 5 vols. London: Pali Text Society.

———, trans. 1932–36. *The Book of the Gradual Sayings*. 6 vols. London: Pali Text Society.

Wyschogrod, Edith. 1990. *Saints and Postmodernism*. Chicago: University of Chicago Press.

Yamaguchi, Susumu, trans. 1964. "Gesshō-zō Shihyakuron-chūshaku Hajōhon no kaidoku. Suzuki Gakujutsu Zaidan Kenkyū Nenpō." *Annual of Oriental and Religious Studies* 1: 3–35.

Yamakami, Sogen. 1912. *Systems of Buddhistic Thought*. Calcutta: University of Calcutta Press.

Zwilling, Leonard. 1992. "Homosexuality in Indian Buddhist Texts."In *Buddhism, Sexuality, and Gender*, edited by José Cabezon, 203–14. Albany: State University of New York Press.

Zysk, Kenneth. 1991. *Asceticism and Healing in Ancient India: Medicine in the Buddhist Monastery*. New York: Oxford University Press.

INDEX

Dharmadāsa 23, 113, 211n23
Dharmapada 14, 20, 21, 22, 34, 138
Dharmapāla 14, 18–19, 112, 210n19
Doniger, Wendy 75–76. *See also* O'Flaherty, Wendy Doniger
Dutt, Nalinaksa 4

emptiness 4–6, 14–19, 67, 154–155
enlightenment 4, 18, 30, 81, 152
eternalism 5, 14
exceptional practitioners (*ārya*) 19, 62, 64, 133

Faure, Bernard 90, 100, 101
five degenerations 190, 220n2
form realm 113
formless realm 113, 196
four classes (*varṇa*) 69, 91, 98, 102, 203–206
four elements 26, 62–63, 133, 145–146
four means of knowledge 15, 193

Garbhāvakrāntinirdeśa 51–52
Garfield, Jay L. 14–15
Gautama Dharmasūtra 95
generosity 12, 17, 96, 188
Glucklich, Ariel 24, 71
Goddess of Good Fortune 129
Gold, Anne Grodzins 39
Gombrich, Richard F. 35
Gonda, Jan 32, 36, 72, 89, 105
gradual path 17, 30
great compassion 4, 18, 30, 152, 160
Griffiths, Paul J. 18–19
Gyatso, Janet 12

hagiography 8–12
Hallisey, Charles 21
Hamilton, Sue 87
Harrison, Paul 29, 61
heaven
  difficulty of reaching 125
  Nanda's journey to 26–27
  result of meritorious action 5, 134
  reward for death on the battlefield 103–104
  temporary pleasures of 60–61
  Vedic rituals and 33, 73, 91
Heesterman, Jan 99
hell
  Aśoka's prison 106
  gods falling from heaven to 61
  king's rebirth in 90–91, 107
  result of harmful actions 120, 148, 194
  unchaste monk rebirth in 81, 207
Horner, I. B. 81
Hsüan-tsang 9

ignorance 8, 18, 46, 124, 151, 180
immortality
  deathless state proclaimed by the Buddha 31
  physical immortality 24, 32–33, 73, 81, 119
  Upaniṣads on spiritual immortality 33–34
impermanence. *See also* momentariness
  death and impermanence 41–42, 46–49
  impermanent nature of things 7–8, 15, 26, 28–30, 62–64
impurity
  of the human body 27–28, 69–70, 86–87, 178–184
  mental 71–72, 79
  of women's bodies 82–86, 166, 177–178
inference 14–16, 20, 23, 193
Indra 40, 56, 89–90, 103
Ingalls, Daniel H. H. 82
inherent characteristic (*svalakṣaṇa*) 66, 156
inherent existence (*svabhāva*)
  Abhidharma conception of 4, 64–66
  Madhyamaka rejection of 11, 15, 17, 155–156
insight 3–8, 26, 154
interpretable discourse (*neyārtha*) 66–67, 160, 162
Isisiṅga 77

Jaiminīya Brahmaṇa 44
Jaini, Paddmanbh S. 61
Jāmadagnya 23, 100, 197–198

Obermiller, Eugene 10–11
Olivelle, Patrick 33–34, 73, 83, 102
outcaste 41, 70, 83 , 100, 102

Pagel, Ulrich 23, 28, 48
Parry, Jonathan 47, 51
Pasenadi 35
perception 8, 15–16, 18, 69, 193–194
pleasure
  divine 60–61, 66, 207
  of meditation 26, 64
  transient nature of 58–61, 135–143
  Vasubandhu's views on 63–67
Pollock, Sheldon 55, 89–90, 97
Prajāpati 33
Prasannapadā Madhyamakavṛtti
  on the aggregates 14
  dedication to Nāgārjuna 13
  on the four illusions (*viparyāsa*) 8
  on the four means of knowledge 15–16
  on pain experienced by exceptional practitioners 62
Prāsaṅgika 11
purity
  brahmanical views on the purity of women 178–180
  Buddhist critique of physical 70, 177–184
  superior, of brahmins 69–72, 17

Rāma
  as the ideal king 90–91
  as Sītā's husband 55, 76–77
Rāmāyaṇa
  Candrakīrti's use of 17, 20, 23
  chastity of women 76–77
  king as compassionate protector of his subjects 92, 97
  on the king's divine nature 89–91
  on kings who retire to the forest 106
  Rāma's grief over Sītā's abduction 55, 136
  on the seduction of young ascetics 78
  Śunaḥśepa's story 40–41, 120
Ratnaśrī 48
Ratnāvalī
  the bodhisattva's compassion 154, 158
  collections of merit and knowledge 17
  on eternalism and nihilism 5
  king's sovereignty 95, 108
  sense perception 155
  women's impure bodies 84
Rāvaṇa 23, 55, 76, 136
Ray, Reginald 47–48
real body (*sātkāyadṛṣṭi*) 11, 71, 116
Red mda' ba 17
rGyal tsab 17
Rig Veda 32–33, 37, 44, 69, 73
Robinson, Richard 9

sacrifice
  Buddhist conception of nonviolent sacrifice 34
  of Śunaḥśepa 40–41
  Upaniṣadic conceptions of 33–34
  Vedic 32–34, 69
  warriors', on the battlefield 103–106, 200–201
Samādhirājasūtra 16, 154
Śantideva 7
Sariputra 50
Śatapatha Brahmaṇa 32
Satipaṭṭhānasutta 25–26
Saundarananda 26, 77
Scarry, Elaine 25, 104
scriptural authority 15–16, 103–104, 119, 193, 197
self
  associated with arrogance, egotism, and selfishness 88–89, 108, 110
  divine self constructed by Vedic sacrifice 32
  heterodox philosophers' view of 159
  identical with brahman 32, 34–35
  not related to the aggregates 17, 71
Seneviratane, H. L. 95
sexuality
  Brahmanical views on 33, 72–74